PUBLICATION NUMBER 19

Duke University Commonwealth-Studies Center

Canada-United States Treaty Relations

Duke University Commonwealth-Studies Center Publications

Canada-United States
Treaty Relations

Robert R. Wilson, John E. Read, Green H. Hackworth, Maxwell
Cohen, G. V. La Forest, Charles E. Martin, Theodore
Ropp, Charles P. Stacey, Edward McWhinney,
Wesley L. Gould, David R. Deener

Edited by

David R. Deener

PUBLISHED FOR THE

Duke University Commonwealth-Studies Center

DUKE UNIVERSITY PRESS, DURHAM, N. C.

CAMBRIDGE UNIVERSITY PRESS, LONDON

1963

L.C.C. number 63-13312

I.S.B.N. 0-8223-0046-X

Second printing, 1971

Printed in the United States of America

FOREWORD

The appearance in the era of two World Wars of the Commonwealth of Nations as the heir to what was once the British Empire has not been given in the United States the attention it merits as a field of study. It was in response to this need that a Commonwealth-Studies Center was created at Duke University in 1955 with financial assistance from the Carnegie Corporation. The Center is devoted to the encouragement of research in Commonwealth affairs by members of the Duke University faculty and graduate students, and to the encouragement of similar research in economics, history, and political science by scholars and graduate students from various Commonwealth countries.

The purposes of the Center are implemented in a number of ways. Among these has been an annual program known as the Commonwealth Summer Seminar and Research Group, which in each of the summers of 1956, 1957, 1958, and 1959 brought to the University for a period of two months groups of scholars already known for their interest and competence in one or another aspect of Commonwealth affairs. During the summer these scholars in residence pursued their own research in their chosen fields. They came together daily around the coffee table for informal discussion of their research projects or of more general commonwealth topics. In addition, the groups met formally at intervals as a seminar for critical analysis of papers prepared by distinguished visiting Canadian and American lecturers.

The Summer Seminars in 1957, 1958, and 1959 had as points of focus central themes relating to Canadian affairs. In 1957 the theme was Canadian federalism; in 1958 it was the economic impact of the United States on Canada; and in 1959 it was the growth of Canadian policies in the field of external affairs.

The Canadian theme was continued in the summer program for 1961. Because of the nature of the particular topic under consideration in 1961, the format of the Program was changed from a two-month seminar and research group to a four-day Conference on Canada–United States Treaty Relations. At the evening sessions of the Conference, formal addresses were delivered by distinguished scholars and practitioners of international law and diplomacy. The day sessions consisted of round-table meetings at which papers presented by six scholars served as bases for discussion. In addition to those presenting addresses and papers, the Conference was attended by twenty-one invited participants from Canada and the United States, representing academic institutions, government, and private organizations. Both the evening and day sessions were joined by interested members of the Duke University faculty.

The Summer Seminar and Research program and the Conference on Canada–United States Treaty Relations have sought to further a number of useful purposes. The Research Group provided a means whereby a limited number of scholars who are university teachers with Commonwealth interests could pursue their research throughout a summer unimpeded by the demands of classroom instruction. It has given them an opportunity for informal association with others of similar interests for the free exchange and stimulation of ideas. The Conference also had exchange and stimulation of ideas as one objective. Both the Conference and the earlier Summer Seminars, in centering attention on a particular theme, have brought to the participants and to the wider audience to which these pages are addressed some of the mature thought of scholars whose understanding of political, economic, legal, constitutional, and social forces, as these have been operating between Canada and the outside world, is penetrating as well as comprehensive.

Since the Commonwealth-Studies Center is concerned exclusively with the encouragement of research, any interpretations of Commonwealth developments appearing in its publications do not represent expressions of the views of the Center or of the Carnegie Corporation; the authors of the several publications are responsible for the conclusions expressed in them.

PAUL H. CLYDE

The year 1923 carries a special significance in the history of Canadian external affairs. It marks the Halibut Fisheries Treaty with the United States, the first treaty to be negotiated by Canada completely on her own. That the "first" Canadian treaty should have been concluded with the United States is appropriate. For among the mass of Canadian treaties, those with the United States are most conspicuous. The reverse also holds. Treaty commitments to Canada comprise a large and vital segment of the totality of United States international obligations. In other ways, too, is this complex of treaty relations impressive. Canada–United States treaty obligations are long-lived, dating to the eighteenth century; numerous, running into the hundreds; encyclopedic, covering a multitude of subjects.

To survey in full and in detail the ambit of Canada–United States treaty relations is not the design of this symposium. It attempts rather a balance and a blend—a balance between depth and breadth, between sharp focus and panorama; a blend of diverse views, approaches, and perspectives.

The symposium opens on a broad theme. Professor Robert R. Wilson of Duke University discusses the significance of Canada–United States treaty arrangements in relation to the development, both adjectival and substantive, of international law. Treaty relations of the two countries have lent emphasis to the peaceful settlement of disputes and to the use of the binational joint commission, and have contributed to fisheries and fluvial law. But some possible developments did not eventuate, such as the projected neutrality "rules" of the *Alabama Claims* and the ten-mile bay principle suggested in the *North Atlantic Coast Fisheries Arbitration*. And there remain areas, Professor Wilson indicates, in which further strengthening of ties seems desirable. These would include inter-American affairs, economic and commercial relations, and defense; plus a wider use of formal means, including compromissary clauses, for adjustments of differences.

Perspective and panorama continue with the contribution of Canada's Judge John E. Read, the fourth paper in the symposium. He cautions against easy expectations that institutions and law, especially international law, familiar to Canadians and Americans will readily adapt *in toto* to the bulk of the peoples of the world, peoples who have not shared the Christian Western tradition. But he argues strongly that the ideals of Western institutions and law do constitute valuable assets in the struggles of the Cold War. Judge Read concludes with some suggestions for strengthening the World Court; and from the viewpoint of Canada–United States treaty relations, it may be noted that some of his points are drawn directly from the experience of the two nations in settling their differences.

The broad view animates the paper by Judge Green H. Hackworth of the United States, the seventh in the symposium. Judge Hackworth lays stress on the factors contributing to the spirit of mutuality underlying Canada–United States treaty relations. Close, effective, and harmonious treaty relations spring from a firm background of mutuality; this is a cardinal point to be gained from the treaty experience between the two North American countries, and a point, Judge Hackworth affirms, that could well be taken into account elsewhere, even in the vast multilateral arena that has grown up in the postwar world.

The symposium closes as it opens, on the broad theme. Professor Maxwell Cohen of McGill University analyzes trends and future problems in Canada–United States treaty relations. He notes and characterizes the several historical periods of treaty relationships between the two nations, that of the postwar period being styled one of concern with joint management of a continent. From the standpoint of joint continental management, Professor Cohen enumerates treaty problem areas of the future. Perhaps the most vital matter of all receives emphasis in his concluding remarks; this is the strongly felt need in Canada to retain a separate national identity.

Depth and focus are given the symposium by contributions dealing with three specific problem areas: boundary waters, defense, and economic relations. In each area a pair of papers is presented, one by a Canadian author, the other by an American.

Boundary waters problems are divided geographically for discussion. Professor G. V. La Forest of the University of New Brunswick takes up those of the Eastern regions. He considers briefly boundary settlement problems, questions of navigation and, in greater detail, the Boundary Waters Treaty of 1909 and the International Joint Commission. The Chicago Diversion, the St. Lawrence Seaway and Power Development, and the Passamaquoddy Tidal Project attract closer scrutiny. In closing, Professor La Forest notes that important matters of joint concern may arise in connection with the continental shelf of the Atlantic. For the Western area, Professor Charles E. Martin of the University of Washington discusses the Columbia River Basin Treaty of 1961. He sets forth the various legal doctrines advanced for the allocation of boundary waters, traces the negotiations involved in drafting the treaty, and sums up its provisions and the principles and practices upon which these are founded. He notes also the objections of British Columbia to the treaty, objections which have operated to defer final ratification of the agreement.

Defense problems come under the pens of two historians. Professor Theodore Ropp of Duke University sketches the historical evolution of Canadian defense and military policy from that of a colonial appendage to that of a mid-twentieth century "middle power." But Canada as a middle power still has Commonwealth ties and, more important, ever more close ties with defense and military decisions made in Washington. Outside of these, Professor Ropp points to problem areas of the international community, Africa and Asia, where Canadian military force may be put to effective use far more readily than either British or American. Discussion of defense matters continues with an analysis of Canadian-American military co-operation since the outbreak of World War II by Colonel Charles P. Stacey of the University of Toronto. Colonel Stacey notes the original difficulties faced by Canada in inserting herself into British-American councils. He details many of the problems that have arisen and still arise in a co-operative task when the partners are so vastly unequal in power and potential. Colonel Stacey's call for greater independence on the part of Canada in defense matters seems tempered with a realization that a parting of the ways between the two countries hardly appears to be in the cards, whatever annoyance springs up in Canada or impatience in Washington.

Commercial and economic affairs perhaps represent an area in which formal treaty ties have been least significant, but in which the informal bonds of commerce play a great role. Yet not a role that precludes economic rivalry between the two North American countries, as the discussion of the Cuban Affair by Professor Edward McWhinney of the University of Toronto illustrates. Canadian prospects for increased trade with Cuba after the Castro ouster of American interests proved short-lived indeed. It is Professor McWhinney's thesis that the immediate Canadian reaction in the Cuban instance was more symptomatic of longer-festering sores related to such things as United States antitrust policy, American investment in Canada, and American policy toward trade with the Communist bloc. Professor Wesley L. Gould of Purdue University deals with Canadian-American collaboration in the specific areas of metals, oil, and natural gas. It has proved easier for the two nations to arrive at agreed measures for conservation of resources, fisheries for example, than at mutually satisfactory rules for their exploitation. Yet exploitation need not necessarily be on an exclusively nationalistic basis even in the absence of formal international agreements. As Professor Gould's analysis shows, one nation's interest in the natural gas field has been presented, sometimes with effect, before the regulatory agencies operating in the other. His suggestion for a more effective treaty arrangement in regard to natural resources reflects a continental approach to joint economic problems.

Such then is the design of blend and balance of this symposium. It is not surprising that differing emphases, values, and interpretations emerge from this collection of papers, representing as they do a diversity of views of historians, jurists, lawyers, and political scientists from both sides of the 49th parallel. Yet from repeated emphasis in paper after paper, certain features and problems of Canadian–United States treaty relations stand out boldly.

In the forefield certainly stands Canadian determination to maintain a distinct national identity and a consequent concern for Canadian sovereignty in particular instances, such as those involving United States antitrust suits, powers of military decision, and the reach of American restrictions on trade with the Soviet empire. Of a different nature is the situation described by a cliché from across the Atlantic: "When the United States sneezes, Europe catches a cold." Unfortunately, Canada oftentimes runs high fevers and suffers severe chills. These factors do not go unrecognized on the American side. But being joint occupiers of a single continent does not automatically guarantee a ready solution for all differences. Even identical twins do not see the world alike, and Canada and the United States are far from identical, particularly as regards the variety of pressures that come to bear on foreign policy decisions.

As somewhat of a counterbalance to the problems before the two countries is the past record of firm accomplishment in their treaty relations, a record again given repeated emphasis throughout the symposium. The boundary settlements, the fisheries agreements, extradition, the work of the International Joint Commission—these and others attest the results to be obtained through patient negotiation and regard for mutual interests.

Still it is unlikely that Canada–United States treaty relations will proceed unruffled through the period of the Cold War and tepid peace to whatever lies beyond,—especially, and I ask to be indulged in a paraphrase of a quip, if it should come to mean co-operation between right-thinking Americans and left-thinking Canadians. But there is some comfort in the fact that occasionally the governments at Ottawa and Washington have been able to reach agreement more quickly with each other on certain items than either has been with its respective provincial and state capitols. In the long run, what the countries share in common—political institutions, law, an immigrant origin, a continent to exploit, a democratic foundation, a tradition of peaceful relations, and others—stand to make for continued workable and satisfactory treaty relations; yet some of these very same factors, particularly federalism and the pressures of domestic democracy, will undoubtedly give rise to plague and provocation in day-to-day diplomacy.

DAVID R. DEENER

CONTENTS

Canada-United States Treaty Relations

Canada-United States Treaty Relations and International Law

Robert R. Wilson

Public international law is based in part upon treaties. The latter may have as their object to *make* legal rules of wide application.[1] In other situations they may only *affirm* what already exists in the form of customary rules. Intended relation of treaty provisions to the body of customary rules may not, of course, be specifically stated in the provisions themselves. In exceptional cases party states have assented to the *non-application,* as between themselves and during the life of their treaty, of certain rules of customary law.[2] A classification widely used by European publicists distinguishes as *particular* law that which is in bilateral form, as *general* law that which is binding upon a considerable number but not all of the states, and as *universal* law that which is binding upon substantially all the states of the world.

It has sometimes happened that rules originally expressed in conventional (multilateral) form have at length come to be regarded as parts of customary international law. A state might then be considered to have become bound by them, although it had not formally accepted the multilateral treaty.[3] In the making of some multi-

[1] As illustrated in the treaty concerning the Antarctica signed by twelve states on December 1, 1959; text in *Amer. Jour. Int. Law,* vol. 54 (1960), 477-483. The avowed object of a multilateral treaty may be a complete modernization of international law on a particular subject. See, for example, *Proceedings of the International Civil Aviation Conference,* Chicago, Nov. 1–Dec. 7, 1944, Dept. of State Pub. 2021 (1948), 3.

[2] A familiar illustration is the provision sometimes found in claims conventions whereby no claim is to be rejected by reason of the rule, based upon international law, that local remedies have not been exhausted.

[3] Speaking of certain rules in the Annex to Hague Convention IV of 1907, the Nuremberg Tribunal in 1946 said that "by 1939 these rules laid down in the Convention were recognized by all civilized nations, and were regarded as being declaratory of the laws and customs of war. . . ." *Trial of the Major War Criminals*

lateral instruments there has been specific intent to preclude denunciation at some later date.[4] Recent research has led to the conclusion,
however, that even so-called "law making" treaties may be subject
to denunciation by the parties to them.[5] To adjective law on the
subject of reservations to multilateral instruments, the International
Court of Justice has made a notable contribution in its *Advisory
Opinion on Reservations to the Genocide Convention.*[6]

Having in mind what has been suggested concerning the differing
legal purposes of treaty-making, it is possible to consider the treaty
relations between states such as the United States and Canada from
the point of view of their effect upon the body of international law.
The sheer quantity of this treaty material is impressive. As of
January 1, 1961, there were no less than 187 separate bilateral
instruments in force between the two states (this number comprising
treaties, agreements, and amendments to earlier agreements). The
subjects included amity, atomic energy, aviation, boundaries, boundary
waters, claims, consuls, customs, defense, economic co-operation, extradition, finance, fisheries, health and sanitation, highways, judicial
procedure, labor, maritime matters, migratory birds, military affairs,
naval vessels, pacific settlement of disputes, patents, postal arrangements, property, smuggling, surplus property, taxation, telecommunication, territorial acquisition, tracking stations, trade and commerce,
and weather stations.

Of the 187 bilateral treaties, 28 were inherited by Canada from
Great Britain. In this list were parts of the Jay Treaty (Arts. 9 and
10), the 1818 convention on fisheries and boundary matters, the
Webster-Ashburton Treaty, the Oregon Treaty of 1846, the Northwest Boundary Treaty (declaration adopting maps) of 1870, protocol respecting northwest boundary waters (1873), Alaskan boundary
(1903), report of Alaskan boundary commissioners (1905), demar-

---

*before the International Military Tribunal, Nuremberg, 14 November 1945—1 Octo-
ber, 1946* (Nuremberg, 1947-1949), I, 253-254.

[4] On the point with reference to the banning of the use of bacteriological warfare,
in the Protocol of June 17, 1925, for the Prohibition of the Use in War of Asphyxi-
ating, Poisonous or Other Gases, and of Bacteriological Methods of Warfare, see
Cmd. 3604 (1930), *Cmd.* 3757 (1931), *Cmd.* 4279 (1933).

[5] Edwin C. Hoyt, *The Unanimity Rule in the Revision of Treaties: A Re-Examination* (The Hague, 1959), 46, 47.

[6] I.C.J. *Reports*, 1951, 15-30. See also Hersch Lauterpacht, *The Development
of International Law by the International Court* (London and New York, 1958),
313, 372, 374.

cation of boundary (1908), Boundary Waters Treaty (1909), boundary of Passamaquoddy Bay (1910), part of the commercial treaty of 1815 (Art. IV only), extradition (1889, 1900, 1905, 1922, and 1925), reciprocal rights in conveyance of prisoners, wrecking and salvage (1908), migratory birds (1916), Rush-Bagot Agreement (1817), money order agreement (1901), tenure and disposition of real and personal property (1899—made applicable to Canada in 1922), supplementary convention on real and personal property (1921), telecommunication (for Canada and Newfoundland, 1925), protocol on cession of Horseshoe Reef (1850), and treaty for the advancement of peace (1914).

As of January 1, 1961, there were 153 multilateral treaties to which both the United States and Canada were parties, either as original signatories or adherents. Among these, in addition to the United Nations Charter and the NATO treaty, are basic instruments of the specialized agencies of the United Nations system, the General Agreement on Tariffs and Trade (both the countries having accepted 35 of the 42 separate agreements), the 1929 Prisoners of War Convention, a whaling agreement and protocol thereto, several fisheries agreements (Northwest Atlantic, 1949, and 1956 protocol thereto, North Pacific, 1952, an interim convention on conservation of North Pacific fur seals, a NATO status of forces protocol, declaration on atomic energy (1945), an agreement as to disposition of atomic energy inventions (1956), and co-operation between NATO parties concerning atomic information (1955).[7]

The limitations of a brief inquiry necessitate considerable selectivity, the object being to discern treaty commitments that have some significance from the point of view of the development of international law. It seems appropriate to note, as a preliminary, special factors that seem to influence legal relations between these two states. It is also instructive to look at recent and contemporary treaty-making in the light of certain prior adjudications of questions involving treaties between Great Britain and the United States. In the period following Canada's assumption of full power with respect to making its own treaties, there will be consideration, again on a selective basis, of treaty law under broad subject classifications.

[7] *Treaties in Force, A List of Treaties and Other International Agreements of the United States in Force on January 1, 1961*, Dept. of State Pub. 7132.

1. SPECIAL FACTORS

That there has come to be a great measure of understanding between the two countries may be acknowledged without indulging in what have been called the "customary sentimentalities." The principal basis for this understanding is interdependence. The latter does not, of course, imply political unity, and the Castro regime in Cuba hardly used the best descriptive technique when in an official note early in 1961 it referred to *"the* North American Government."[8] Nevertheless, the community of interests between the two countries is such as might reasonably be expected to support a practical, constructive treaty relationship. Recognition of a common danger undoubtedly plays a large part. "Your country, my country—each is a better and stronger and more influential nation," said the then President of the United States in an address to the Canadian Parliament in 1953, "because each can rely upon every resource of the other in days of crisis."[9] The idea was not new when in 1951 an American Secretary of State said that from a military point of view the defense of the United States could not be worked independently of the defense of Canada. Official recognition of the fact had come in 1940 when there came into being the Permanent Joint Board on Defence, an agency which continued in existence after the Second World War.[10]

The necessity for co-ordinated defense arrangements has, of course, by no means been the only unifying force. In the introductory paragraph of their 1955 agreement upon cooperation concerning civil uses of atomic energy, for example, the two Governments set forth that

There exists a unique tradition of cooperation between Canada and the United States. Based on similar national interests, this cooperation produces special industrial and economic inter-relationships. Consequently, progress in each country toward the full benefits of the peaceful uses of atomic energy will be accelerated through an arrangement which is consistent with the cooperation existing in other areas.[11]

President Kennedy summarized various relationships when, in a speech before the Canadian Parliament on May 17, 1961, he said that

---

[8] *New York Times*, Jan. 5, 1961, 6 (italics inserted). The same note referred to "North American citizens."

[9] *Dept. of State Bulletin*, vol. 29 (1953), 735.

[10] *Ibid.*, vol. 24 (1951), 434.

[11] 6 U.S.T. 2595.

"Geography has made us neighbors. History has made us friends, Economics has made us partners. And necessity has made us allies."[12]

The economic development of the continent has played a major part. In this area, it was inevitable that the fact of separate sovereignty would affect the making of a common policy. There have naturally been conflicting points of view and consequent resentments. Tax laws, alleged extraterritorial enforcement of American antitrust legislation, foreign assets control laws of the United States that have affected Canadian subsidiaries of American companies, have been subjects of much discussion.[13] Wheat surpluses and problems relating to oil and gas have also had their effect. These, however, have not prevented a great volume of trade. There has been an enormous increase in interchange, along with substantial improvement in material standards of living, which have justified a recently expressed conclusion that "the two economies are more interdependent than at any time in their history."[14]

In the realm of jurisprudence the two countries, with their common British heritage, have a tradition of international law as a part of the common law, with the result that the law of nations is regarded as a part of the law of the land. A result is that in the case of different possible constructions of statutes, interpretations that are in accord with international law will be preferred rather than those not in accord.[15] With respect to legal qualities of treaties in general, there have developed constitutional problems of different kinds in the two countries. In the United States, by express provision of the Constitution a treaty is a part of the "law of the land," although even within this broad proposition there has developed a doctrine of self-executing and non-self-executing agreements.[16] In Canada, after the much-publicized decision of the Judicial Committee of the Privy

[12] *Dept. of State Bulletin*, vol. 44 (1960), 840.

[13] Kingman Brewster, Jr., *Law and United States Business in Canada* (Washington, 1960), *passim*.

[14] Constant Southworth and William W. Buchanan, *Changes in Trade Restrictions between the United States and Canada* (Washington, 1960), 5.

[15] Hersch Lauterpacht, "Is International Law a Part of the Law of England?," *Transactions of the Grotius Society*, vol. 25 (1940), 51-88; D. C. Vanek, "Is International Law a Part of the Law of Canada?," *U. of Toronto Law Jour.*, vol. 8 (1949-1950), 251-297. On recent practice of the United States Supreme Court with respect to language found in the older cases on the point that international law is a part of municipal law, see Philip C. Jessup, *The Use of International Law* (Ann Arbor, 1959), 73.

[16] Alona E. Evans, "Self-Executing Treaties in the United States of America," *Brit. Year Book of Int. Law*, vol. 30 (1953), 178-205.

Council in the *Labour Conventions Case*,[17] there was considerable advocacy of the transfer from the Parliament at Westminster to Canada of the power to amend the British North America Act. As recently as 1960, at a Dominion-Provincial Conference on this matter, all participants seemed to favor such a transfer, although the Quebec Premier and the representation from Saskatchewan opposed the idea of weakening "entrenched" clauses in the basic Act.[18]

Some difficulties over the form and scope of treaties as municipal law thus continue on each side of the border. In Canada there is the requirement of legislation in order to give treaties effectiveness as municipal law, and in the United States the division of powers between the states and the federal government which, some would argue, makes it politically inadvisable for the executive to conclude treaties on certain subjects (such as the right of foreigners to own land in the states or to practice professions therein). As has been seen, such considerations have not impeded the making and enforcement of numerous international engagements between the two countries. As a preliminary to examining some of these instruments from the point of view of the international law standard, it will be useful to recall some of the celebrated cases in which, before Canada began to make her own treaties, situations developed that involved the interpretation and application of international law in the form of custom or conventional rules.

II. Some Prior British-American Resort to Law

Of the "leading" treaties made by the United States in the first century and a half of its existence as an independent entity, a very large proportion were with Great Britain.[19] The making, interpretation, and application of these instruments involved, for the Americans, formal interchange with the Government in London, but the British parties chiefly in interest were often Canadians. This was not so true of the first of the celebrated arbitrations to be mentioned, the *Alabama Claims*, although even in that instance the intelligence and

---

[17] [1937] A.C. 326.

[18] *Globe and Mail* (Toronto), Dec. 3, 1960, 4. On the point that some years earlier there had been "renewed" agitation in Canada to acquire control over the Constitution of Canada, see C. E. Carrington, "Disputes between Members of the Commonwealth," Chatham House Memorandum, July, 1960, 5.

[19] See Charles E. Hill, *Leading American Treaties* (New York, 1922), *passim.*

diplomacy of a Canadian-American had an important part in the effort leading up to the actual submission to arbitration.[20]

In the matter of the *Alabama Claims*, a particular suggestion made by Senator Sumner at one point (concerning the so-called "indirect" claims of the United States) would, if adopted, have precluded later *international* agreement-making between the United States and Canada, for the Senator mentioned a hemispheric flag withdrawal by the British![21] In the proceedings at Geneva there was more talk of customary law than there was clear exposition of it. The British denied that the "agreed" rules were expressive of what had already come to be accepted as custom. At any rate the *Alabama* settlement was hailed as a victory for law even if the latter comprised negotiated rules and not just discovered custom. The sequel did not involve the parties' persuading the principal maritime powers to accept the "rules," for they were not able to agree upon the form of proposal to the other powers, notwithstanding a determined American effort to this end.[22] It is possible that some direction was given to the subsequent development of international law on the subject of neutral duties, although the relevant part of Hague Convention XIII of 1907 was written in terms of the means at the neutral's disposal rather than in terms of "due diligence." At any rate, there had been a demonstration that serious questions between major states could be settled on the basis of respect for law.

In the case of the *Bering Sea Arbitration*, the victory of the British over the Americans involved a situation that, at the time, had not been a matter of great concern to the international community as a whole, i.e., the conservation of the products of the sea for the good of the human community in general. A rigid interpretation and application of the existing law could mean only that the Americans would lose the case. However, as has subsequently been suggested, the Americans were soon to realize that in securing the regulations which they desired they had in fact won.[23] A leading British publicist has taken the position that the tribunal need not have denied the right of protecting resources. American invocation of the law of

[20] The Canadian-American referred to was Sir John Rose.

[21] J. B. Moore, *History and Digest of the International Arbitrations to Which the United States Has Been a Party* (Washington, 1898), I, 525-526.

[22] Robert R. Wilson, *The International Law Standard in Treaties of the United States* (Cambridge, Mass., 1953), 214-220.

[23] Hugh L. Keenleyside and Gerald S. Brown, *Canada and the United States: Some Aspects of Their Historical Relations* (New York, 1952), 208, 209.

nature did not persuade the tribunal, yet the manner in which American counsel urged upon the arbitrators the necessity of having regard for the general principles of law and justice has been described as "the most spirited defence ever officially undertaken by a Government of the law of nature as the foundation of international law." The same author feels that the claim of freedom of action by the Americans (to which was opposed the rigid conception of the completeness of international law) might legitimately have been subsumed to "an overruling principle more comprehensive than that of the freedom of the sea itself."[24] Furthermore, if the principle of the freedom of the seas as applied by the tribunal meant that "the United States was bound to be a passive witness to the destruction of a valuable industry closely connected with its territory and of importance to the world at large," the holding was questionable.[25]

Within two decades there was an international agreement designed to accomplish what invocation of natural law had failed to do. To the Convention on Pelagic Sealing, signed July 7, 1911, the United States, Great Britain, Russia, and Japan were parties. Recognition of the interest of the international community as a whole in conservation of the resources of the sea has subsequently figured prominently in the development, although the reconciliation of conflicting points of view has not always been easy.

The *Alaskan Boundary Arbitration* of 1903 assumes significance not because of the relative importance of international law involved, but because there seems to be a unanimous or near-unanimous Canadian opinion that the outcome looked more to the preservation of good Anglo-American relations than to protection of Canadian interests. The tribunal included the Lord Chief Justice of England (Alverstone), A. B. Aylesworth, K.C., of Toronto, and Sir Louis Jetté, Lieutenant-Governor of Quebec. The American members were Elihu Root, Henry Cabot Lodge, and George Turner. The decision of four to two (Alverstone voting with the Americans) awarded to the United States the heads of certain inlets that had been in question, and also Sitklan and Kannaghunut Islands. The effect of awarding the islands was, according to the Canadian view, to deprive Canada of much of the advantage that she would otherwise have had from controlling

[24] Hersch Lauterpacht, *The Function of Law in the International Community* (Oxford, 1933), 98, 99.
[25] *Ibid.*, 309.

the Portland Channel. In the more than half a century since this arbitration there has continued to be, on the part of the Canadian publicists, expression of opinion that the Lord Chief Justice was more concerned to conciliate the United States than to respect the legitimate interests of Canada.[26] The case has lived in memory more because of this reaction than because of the relative importance of such international law as was involved.

In contrast, the *North Atlantic Coast Fisheries Arbitration* did deal with various matters of substantive international law, as, for example, servitudes, the manner of determining the extent of territorial waters inside of and out from bays, and the interpretation of treaty clauses that confer rights upon aliens. The tribunal declined to recognize as establishing a servitude the language of a treaty made when the concept of servitude apparently was not known to, or recognized by, the treaty makers. Concerning bays, the tribunal projected the ten-mile rule on the distance from headland to headland in cases where the same state controlled both headlands. Some four decades later the International Court of Justice decided that the rule, although it had found application at various times in the intervening period, had not come to be so regularly followed as to enable the Court to rule that it had become a part of customary international law.[27]

The conclusion of the tribunal in the *North Atlantic Fisheries Case* that certain rights accorded to Americans by the provisions of treaties in 1818 were "regulated" (rather than absolute) rights provides practical guidance for treaty draftsmen and for treaty interpreters of such treaties as those on friendship, commerce, and navigation in which some rights are commonly mentioned without specific qualification rather than on a national-treatment or most-favored-nation-treatment basis. In general, the contribution of the *North Atlantic Fisheries Arbitration* to clarification of international legal concepts stands out as above that of the other arbitrations with Great Britain that especially affected Canadian interests.

The examples cited, all touching in some measure upon substantive international law—whether of neutral duties, freedom of the high seas, boundary determinations, or alien rights in territorial waters—provided background for more modern Canadian-American

[26] For a recent example, see Maurice Pope, ed. and comp., *Public Servant: The Memoirs of Sir Joseph Pope* (Toronto, 1960), 144-147, 250-255, 296-299.
[27] I.C.J. *Reports*, 1951, 131.

relations. The sequel has been the growing realization of interdependence, as already noted. Invocation of legal principles, as well as assertion of interests on other bases, has, in this sense, been a natural development for the two countries in their relations with each other. The development was to continue when Canada began to make her own treaties.

III. Canada's Assumption of Full Treaty-Making Power

It is striking, but perhaps not unnatural, that the emergence of Canada as an entity with full statehood took place under circumstances wherein the capacity to conclude treaties figured importantly. The problem of regulating halibut fisheries furnished the occasion. This is not to underrate the importance of formal steps such as those taken in 1926 and 1931 to define the position of the self-governing Dominions in the Commonwealth. Nor does it overlook the matter of representation at the Paris Peace Conference or at the Washington Conference on the Limitation of Armament. It is to assert that the need for regulation through bilateral agreement of a practical problem of Canada and the United States first furnished occasion for Canada to exercise full contractual power. It was with the signing of the Halibut Treaty in 1923 that, in the picturesque language of an Irish editor, Canada really began to "sign her own cheques."[28]

For the present purpose one feature of the process of making the treaty invites special attention. This is the Canadian reaction to wording which the United States Senate added when giving its advice and consent to ratification:

Subject to the understanding, which is hereby made a part of this resolution of ratification [sic], that none of the nationals and inhabitants and vessels and boats of any other part of Great Britain shall engage in halibut fishing contrary to any provision of this treaty.

To the British Ambassador's question as to what meaning the words "any other part of Great Britain" was intended to have, the

[28] *Irish Times*, issue of June 30, 1923. Cf. Alfred LeRoy Burt's statement that "during the transition from empire to commonwealth . . . political reality was trampling on the heels of outmoded legal technicality." *The Evolution of the British Empire and Commonwealth from the American Revolution* (Boston, 1956), 748.

Secretary of State replied frankly. Senator Lodge, Chairman of the Senate Committee on Foreign Relations, had conferred with Senator Jones of the state of Washington (who had introduced the resolution in the Senate) and found that the "intention was undoubtedly to cover any part of the British Empire."[29] To Senator Lodge, who had secured approval of the treaty from the Senate on the last day of the session, the resolution seems to have been regarded as harmless.[30] The Department of State did not welcome the reservation. In a letter to the President the Undersecretary of State (Phillips) pointed out that the treaty, which had been drafted in Washington, "was an American document with only one or two insignificant and verbal changes offered by the Canadians." Furthermore, the omission of the British Ambassador's signature from the document had "caused a great deal of unfriendly debate in London and many of the leading British newspapers had condemned Canada for taking the course that it did in dealing with the Secretary of State."[31]

The outcome of the matter, as between the Executive and the Senate, was that the treaty was resubmitted to the latter body and there was consent to the conclusion of the treaty as it had originally gone to the Senate. It was signed by Mr. Hughes and by the Canadian Minister of Marine and Fisheries, Ernest Lapointe. It was obviously a better type of international agreement for the purpose of Canada's assuming her right to make her own commitments than a more political type of treaty would have been. The application of the rules of the Halibut Treaty were soon to provide impressive evidence of the value of this type of co-operation.[32]

[29] Dept. of State file (National Archives) 711.428/729.

[30] Ibid., 711.428/730.

[31] Ibid., 711.428/735. In later discussion Mr. Meighen for the Opposition said: "In the conduct of our . . . treaty and other relations with other . . . nations of the world, it is essential, so long as the British Empire exists—whether you call it a commonwealth of nations or the British Empire . . . that in all these relations there shall exist harmony and a unity of purpose; in a word that all our outside relations are harmonized so that we present to the world not a discordant but a united front." Canada, Parl. Deb. (Commons), vol. 159 (June 27, 1923), 4481-4482.

On the part taken by the Canadian Prime Minister in connection with the Halibut Treaty, see R. MacGregor Dawson, William Lyon Mackenzie King: A Political Biography, Vol. I, 1874-1923 (Toronto, 1958), 430-439. The principal correspondence between Ottawa and the British Ambassador at Washington on the treaty is reproduced in R. MacGregor Dawson, ed., The Development of Dominion Status, 1900-1936 (London, New York, 1937), 254-257.

[32] See note 50, infra.

iv. Internationally Agreed Legal Rules

Space limitations of the present study permit consideration only of selected subjects on which the United States and Canada have through their contractual power sought to apply the international law standard. This has taken place particularly with respect to boundary matters, water diversion, and fisheries.

Non-fortification of the boundary line did not have any special significance for the substantive law of nations, and indeed has provided occasion for some derogatory comment concerning actual practice.[33] Uses of boundary waters (and also waters tributary thereto, and those flowing from boundary waters) have, on the other hand, provided occasion for considerable making of law through treaties. In what is a remarkable example of technical drafting, the Boundary Waters Treaty of 1909 provided for commission handling of problems of mutual concern. Machinery set up was available for reference, at the option of the party states, of other-type disputes which might arise, but there was no advance commitment to refer such disputes. A principal question that has arisen concerning the use of waters is that of whether an upper state may divert such waters to the detriment of a lower state. A related question is that of remedies in case of serious detriment, and specifically, whether only the law of the place where the diversion occurs is to apply.[34]

The so-called Harmon Doctrine was not new in 1909. It had found expression in relations between the United States and Mexico, when Attorney-General Harmon ruled that what the United States did on the upper stretches of a river to which both states had rights of use was not a matter with respect to which Mexico could have a valid claim against the United States.[35] Article II of the Boundary

[33] Cf. James Eayrs, quoting Mackenzie King on the point, in Hugh L. Keenleyside *et al.*, *The Growth of Canadian Policies in External Affairs* (Durham, N. C., 1960), 64.

[34] For an argument that Article II of the Boundary Waters Treaty *supplants* remedies that would be available under international law, see C. B. Bourne, "Columbia River Diversion: The Law Determining Rights of Injured Parties," *U. of British Columbia Legal Notes*, vol. 2 (1958), 610-622. Compare Charles E. Martin, "The Diversion of Columbia River Waters," *Proc. Am. Soc. Int. Law*, 1957, 2-10.

[35] In his opinion the Attorney-General took the position that if Mexico's claim to rights in the subject matter should be upheld, this would in effect be a servitude, would put the upper country at great disadvantage, and would cause it to arrest its development and deny to its people the resources which nature had supplied. He thought that the "right" for which Mexico contended would be inconsistent with the

Waters Treaty has, in the half century since its acceptance, been the subject of considerable discussion, one of the points raised being that of the Doctrine's consistency with established international law.[36]

When the treaty was under discussion in the House of Commons, the Minister of Public Works (Pugsley) characterized Article II as "simply an affirmance of what has always been contended by the United States to be international law, and of what I do not think has been disputed by the jurists of this country...that so far as the waters which are wholly situate within the country are concerned, that country may make a diversion of these waters and prevent them from flowing into the boundary waters."[37]

The Opposition Leader (Borden) thought that the Canadian Government had been too much influenced by an opinion of a United States Attorney-General when they "accepted [it] as a thoroughly reliable statement of international law...." He was "inclined to think that the government in entering into this treaty have had a wrong impression as to the international law on this subject." Borden suggested that not international law, but a very different principle was incorporated into the treaty. He submitted that the Canadian Government in entering into the treaty had "done so with not very much regard to international law, and as far as they did have any regard thereto, under a very thorough misapprehension as to the rules of civilized nations with regard to this subject."[38] Prime Minister Laurier said that he would have regarded the international law the same as did Borden, i.e., would have felt that the same principle should prevail as in the common law and the civil law—namely, that one "may make such use as he pleases of the water which flows over his property so long as he does not do so to the detriment of anybody else." He went on to say, however, that he had no choice but to accept the Harmon Doctrine if the treaty was to be obtained. Under the circumstances he had taken this course, saying in effect to the Americans, "Very well, if you insist upon your view of it we want

sovereignty of the United States; as for comity, he thought this should be a matter of policy, not a matter of law.   21 *Ops. Atty. Gen.* 280-283; *For. Rel.*, 1894, 395, 397.   See also discussion in David R. Deener, *The United States Attorneys General and International Law* (The Hague, 1957), 253, 254.

[36] See, generally, Don C. Piper, "International Law of the Great Lakes," a doctoral dissertation accepted at Duke University in 1961.

[37] Canada, *Parl. Deb.* (Commons) vol. 98 (1910-1911), c. 870 (Dec. 6, 1910).

[38] *Ibid.*, c. 904-905.

our law the same as your law and the consequences will be the same on either side."[39]

During the life of the Boundary Waters Treaty, the Harmon Doctrine has not been consistently applied. Canadian argument against the application by the Chicago Sanitary District (for increased diversion) invoked, for example, international law; and the Doctrine was not applied in the Lake of the Woods Treaty—by which approval of the International Joint Commission was required for potentially injurious diversions or other uses of border waters flowing into the Lake, and of some waters tributary to boundary waters.[40] It would appear that the trend of the development has definitely been against the acceptance of the Harmon Doctrine as a rule of general application apart from conventional arrangement.

The essential principle was to receive extended consideration when the Columbia River Treaty between Canada and the United States came under discussion. In this connection there arose the question of whether law on the point had been established, or whether it was still in the making.[41] A State Department spokesman inclined to the view that while the principle opposed to the Harmon Doctrine was entirely defensible, the fact of the 1909 Treaty with its Article II would put Canada and the United States in a different position from that of countries between which "there are no rules whatsoever."[42] This was presumably meant to suggest a situation in which there were

[39] *Ibid.*, c. 911-912.
[40] See Jacob Austin, "Canadian-U.S. Practice and Theory Respecting the International Law of International Rivers: A Study of the History and Influence of the Harmon Doctrine," *Can. Bar Rev.*, vol. 37 (1959), 393-445.
[41] A State Department memorandum said, concerning the Harmon Doctrine and Article II of the 1909 Treaty, that "There is no evidence in the record that the United States negotiators intended the general reservation of jurisdiction and control to incorporate the Harmon opinion into the treaty. If the Harmon opinion is legally sound, it applies to all categories of waters. . . ." The point was made that the written record provides no evidence that the doctrine was cited by the American negotiators, although it may have been mentioned orally. *Legal Aspects of the Use of Systems of International Waters,* Sen. Doc. 118, 85th Cong., 2nd Sess. (1958), 60-61.
[42] In further statement the Assistant Legal Adviser said that the trend in international law was strongly toward the establishment of the principle that an upstream riparian state cannot deal with the waters which cross its boundary to a downstream riparian state in such a way as seriously to impair the "rights or interests of the downstream riparian state." The Deputy Assistant Secretary (White), while deferring to his colleague on the extent to which the particular treaty provision might serve as a precedent, drew attention to the fact that under the terms of reference the negotiators had dealt solely with the Columbia River basin. *Columbia River Treaty, Hearings before the Committee on Foreign Relations,* U.S. Senate, 87th Cong., 1st Sess., March 8, 1961, 39.

no *conventional* rules whatsoever. At one point in the Senate hearings on the Columbia River Treaty a member of the Senate inquired whether the principle in mind for the treaty was on an *ad hoc* basis, or whether there was to be a principle that would be uniformly applied. While saying in reply that the Senator would want to pursue this subject with the State Department, Secretary of the Interior Udall expressed his view that what had been established was a "good principle of international relations."[43] At another point in the hearings, when asked about international law governing the right of one country to affect the flow of waters in a manner that has an adverse effect on the natural flow in an adjoining country, an Assistant to the State Department's Legal Adviser said that "this is a branch of international law which is currently in the process of evolution. It is very active at the moment, and this treaty . . . is going to be one of the major points of development for international law in this respect."[44]

What may be described as the decline of the Harmon Doctrine—in the sense that it would not apply unless written into a conventional agreement—seems to have been due in part to technological changes. Earlier fluvial law had developed in the light of uses of river waters that did not materially affect water *flow*. When this situation changed there was need for bringing international law on the subject into line with newly recognized needs of states having rights in

[43] *Ibid.*, 12.
[44] *Ibid.*, 38.

As early as 1945, in Senate hearings, the validity and utility of the Harmon Doctrine had been in question. An Assistant to the Legal Adviser of the Department of State (B. M. English) said that the Doctrine was doubtful when viewed in the light of (1) practice of states as evidenced by treaties between various countries, including the United States, providing for the equitable apportionment of waters of international rivers, (2) decisions of domestic courts giving effect to the doctrine of equitable apportionment, and rejecting, as between the parties, the Harmon Doctrine, and (3) the writings of authorities on international law in opposition to the Doctrine. Mr. Acheson, then Assistant Secretary of State, referred to the Harmon Doctrine as "hardly the kind of legal doctrine that can be seriously urged in these times." *Hearings on Water Treaty with Mexico*, Committee on Foreign Relations, U.S. Senate, 79th Cong., 1st Sess. (1945), 1751, 1762.

In 1958 the Acting Legal Adviser of the Department of State (Raymond) had said in a letter (dated July 29): "The Department of State believes that a reiteration of the Harmon doctrine by any branch of the United States Government would not be in the best interests of this country or in line with the progressive development of international law during the last 60 years." *Hearings on Diversion of Waters from Lake Michigan*, Subcommittee of Committee on Public Works, U.S. Senate, 85th Cong., 2nd Sess. (1958), 109.

flowing waters.[45]   It is natural that this development should be reflected in treaties, such as that concerning the Columbia River.

In another situation involving movement across the boundary, suggestive language in a Canadian–United States treaty did not produce very startling results.   In a convention signed April 15, 1935, the two states agreed to arbitrate the question of damage done in the United States by reason of fumes wafted across the border from a smelter at Trail, in British Columbia.   By Article IV commissioners were to apply the law and practice followed in dealing with "cognate cases" in the United States.   The same article envisaged a solution that would be "just" to all concerned.   Considering whether the question of damages could be settled on the basis of law applied in the United States or on the basis of international law, the commissioners found no real problem.   They said that "the law followed in the United States in dealing with the quasi-sovereign rights of the States of the Union, in the matter of air pollution, whilst more definite, is in conformity with the general rules of international law." The arbitrators did not know of any case of air pollution that had been dealt with by an international tribunal.   They found it reasonable, in a situation where no contrary rules prevailed in "generally applicable law," to follow precedents established by the United States Supreme Court—"where no contrary rule prevails in international law and no reason for rejecting such precedents can be adduced from the limitations of sovereignty inherent in the Constitution of the United States."   They quoted the Supreme Court's statement in New York v. New Jersey[46] to the effect that "before this Court can be moved to exercise its extraordinary power under the Constitution to control the conduct of one State at the suit of another, the threatened invasion of rights must be of serious magnitude and it must be established by clear and convincing evidence."   Again referring to the same case, the tribunal said that "What the Supreme Court says there of its power under the Constitution equally applies to the extraordinary power granted this Tribunal. . . .   What is true between States of the Union, is at least equally true concerning the relations between the United States and the Dominion of Canada."   The tribunal then proceeded to find applicable, under principles of inter-

---

[45] See Jacob Austin, loc. cit. and cf. Herbert A. Smith, The Economic Uses of International Rivers (London, 1931), 40-43.
[46] 256 U.S. 296, 309 (1921).

national law as well as under United States law, the rule that "no State has the right to use or permit the use of its territory in such a manner as to cause injury by fumes in or to the territory of another or the properties or persons therein, when the case is of serious consequence and the injury is established by clear and convincing evidence."[47]

v. Commercial Relations and Economic Development

In 1959 the United States sold approximately $3,700,000,000 worth of goods to Canada and bought approximately $3,000,000,000 worth from that country. The reciprocal trade agreement program has had much to do with this interchange. The two countries concluded four major trade arrangements, bilateral ones in 1935 and 1938, multilateral ones under GATT at Geneva in 1947 and at Torquay in 1951. American agricultural policy has occasioned concern and complaint on the Canadian side. While making extensive tariff concessions, the United States has secured general escape clauses for the suspension or termination of concessions when they can be shown to cause or threaten serious injury to domestic industry. These safe-guarding provisions have come to be included in GATT as well as in the earlier bilateral arrangements.[48] Such protective devices have little if any significance for international law, since the latter has traditionally allowed states to fix their own tariffs. Although the United States has signed nearly a score of bilateral treaties of friendship, commerce, and navigation since World War II, there has been no such treaty between Canada and the United States. If one should be concluded, it would presumably include provisions on some subjects to which customary international law applies, such as compensation for alien-owned property taken for public use, non-discrimination against aliens and alien companies in taxation and exchange control. The need for a treaty of this type is presumably not so great as would be the case were the two countries farther apart in their general standards of treatment for aliens and alien-owned or controlled enter-

[47] *Trail Smelter Arbitration between the United States and Canada under Convention of April 15, 1935, Decision of the Tribunal Reported March 11, 1941*, Dept. of State Arbitration Series No. 8 (1941), 33-36.

[48] Irving Brecher and S. S. Reisman, *Canada-United States Economic Relations*, prepared for the Royal Commission on Canada's Economic Prospects (Ottawa, 1957), 178.

prises. Canadian sensitivity to American investors' ownership of subsidiaries in Canada would also seem to be a deterrent to the conclusion of long-term treaty rules on rights with respect to companies.

In 1960, under American initiative, the United States and Canada joined with eighteen European states (those that had composed the Organization for European Economic Co-operation) to form the Organization for Economic Cooperation and Development. The two North American members thus became partners in a plan to "promote orderly economic growth within its 20 member community, and to assist more effectively the less developed countries."[49] Discussion of the new Organization brought out that the latter was not a trade organization and had no effect upon GATT. For international law this development would seem to be significant more because of its promotion of international co-operation than because it marked projection of any new substantive law.

VI. FISHERIES

The development of fisheries through Canadian–United States co-operation appears to have had considerable influence upon international law and usage. Illustrative are the 1923 Halibut Treaty, already referred to, the Great Lakes Fisheries Convention, signed September 10, 1954, and the International Convention for High Seas Fisheries of the North Pacific Ocean, signed May 9, 1952.

That from the point of view of mere conservation the application of the Halibut Treaty is impressive, appears clearly from the record of growth. In 1939 the United States–Canadian Pacific halibut catch was 49.6 million pounds, valued at $3,671,000. That for 1958 was 64.9 million pounds, valued at $13.7 millions. Landing by the Canadian fleet in 1958 was the largest in history.[50]

At times in the past there have been public references to "law" in this subject matter without distinguishing "particular" law from law of wider application. In 1888, for example, Sir Charles Tupper, referred in Parliament to the 1818 treaty as having "distinctly laid down the International law as between the two countries."[51] The

[49] Ex. Rept. No. 1, 87th Cong., 1st Sess. (1961), 3.
[50] *Fishery Statistics of the United States, 1939* (1942), 192; *ibid., 1958* (1960), 359-360.
[51] Canada, *Parl. Deb.* (Commons), vol. 25 (1888), 674.

context would seem to indicate that what the speaker had in mind were special rules in the nature of particular international law (rather than affirmations of principles already established). Of the same nature have been some recently established rules with respect to Great Lakes fisheries. In 1954 the two countries concluded an agreement to facilitate methods of destroying the parasitic sea lamprey of the Lakes. A second objective of this convention was the co-ordination of research on fisheries of the same water. There was provision for a Great Lakes Fisheries Commission composed of two national sections, the approval of each section being required for decisions and recommendations.[52]

In the post-World-War-II period coastal fisheries have assumed much importance, and there has naturally been reference to generally applicable law. Thus in 1952 a spokesman for the Department of State was hardly indulging in overstatement when he observed that the "general situation in the field of international law respecting fisheries" was "somewhat unsettled as a result of various claims and pressures. . . ." He went on to say that the policy of the United States was to work toward the stabilization of international law in the field.[53] The international conferences of 1958 and 1960 have presumably made some progress toward such stabilization. Canada and the United States, with extensive coast lines as well as interests in high seas fisheries, are among the parties especially concerned.

A recent move in the direction of conservation and development of sea life has involved the co-operation of Canada, Japan, and the United States. The convention which became effective on June 12, 1953, seeks to arrange a situation resulting from the fact that salmon, halibut, and herring from a certain part of Asia intermingle with those from North America. Japan agreed to prevent its fishermen from taking such fish within a specified zone, while the United States and Canada agreed to carry on conservation measures in this zone. The parties agreed upon a provisional dividing line (on or near 175° W. Longitude). The International North Pacific Fisheries Commission created by the convention has power to determine that a particular area no longer needs to be within the agreed zone—al-

[52] See Charles B. Selak, Jr., "The United States–Canadian Great Lakes Fisheries Convention," *Amer. Jour. Int. Law*, vol. 50 (1956), 122-129.
[53] *Dept. of State Bulletin*, vol. 26 (June 30, 1952), 1021-1023 (remarks of William C. Herrington).

though the Commission was not to make decisions or recommendations within three years of the effective date of the convention.[54]

As in the case of certain agreements on other subjects, there has sometimes been in connection with fisheries indirect acknowledgment of the customary law against the background of which treaties are made. Thus in the agreement which the United States, Canada, and Japan signed on December 14, 1951, there was provision that nothing therein should be deemed to affect adversely (prejudice) the claims of any contracting party with regard to the limits of territorial waters or the jurisdiction of a coastal state over fisheries.[55]

VII. INTERNATIONAL ORGANIZATION LAW IN THE WESTERN HEMISPHERE

While the Organization of American States has since its inception been open to Canada, that state being within the defense zone which the American Republics drew in the Treaty of Rio de Janeiro, 1947, Canada has not become a member of the OAS. Through interlocking defensive arrangements, however, Canada, as a member of NATO, is in a sense related to other states in the hemisphere through the United States.[56]

In April, 1961, Mr. Pearson suggested in the Canadian House of Commons that the time had perhaps come for Canada to assume responsibilities as an OAS member. Government spokesmen indicated that the matter was under consideration. The Minister of External Affairs (Green) said that there would be a decision to join when a majority of Canadian people indicated that Canada should be a member. The position that Canada should join the OAS has been taken by the CCF and Liberal Party.[57]

The Bogotá Conference of 1960 furnished occasion for expression of American opinion on the matter of Canada's entry. The report to the United States Senate by its members who attended the Conference contained the following statement:

[54] See, concerning this convention, Canada, Department of Fisheries, *30th Annual Report* (1959), 74-77; Shigera Oda, "Japan and the International Fisheries," *Japan Ann. of Int. Law*, No. 4 (1960), 50-63.

[55] See *Dept. of State Bulletin*, vol. 26 (March 3, 1952), 343.

[56] Arthur P. Whitaker, "The Organisation of American States," *Year Book of World Affairs*, 1959, 115, 117.

[57] *The Gazette* (Montreal), May 6, 1961, 45.

There has also existed in Latin America for a long time a desire for closer association with Canada and for Canadian membership in the Organization of American States and its specialized agencies. This, too, is a desire which the United States can heartily second. Canada is geographically a part of the Western Hemisphere. It has substantial investments and other commercial interests in Latin America. A bigger Canadian role in hemispheric affairs would be welcomed by all concerned and would not be inconsistent with Canada's position as a leading member of the Commonwealth.

It needs to be recognized in Canada that if freedom is not strengthened in Latin America freedom may very well become endangered in the entire Western Hemisphere. The United States should not be considered by Canada as a buffer zone between Canada and churning unrest in many parts of Latin America. Rather, Canada and the United States should consider themselves to be hemispheric partners with those countries in Latin America who seek to make available to their people the blessings and benefits of economic and political freedom of choice for each individual citizen. A Western Hemisphere divided between freedom and communism, between a decent standard of living for the people of the United States and Canada and poverty and great human want for millions of people in Latin America, is a hemisphere which threatens its own security and survival.[58]

VIII. FURTHER STRENGTHENING OF LEGAL TIES

The foregoing examples have indicated that in the course of their treaty-making the United States and Canada have on a number of occasions moved to relate their compacts to the body of international law. The prospect for further emphasis upon that law in their mutual relations would appear to be fairly bright.

One way in which this might be done would be habitual inclusion of a compromissary clause in their treaties. Such clauses as that in the agreement on air transport services signed June 4, 1949,[59] are now exceptional. Particularly in view of the reservations which the

[58] *The Bogotá Conference*, September, 1960, Report of Senators Wayne Morse and Bourke B. Hickenlooper to the Committee on Foreign Relations, U.S. Senate, 87th Cong., 1st Sess. (1961), 8-9. In his address to the Canadian Parliament on May 17, 1961, cited in note 12, *supra*, President Kennedy expressed his belief that "all of the free members of the Organization of American States would be heartened and strengthened by any increase" in Canada's hemispheric role. "Your country and mine," he said, "are partners in North American affairs. Can we not now become partners in inter-American affairs?"

[59] 63 *Stat.* 2489.

two states have made in their respective acceptances of the Optional Clause for obligatory jurisdiction of the International Court of Justice, greater use of compromissary clauses in bilateral agreements would seem to be desirable. By the provisions of the Boundary Waters Treaty the two states *may* refer to the International Joint Commission questions other than those relating to boundary waters, but they are not committed in advance to do so, and practice does not suggest great utility in this part of the treaty.

There have been some suggestions that "principles" be laid down. Thus in the Canadian House of Commons on February 26, 1959, Lester B. Pearson said that he supposed there were then more problems with the United States than there had been at any time since the Canadians through a Canadian government became solely responsible for their relations with the United States.[60] He went on to suggest a "top level" conference between United States and Canadian leaders to consider whether some agreement could be reached and set out in a formal convention, perhaps for approval by legislative bodies and "embodying principles that should govern our relations." Referring to the Hyde Park agreement as the kind of thing he had in mind, he said a formal arrangement was needed. He added that when one government, with or without consultation, should take action that seemed to the other to be contrary to principles in the formal agreement, that other could appeal. Apparently in mind were such subjects as defense, commercial relations, and economic activities. A reply from the Government members suggested that to do this would result in "over-formalisation" of relations with the United States.

On the same subject some three weeks later Mr. Pearson again suggested a conference to see whether a formal agreement could not be drawn up, debated in Parliament and in Congress and, if approved by those bodies, made effective as a statement of principles to which either state could appeal. He did not, however, suggest any kind of obligatory arbitration to be set in motion at the instance of either state.

There already exists some machinery, aside from the regular diplomatic channels, that provides opportunity for exchange of views on problems of common concern. There is, for example, the Canada–United States Interparliamentary Group. The fourth meeting of

[60] Canada, *Parl. Deb.* (Commons), 1959, II, 1409, 1410, 1435, 1974.

this body, which includes twenty-four members of the Congress and an equal number from the Canadian Parliament, was held in Ottawa and at Quebec City in February, 1961. A variety of subjects were under informal, off-the-record discussion. There was a committee on defense co-operation and disarmament, one on trade and economic matters, and one on boundary waters, cultural affairs, and foreign policy matters of common concern. The combined group left it to each national delegation to make reports and recommendations to its own legislative body. Concerning the third committee mentioned above, American participants reported that, *inter alia*, there was general agreement on the need to give continued support to the United Nations, to the resolution concerning intervention in the Congo, to the Secretary-General, and to the course pursued by the United States in the Security Council during the period just prior to the meeting of the Interparliamentary Group.[61]

In the month following this meeting of the Interparliamentary Group came the sixth annual meeting of another Canadian–United States body. This was the Committee on Trade and Economic Affairs. The conferees from Canada included the Ministers of Finance, Trade, National Revenue, and Agriculture. For the United States the Secretaries of State, Treasury, Interior, Agriculture, and Commerce participated, also the Undersecretary of State for Economic Affairs. Topics reported to have been under discussion included the general wheat surplus, the recession, the balance-of-payments difficulties facing each government, and the tax advantage that Canada was reported to have been giving to Canadian companies but not to Canadian subsidiaries of American companies.[62]

In the every-day relations between the two countries it is inevitable that there will arise, with relative frequency, claims of the nationals or firms of one country against the federal government of the other country. There would therefore seem to be merit in the suggestion recently made by Professor (now Judge) Philip Jessup that there be a treaty establishing a permanent international commission for the handling of such cases. There might, if this were desired, be a requirement that preliminary recourse must have been had to the United States Court of Claims or the Exchequer Court of Canada.

[61] *Canada–United States Interparliamentary Group*, 87th Cong., 1st Sess. (1961), Senate Doc. 27, 6.
[62] *New York Times*, March 14, 1961, 8.

In more important cases, it was suggested, there might be appeal to the International Court of Justice from the claims tribunal's awards.[63] This would indeed appear to be a constructive step toward routine applications of the international law of responsibility. It would also serve to minimize the traditional rule of the law of nations concerning sovereign immunity.

Such an international claims machinery, not on an *ad hoc* basis, but on a continuing one, would be an evidence of political maturity and belief in the rule of law. It would seem desirable, in any case, to have between the two countries something more committal than the old Advancement-of-Peace Treaty for commissions of inquiry, made with Great Britain nearly a half century ago and inherited by Canada.

The mere number of treaties in force between Canada and the United States does not necessarily indicate adequacy of arrangements for the application of principles and the normal growth of the law. In this direction, however, would seem to lie the possibility of much improvement. To achieve it will require a spirit of accommodation and of striving for understanding. Not merely idealism, or a common peril, but rational estimation of mutual advantage may provide adequate motivation. In this spirit a Congressional Committee, reporting in 1958, said in part:

United States–Canadian relations . . . are not a one-way street. If the United States has at times acted arbitrarily and unilaterally, so has Canada. If the United States has taken economic action which infringes on Canadian interests, so has Canada infringed on United States interests. If the United States has initiated tariff and tax actions which are unfair, so has Canada.

. . . .

Canadian and United States interdependence demands a new category of relationship. . . . The concept to be realized in the best interests of both countries is that of free and powerful nations of different background and capabilities, united through a basic agreement in values and aspirations, and voluntarily joined in enterprises, domestic and foreign, calculated to strengthen the chances for a world reflecting their common values.[64]

---

[63] Jessup, *op. cit.*, 114. See also, for views on the desirability of having international law govern in international relations, J. T. Thorson (President of the Exchequer Court of Canada), "A New Concept of the Rule of Law," *Can. Bar. Rev.*, vol. 38 (1960), 238-257.

[64] *Report of the Special Study Mission to Canada* (Hays-Coffin Report), 85th Cong., 2nd Sess. (1958), Rept. No. 1766, 1, 15.

Greater and more effective effort for the understanding and further development of international law would seem to be entirely consistent with the view that "many of the issues which arise in Canada–United States relations can only be understood from the perspective of what is essentially a basic Canadian decision to maintain a distinct political entity."[65]

[65] Brecher and Reisman, *op. cit.*, 6.

2

Boundary Waters Problems
in the East

G. V. La Forest

"A river," said Mr. Justice Holmes, "is more than an amenity, it is a treasure."[1] This truth, which applies to other bodies of water, has long been known. Most of the great civilizations of the world are associated with a river—the Tiber, the Rhine, the Seine, the Thames in Europe, and on this continent the Mississippi and the St. Lawrence. Rivers have from earliest times been used for domestic and sanitation purposes, for fishing, for navigation, and later for irrigation and for operating mills. But it was left to modern technology to unlock even greater riches from waters. Traditional uses have been vastly expanded and new uses such as hydroelectric power have been developed. But modern technology is not an unmixed blessing. A use of water for one purpose is often inconsistent with its use for another purpose. Thus diversion for irrigation and other uses may seriously diminish or exhaust the flow downstream. And pollution from sewage and industrial waste has become a most serious problem.

There then arises the necessity of selecting the most profitable uses of waters, a matter made all the more difficult because the necessary engineering work is costly. All this raises sufficiently complex difficulties where a body of water is wholly within one country. But these are greatly multiplied where more than one state is involved; particularly federal states like Canada and the United States where local interests may have views opposed to those of the general government, as witness the present controversy between the Government of British Columbia and the Canadian Government now that the Columbia River Treaty has been signed.

Even a fleeting look at the map of North America reveals how important the settlement of conflicting interests regarding interna-

[1] *New Jersey v. New York et al.*, 283 U.S. 336, 342 (1931).

tional waters is to Canada–United States relations. Of the 3,500 mile boundary extending from Passamaquoddy Bay on the Atlantic Ocean to the Strait of Juan de Fuca on the Pacific, at least 2,000 miles consist of waters. Most of these are located on the eastern half of the continent, the area with which I am concerned, and include the Great Lakes–St. Lawrence River system, by far the largest fresh-water system in the world. Add to these the many rivers crossing the boundary and one begins to visualize the extent and variety of the problems that may arise.

I. THE SETTLEMENT OF THE BOUNDARY[2]

From the founding of the United States, boundary and trans-boundary waters have loomed large in Canadian-American treaty relations. For the first hundred years or so the problems were closely associated with the settlement of the boundary. For, despite the optimism revealed by the words introducing the boundaries of the United States in the Definitive Treaty of Peace of 1783—"And that all disputes which might arise in future, on the subject of the boundaries of the said United States may be prevented"—disputes regarding the boundary began to arise almost immediately after the ratification of the treaty. This resulted from the fact that many of the topographical features relied on in the description of the bound-aries either did not exist or there was disagreement as to where they were. Thus the St. Croix River was referred to in describing the point from which the boundary line began and as forming part of the boundary, but there was no river then commonly known as the St. Croix and there were two separate streams falling in the Bay of Fundy, the Magaguadavic and the Scoudiac, that might possibly fit the description. The northwesternmost head of the Connecticut River was equally difficult to locate, and there were numerous diffi-culties of a similar nature.

The device of referring these problems to commissions was early adopted. The Jay Treaty of 1794 provided that the St. Croix dis-pute be referred to the final decision of commissioners, one to be named by the British sovereign, one by the President of the United States, and the two to appoint a third. Similarly, under the Treaty

[2] See Moore, *Int. Arb.*, I, chaps. 1-6.

of Ghent ending the War of 1812, four different groups of commissioners were appointed to decide upon the ownership of the islands in the Bay of Fundy and to determine the boundary from the source of the St. Croix to the Lake of the Woods.

The commissioners arrived at their decisions by a close examination of old maps and historical documents and surveys and investigations on the scene, and compromised on matters where information was missing. Sometimes they worked in a most amicable fashion. Thus Mr. Sullivan, the agent of the United States before the St. Croix Commission, commented that "The whole business has been proceeded upon with great ease, candor and good humor."[3] But at other times, as for example during the settlement of the boundary from the source of the St. Croix to the St. Lawrence, the arguments were characterized by not a little acrimony. Indeed this particular boundary and that from Lake Huron to the Lake of the Woods were not settled until the Ashburton-Webster Treaty of 1842. These disputes over land and water boundaries continued into this century, ending with the final settlement of the water boundary in Passamaquoddy Bay.[4] Apart from their intrinsic importance they provided both parties with invaluable experience in negotiated settlements.

II. Freedom of Navigation[5]

In addition to the determination of the boundaries, the period extending from the founding of the United States until the twentieth century saw the making of numerous treaty provisions affecting the navigation of boundary waters. These were often arrived at to facilitate the making of a decision on the boundary. The first of these provisions appears in the Treaty of Paris itself, which provided that the Mississippi, then thought to have its source near the international boundary, should be free and open to British subjects and American citizens. Shortly afterwards the Jay Treaty of 1794 provided in Article III that the same persons and Indians on either side of the boundary might navigate all the lakes, rivers, and streams of either country, but the bulk of this treaty expired in 1807. Other agreements became permanent. Thus the Ashburton-Webster Treaty

---

[3] *Ibid.*, 17, citing Amory's *Life of Sullivan*, I, 325.
[4] TS 551, 720.
[5] See Moore, *op. cit.*, chaps. 1-6.

provides in Article II that all water communications and portages from Lake Superior to Pigeon River shall be free and open to the use of citizens and subjects of both nations. A similar arrangement is made in this treaty regarding the channels in the St. Lawrence River on both sides of the Long Sault Islands and Barnhart Island, the channels in the Detroit River on both sides of the Island Bois Blanc and between that island and the Canadian-American shores, and all the channels and passages between the islands lying near the junction of the River St. Clair with Lake St. Clair. So, too, under Article III the St. John River where it forms the boundary between New Brunswick and Maine became free and open for navigation, and in addition the unusual provision is made that forest and agricultural produce grown in parts of Maine watered by the river or its tributaries are to have free access on the river to the seaport at its mouth and while within New Brunswick such produce is to be treated as if it were New Brunswick produce; similar treatment is accorded in Maine to Canadian produce from the upper St. John. Then followed the Reciprocity Treaty of 1854 giving American citizens freedom of navigation on the St. Lawrence River and canals, subject, however, to the right of the British Government to suspend the privilege. This power of suspension does not appear in the Treaty of Washington, 1871, which now governs the matter. That treaty provides that the navigation of the river is made perpetually free and open for the purposes of commerce to the citizens of the United States, subject to any laws and regulations not inconsistent with such privilege of free navigation. Under another Article the British Government engaged to urge upon the Canadian Government to secure to Americans the use of the Welland, St. Lawrence, and other Canadian canals on terms of equality with Canadians; and the United States agreed to give British subjects the use on terms of equality with Americans of the St. Clair Flats canal and to urge on the state governments to secure to British subjects the use of state canals connected with boundary and trans-boundary waters.

The meaning of "free and open" has given rise to some differences of opinion. The matter was raised before the International Joint Commission in the St. Lawrence River Power Company reference in 1918.[6] Counsel for the United States argued that it was a sufficient

[6] Chirokaikan Joseph Chacko, *The International Joint Commission between the United States and the Dominion of Canada* (New York, 1932), 191 ff.

compliance with this clause in Article VII of the Ashburton-Webster Treaty that both parties are treated equally; there was no obligation to keep the waters open perpetually. But as counsel for Canada pointed out, this is in effect to suggest that the words can mean equality of non-user which, if it may be said to be consistent with the word "free," is certainly an odd meaning to attach to "open." However, as the commission indicated, the words "free and open" permit reasonable interference with navigation. And though there has been some conflict of opinion on the point in Canadian cases,[7] Canada and the United States have, in connection with the St. Lawrence Seaway, acted on the basis that tolls may be charged for use of improvements so long as the citizens of both countries are given equal treatment.

III. The Boundary Waters Treaty of 1909 and the International Joint Commission[8]

Up to the twentieth century, then, boundary waters disputes between Canada and the United States centered largely on the actual location of the boundaries and problems of navigation. In this century, while problems respecting navigation continued, especially on the St. Lawrence, many others have arisen from the new uses of waters made possible by modern technology, particularly hydroelectric developments. But the problems of this century may also be contrasted with earlier disputes in the manner in which they are solved. Earlier disputes had been left to be settled by *ad hoc* com-

[7] Lamont, J. (Cannon, J. concurring) in *Arrow River and Tributaries Slide & Boom Co. v. Pigeon River Co.*, [1932] S.C.R. 495, held tolls could not be imposed under the words, but Anglin, C.J.C., held as had Wright, J., in the court below, [1931] 1 D.L.R. 260, that the treaty did not prevent the imposition of tolls applying equally to citizens of both countries. Mullock, C.J.O., expresses a view similar to Lamont, J.'s in *Rainy River Boom Corp. v. Rainy River Lumber Co.*, (1912) 6 D.L.R. 401. In the United States, the Supreme Court has held that tolls may be valid under the treaty if reasonable and nondiscriminating; see *Pigeon River Improvement, Slide & Boom Co. v. Charles W. Cox*, 291 U.S. 138, 158 (1931).

[8] See Chacko, *op. cit.*, 72 ff.; L. M. Bloomfield and Gerald F. Fitzgerald, *Boundary Waters Problems of Canada and the United States (The International Joint Commission 1912-1958)* (Toronto, 1958), 9-14; Jacob Austin, "Canada-United States Practice and Theory Respecting the International Law of International Rivers: A Study of the History and Influence of the Harmon Doctrine," *Can. Bar. Rev.*, vol. 37 (1959), 393, 417-423; Robert A. MacKay, "The International Joint Commission between the United States and Canada," *Am. Jour. Int. Law*, vol. 22 (1928), 292; see also Clyde Eagleton, "Use of the Waters of International Rivers," *Can. Bar Rev.*, vol. 33 (1955), 1018; Robert D. Scott, "The Canadian-American Boundary Waters Treaty: Why Article II?," *Can. Bar Rev.*, vol. 36 (1958), 511.

missions and the give and take of separate treaty negotiations. These methods had the obvious disadvantage that extrinsic political considerations might sometimes have more weight than matters immediately relevant to a controversy. This disadvantage has been obviated in this century by the establishment of a permanent body for the settlement of disputes, the International Joint Commission.

The idea that there should be an international organization having jurisdiction over international streams took root at an Irrigation Congress held at Denver, Colorado, in 1894. The congress was convened by the United States and was attended by representatives of the United States, Canada, and Mexico. The Canadian delegate, Colonel J. S. Dennis, introduced a resolution urging on the United States "the appointment of an international commission to act in conjunction with the authorities of Mexico and Canada in adjudicating the conflicting rights which have arisen, or may hereafter arise, on streams of an international character." The resolution was unanimously adopted by the congress and was followed by a similar resolution at the Fourth Annual Session of the International Irrigation Congress held the next year at Albuquerque, New Mexico. Shortly afterwards, Canada informed the American authorities that it would be glad to co-operate with the United States and Mexico in the establishment of an international commission for regulating streams flowing from one country to the other, but the American authorities were not prepared to act at the time.

In 1902, however, the United States passed a Rivers and Harbors Act under which the President was requested to invite the British Government to join in the formation of an international commission to be composed of three members from the United States and three representing Canada to investigate and report on the conditions and uses of waters adjacent to the boundary, the maintenance and regulation of suitable levels therein, and the effect on the shores and navigation from the diversion of these waters, and to make suitable recommendations thereon. The American commissioners were appointed the same year, but the Canadian commissioners were not named until 1905. This International Waterways Commission made several valuable reports, but it was a purely investigative body and was not empowered to act upon or enforce its decisions. This prompted the Commission in 1906, and again in 1907, to recommend the creation of a permanent commission with power to supervise and enforce decisions and rules. The recommendation came at a psychological moment. A controversy concerning the Lake of the Woods had been pending since 1888 and there were other disputes relating to the St. Mary and Milk rivers. Consequently negotiations began in 1907 and culminated in the Boundary Waters Treaty, 1909.

The Boundary Waters Treaty, 1909, is by far the most important of the many treaties respecting boundary and trans-boundary waters of Canada and the United States. Not only does it establish the International Joint Commission, a body possessing wide judicial, investigative, and administrative powers; it adopts a number of fundamental principles regulating international waters. Thus Article I provides that boundary waters (defined by the preliminary Article as "waters from main shore to main shore of the lakes and rivers and connecting waterways . . . along which the international boundary . . . passes"), canals connecting boundary waters and Lake Michigan shall forever continue to be free and open for the purposes of commerce to the inhabitants of both countries, subject to the laws of each country within its territory not inconsistent with the privilege of navigation and applying without discrimination to the inhabitants of both countries. It is further provided by Article VIII that each country on its own side has equal and similar rights to the boundary waters. But the following order of precedence must be observed in the use of these waters: (1) uses for domestic and sanitary purposes; (2) uses for navigation; and (3) uses for power and irrigation. As to waters crossing the boundary, Article II adopts the Harmon Doctrine by providing that each contracting party has exclusive jurisdiction and control over waters on its own side which in their natural channels would flow across the boundary or into boundary waters, and so may make any interference with such waters; but it further provides that persons injured by such interference on the other side of the line shall have the same rights and remedies as if the injury occurred in the country where the interference took place. Further, the exclusive jurisdiction mentioned in Article II would appear to be subject to the provision in Article IV that boundary waters and waters flowing across the boundary shall not be polluted to the injury of health or property on the other side. Other principles are directly connected with the powers of the International Joint Commission, to which we must now turn.

The International Joint Commission is composed of six commissioners, three from Canada and three from the United States, each national section having its own chairman and secretary. It has power to make rules governing its procedure, and in doing so it has adopted to a considerable extent procedures followed in the courts of law. A majority has the power to render a decision, but if the Commission is equally divided each section reports to its own government. But when the Commission gives a decision in the exercise of its judicial powers, it is binding on both countries.

No similar organization possesses such broad powers as the Commission. Under Article III of the Boundary Waters Treaty it is agreed that, in the absence of special agreement between the parties, no uses, obstructions or diversions of boundary waters affecting the natural level or flow of boundary waters on the other side of the line shall thenceforth be made except by the authority of the United States or Canada within their respective jurisdictions and with the approval of the Commission. This provision does not, however, apply to the governmental works of either government on its own side of the line for the benefit of commerce and navigation that do not materially affect the level or flow of boundary waters on the other side, nor does it apply to the ordinary use of such waters for domestic and sanitary purposes. Article IV provides that in the absence of special agreement between them, neither party to the treaty will permit the construction or maintenance on its side of the boundary of remedial or protective works, dams, or other obstructions in waters flowing from boundary waters or in waters at a lower level than the boundary in rivers flowing across the boundary that have the effect of raising the natural level of waters on the other side of the boundary, except with the approval of the Commission. Article VIII gives the Commission important discretionary powers: the power to suspend, in the cases of temporary diversion, the equality of rights of each contracting party on its own side of the boundary in the use of boundary waters; and the power to give approvals conditional on the construction of remedial or protective works and for the protection and indemnity against injury to interests on either side of the boundary. Again, where the elevation of the natural level of waters results on one side of the boundary from the construction of any obstruction in boundary waters or waters flowing therefrom or waters below the boundary in rivers flowing across the boundary, the Commission must require as a condition of approval that adequate provision be made for the protection and indemnity of all interests on the other side.

In exercising the powers just enumerated, the Commission is in effect a final court. Only the agreement of both countries can override its decision. In addition to these judicial powers, Article IX gives the Commission broad investigative powers. It provides that both governments agree to refer to the Commission any matters of difference involving rights, obligations, or interests of either country in relation to the other or its inhabitants along the frontier, and the Commission is authorized to examine and report thereon, but such reports are merely recommendations; they are in no way arbitral awards. While the Article permits references contrary to the desires of either government, in practice all references have been desired by both governments. Under Article X any other matter may be referred jointly to arbitration by the Commission, but the provision has never been used. Finally, the Commission has special powers relating to particular waters under Article V and under the Lake of the Woods Treaty, 1925, the Rainy Lake Convention, 1938, and the Niagara River Diversion Treaty, 1950.

The Commission has interpreted the treaty in a very flexible manner. Thus it sometimes retains jurisdiction after giving its approval to works to ensure that the conditions it has laid down are followed. Again, it often appoints boards to study technical questions or to supervise works it has approved in order that the conditions it has laid down are followed, and in the latter case, it sometimes provides for appeals to the Commission.

Since its establishment the Commission has had over seventy matters referred to it, and it has proved to be a strong and flexible instrument for the settlement of international disputes. In performing its judicial functions it has, in relation to matters on the eastern side of the continent, been concerned with such matters as booms on the Rainy River, a bridge across the Niagara, numerous dams, fishways on the St. Croix, dredging a channel in the St. Clair, diversions from boundary waters, protection of navigation, power works, and weirs at Massena, New York. Under its investigative powers, it has examined such matters as the apportionment of waters, dams, drainage, diversions of upstream waters in trans-boundary rivers, pollution, and the resources of the St. Lawrence, St. John, and St. Croix rivers.

Some of the matters have been of the highest importance and of the utmost complexity. Thus its study of the pollution of boundary waters is the most extensive bacteriological examination of waters ever made. It has also played a vital role in the development of the St. Lawrence Seaway, one of the most remarkable navigation and power projects ever attempted. And it recently completed an extensive investigation of a gigantic project for harnessing the tides in the Passamaquoddy Bay area. Yet this great international body has also found time to deal with such minor problems as that raised by a farmer who had constructed a small dam on the St. John River between Quebec and Maine in ignorance of the requirements of the treaty.

The transcendent importance of the Commission in Canadian-American relations may perhaps best be seen by a consideration of three of the most important boundary waters problems of the eastern part of the continent, the Chicago Diversion, a dispute not involving the Commission, and the St. Lawrence Seaway Project and the Passamaquoddy tidal project, in which the Commission is closely involved.

IV. THE CHICAGO DIVERSION[9]

The controversy known as the Chicago Diversion is a by-product of Chicago's rapid development as one of the world's great cities. It arose out of the fact that Chicago used Lake Michigan for two inconsistent purposes: as a place to dispose of its sewage and as a source of water for drinking purposes. The inevitable result was a serious health problem. To remedy the situation it was decided to build a drainage canal to withdraw from Lake Michigan sufficient water to dilute the sewage and carry it to the Mississippi River. Accordingly, the Sanitary District of Chicago was established by the Illinois Legislature in 1889, and the canal was opened in 1900. In 1899 the United States Congress took action in the matter by passing an act prohibiting obstructions to navigable waters except with the authorization of the Secretary of War. In 1901 the Secretary of War authorized the Sanitary District to divert from Lake Michigan 4,167 cubic feet per second but the Sanitary District, acting under the

[9] See H. A. Smith, "The Chicago Diversion," *Can. Bar Rev.*, vol. 8 (1930), 330; James Simsarian, "The Diversion of Waters Affecting the United States and Canada," *Am. Jour. Int. Law*, vol. 32 (1938), 488; Austin, *loc. cit.*

Illinois legislation, did not abide by this limitation and diverted close to 10,000 cubic feet per second. The importance attached to this action by Canada can be seen from the fact that the diversion was believed to reduce the level of the Great Lakes and the St. Lawrence River by over four inches. Such a lowering of the water level could result in a serious hazard to navigation and tend to nullify the benefits of improvements to navigation made by Canada at great cost. The diversion was also capable of causing extensive losses of potential hydroelectric power on the St. Lawrence and detracting from the scenic grandeur of Niagara Falls.

At first Canada appears to have had rather uncertain views on the diversion. In 1906 the International Waterways Commission recommended that Chicago be permitted to withdraw 10,000 cubic feet per second. However, in 1912 Canada argued before the Secretary of War against an application by the Sanitary District for an increased withdrawal, and thereafter it continued to protest that the action was contrary to international law. The United States has never admitted that the diversion was in violation of international law, but it took steps at an early date to prevent the contravention of American federal law.

In 1913 it took action in the Federal District Court of Chicago against the Sanitary District, but it was not until 1923 that a decree enjoining the Sanitary District from withdrawing more than 4,167 cubic feet per second was entered, and a further delay of two years took place before the Supreme Court of the United States affirmed this decree.[10] But no sooner had this been done than the Secretary of War granted a permit for the withdrawal of 8,500 cubic feet per second until December 31, 1929, provided sewage works were built to allow a gradual reduction in the diversion after 1929.

Canada was not alone in being disturbed by Chicago's action. In 1906 Missouri had claimed before the Supreme Court of the United States that the Mississippi River was being polluted by the sewage, but the Court dismissed the claim on the ground that the project did not have that result.[11] But a successful action was finally brought in 1922 by those states (Wisconsin, New York, Pennsylvania, Ohio, Michigan, Indiana, and Minnesota) which, like Canada, suffered from the lowering of the level of the Great Lakes. By its decision of

[10] *Sanitary District of Chicago v. United States*, 266 U.S. 405 (1925).
[11] *Missouri v. Illinois*, 202 U.S. 598 (1906).

1929, the Supreme Court enjoined the diversion and ordered it to be reduced in several stages to not more than 1,500 cubic feet by the end of 1938.[12] There the matter has remained, but recent events indicate that the controversy is still very much alive.[13]

The question wh ther the diversion was contrary to international law raises considerable difficulties. It is excluded from the operation of the Boundary Waters Treaty by the provision exempting existing situations. Canada has maintained that the diversion was contrary to international law on the grounds that boundary waters cannot be reduced without consent, that it interferes with Canada's rights of navigation under the Ashburton-Webster Treaty and the Treaty of Washington, and that no permanent diversion should be permitted from a watershed naturally tributary to waters forming the boundary. The United States has never agreed with the Canadian position. Whatever the correct view may be, there seems little doubt that controversies of this kind are less likely to cause strained relations when dealt with through the instrumentality of the International Joint Commission.

v. THE ST. LAWRENCE SEAWAY AND POWER DEVELOPMENT[14]

One of the best examples of the ability of Canada and the United States to co-operate with each other, despite legal and technical difficulties, and the vital role played by the International Joint Commission in achieving this co-operation is the development of the St.

[12] *Wisconsin et al. v. Illinois et al.*, 278 U.S. 367 (1929).

[13] In 1954 President Eisenhower vetoed a bill which would have permitted an additional diversion of 1,000 c.f.s.; 100 *Cong. Rec.* 15,569; and a similar bill was vetoed in 1956; 102 *Cong. Rec.* 15,304. In both instances Canada had lodged protests against the bills involved. For later Congressional consideration of the matter, see *Water Diversion from Lake Michigan*, Hearings before a Subcommittee of the Committee on Public Works, United States Senate, 86th Cong., 1st Sess. (1959).

Action has also been commenced in the Supreme Court for a reopening and amendment of the decree of April 21, 1930, 281 U.S. 696; *Wisconsin et al. v. Illinois et al., Michigan v. Illinois et al., New York v. Illinois et al.*, 358 U.S. 914 (1958), 359 U.S. 902 (1959). The petitions have been referred to a special master, 361, U.S. 950 (1960), and the United States granted permission to intervene, 362 U.S. 957 (1960).

[14] See Maxwell Cohen and Gilbert Nadeau, "The Legal Framework of the St. Lawrence Seaway" (1959), *U. of Illinois Law Forum*, vol. 1959, 29; Gen. A.G.L. McNaughton, "The Development of the International Section of the St. Lawrence River for Navigation and Power" (an address to the Royal Canadian Institute, Toronto, March 4, 1961, mimeographed).

Lawrence Seaway. The St. Lawrence River and Great Lakes system form a highway leading into the heart of the continent. The river has always been navigable up to the City of Quebec for the largest ocean-going vessels, but above Quebec the channels were originally restricted to a depth of about ten feet. However, as a result of a policy of improving navigation pursued by succeeding Canadian governments from the days of New France onward (and particularly by the Federal Government), the channels had been dredged to a depth of about thirty-five feet up to Montreal, a thousand miles from the sea. Above Montreal Canada had by 1900 completed a series of canals giving access to the upper St. Lawrence and Lake Ontario, but navigation was restricted to a fourteen-foot draft.

At the other end of the system, the United States had improved the Great Lakes connecting channels above Lake Erie to provide navigation up to twenty-five feet in depth. The large lake vessels were permitted to navigate still further with the opening by Canada in 1932 of the present Welland Canal (having a channel of twenty-five feet and locks thirty feet in depth) and the creation by the United States of a channel of twenty-five feet from Lake Ontario to Ogdensburg-Prescott. Thus, by the action of both countries each on its own side a substantial part of the St. Lawrence–Great Lakes system had been developed to provide for deep navigation, but the fourteen-foot canal system from Montreal through the international section of the river now created a bottleneck. The deepening and broadening of this part of the river was all that was necessary to provide an uninterrupted highway for large lake and ocean vessels.

Strong pressure to have the bottleneck removed by the construction of a deep waterway through the remaining section of the St. Lawrence began to emanate from the American Midwest and the Canadian Prairie provinces. The inhabitants of these regions saw in the project an outlet for their products at a considerable reduction in cost and, on the American side, a remedy to the inadequate railway facilities. But the project raised difficulties of great magnitude. In the first place, powerful rail and shipping interests in both countries opposed the Seaway. In the United States, New York, Buffalo, Baltimore, and Philadelphia feared the diversion of American traffic to Canadian ports. In Canada, Montreal saw its position as the major eastern Canadian port challenged. There were even sections of Manitoba and Saskatchewan that saw in the Hudson's Bay route a

preferable outlet for the western provinces. To complicate the matter
the project was not economically feasible unless accompanied by concurrent development of hydroelectric power; but for a considerable
period there was an adequate supply of power in Quebec and Ontario, and there were fears in those provinces that the navigation
costs would be absorbed by the power developed. And, of course,
other present and potential water uses—domestic, sanitary, flood control—to say nothing of the varying riparian and other interests along
the river, had to be protected or indemnified. Thus when the project
was finally carried out, some 6,000 persons in Ontario and about 1,500
in New York State had to be moved. All these problems, complex
as they were, were multiplied by the fact that close co-operation was
required not only on the international plane but also with the provinces of Ontario and Quebec and the state of New York, all of which
were vitally concerned.

To obtain an impartial study, the United States and Canada in
1920 asked the International Joint Commission, under Article IX in
the Boundary Waters Treaty, to make a comprehensive investigation
of the whole matter: the improvements necessary to make deep draft
navigations possible between Montreal and Lake Ontario independently of, and in conjunction with, power development; the estimated
cost, and the apportionment of capital costs and maintenance between
the two countries; methods of control; the traffic likely to be carried;
and the economic impact of the project in both countries. At about
the same time the preparation of actual plans for the proposed project
was referred to a Board of Engineers.

The Commission reported on December 19, 1921, recommending
that Canada and the United States should enter a treaty for a scheme
of improvement between Montreal and Lake Ontario and that further engineering studies be made on the basis of the plans presented
by the Board of Engineers. The costs of the project, it was recommended, should be apportioned, in so far as navigation works were
concerned, between the two countries on the basis of the benefit
derived by each country (the Welland Canal being credited to
Canada) and as regards power, the cost and maintenance should be
borne by the country in which a plant was situated and that country
should also own the power.

In May, 1922, the United States Government advised the Canadian Government that it would be happy to negotiate a treaty on the

basis of the Commission's report. Canada replied in January, 1924, calling attention to the fact that the Commission had recommended further technical studies. It was not until July 18, 1932, that the St. Lawrence Deep Waterways Treaty was signed to provide for the construction of the seaway and incidental water power development. But the treaty was never ratified; it was not until March, 1934, that it came up for a vote in the United States Senate, when it failed to obtain the two-thirds majority required by the Constitution.

Little action on the project took place during the depression years. In 1938, however, the United States made new proposals to Canada, but Ontario and Quebec were reluctant to proceed with the power projects envisioned by the proposals until there was assurance that the market would be able to absorb the power. This situation soon changed with Canada's immediate involvement in the Second World War in 1939, at which time the desirability of the project from the point of view of defense also became evident. As a result an inter-governmental agreement was entered into between Canada and the United States providing for the joint development of the Great Lakes–St. Lawrence Seaway and settling other outstanding questions such as the Chicago Diversion. Since such an "Executive Agreement" requires only a simple majority of both houses of the United States Congress, as compared with the two-thirds majority needed to approve a treaty in the Senate, it was expected that sufficient congressional support would be available to implement the project. But it was again opposed by important United States shipping and railway interests along the Atlantic seaboard, and despite many attempts all during the 1940's, the Agreement failed to obtain the necessary congressional approval.

If the seaway was to be constructed a method had to be found that did not require the co-operation of the United States Congress. The one method was for Canada to build it on its own on the Canadian side of the line, and this it could do without further authorization even in boundary waters by virtue of Article III of the Boundary Waters Treaty. Canada was now prepared to take this step; for since it had at last accepted the principle of charging tolls for use of the seaway for the purpose of liquidating capital expenditure and maintenance, it was no longer as important who should bear the capital cost. The power development could be separated from the navigation project; for the demand for power in New York and Ontario was so great that these authorities were willing to proceed with the power development alone. Here again congressional approval would not be required, for under Article III of the Boundary Waters Treaty these works could be undertaken with the consent of the Canadian and American governments and the International Joint Commission.

Canada took the first step towards implementing this policy in December, 1951, by entering into an agreement with Ontario providing for the construction of the seaway by Canada and for the development of power in the international section of the St. Lawrence by the Ontario Hydroelectric Power Commission on the Canadian side and by an entity to be designated by the United States on the American side. The necessary legislation to implement the agreement was enacted in 1952 by the Canadian Parliament and the Ontario legislature.

Before this legislation was enacted, Prime Minister St. Laurent had already proposed to President Truman that both governments should apply to the International Joint Commission to approve the development of power each on its own side by Ontario and by an entity to be named by the United States, and that Canada should build the navigation works entirely on the Canadian side, not only in the Canadian section of the river but also in the international section. President Truman agreed to the application to the International Joint Commission, but, pending approval by the Commission, he reserved the right to make a last attempt to induce Congress to approve the 1941 Executive Agreement; but this attempt failed. Thereupon, pursuant to an exchange of notes of June 30, 1952, incorporating the proposal made by Mr. St. Laurent, the two governments submitted an application to the Commission for authority to construct the power project in the international section of the St. Lawrence. The Commission gave its approval on October 29, 1952.

All necessary international and Canadian authorization had now been obtained, but there remained one more step to be completed in the United States before the project could begin: the designation of the proper entity to carry out the American share of the power development under American law. This was done on July 15, 1953, when the Federal Power Commission designated the New York State Power Authority, but the action of the commission was challenged by opponents of the project and it was not until June 7, 1954, that the United States Supreme Court upheld the action of the

Federal Power Commission[15] Consequently, the power project did not begin until August 10, 1954.

Now that it was evident that an all-Canadian seaway would be built, the proponents of the project in the United States began to agitate to have the United States proceed with its construction on the American side of the international section of the river. The Wiley-Dondero Bill was introduced for the purpose in 1953 and passed on May 6, 1954, shortly before the Supreme Court decision on the power question. There was now legislative provision for building navigation facilities by each country for the same portion of the river. The problem was solved by an exchange of notes on August 17, 1954, under which the United States agreed to build a canal and locks at Barnhart Island on the American side of the international section and to do the dredging required in the Thousand Islands' section. Canada agreed to build a lock and canal near Iroquois, Ontario, in the international section and to complete the necessary dredging between Cornwall and Montreal in Canada, but Canada reserved the right to build a canal system on the Canadian side opposite Barnhart Island whenever the traffic justifies it. After all the maneuvering, work on the seaway and power development of the St. Lawrence could now be started. Though formally consisting of several separate undertakings by the two countries, it is in fact a joint and co-operative venture between two great neighbors.

VI. THE PASSAMAQUODDY TIDAL POWER PROJECT[16]

One of the most intriguing of all the boundary waters[17] problems is the Passamaquoddy tidal power project, or Quoddy as it is often called. Man has long been fascinated by the dream of harnessing the

[15] *Lake Ontario Land Development Assn. v. F.P.C.*, 347 U.S. 1015 (1954).

[16] See International Passamaquoddy Engineering Board, *Report to International Joint Commission on Scope and Cost of an Investigation of Passamaquoddy Tidal Power Project* (Ottawa, Washington, 1950); *Report of the International Joint Commission on an International Passamaquoddy Tidal Power Project* (Ottawa, Washington, 1950); *Investigation of the International Passamaquoddy Tidal Power Project*, a Brochure summarizing the *Report to the International Joint Commission by the International Passamaquoddy Engineering Board* (Ottawa, Washington, 1959); International Passamaquoddy Fisheries Board, *Report to International Joint Commission* (Ottawa, Washington, 1959); *Report of the International Joint Commission on the International Passamaquoddy Tidal Power Project* (Ottawa, Washington, 1961).

[17] Passamaquoddy Bay, it should be noted, is not a "boundary water" within the Boundary Waters Treaty, 1909, for that term applies only to fresh water.

power of the tides. There is no question that this power is enormous and has several intrinsic advantages over river plants: it is predictable for many years and is unaffected by droughts, floods, ice jams, and silting. There is now no doubt either that tidal power may be achieved; the problem is to do so at rates competitive with other means of generating power.

Electric power from the tides can be produced by a flow of water from a higher to a lower level through hydraulic turbines. Two methods have been suggested. Under one method, the one-pool system, water is trapped when coming in at high tide and discharged through turbines into the ocean at low tide, or the water is permitted to enter the pool through turbines at high tide and drained out at low tide. In either case, the one-pool system has the serious disadvantage that it is not able to generate continuous power; it operates for only a fraction of each day. This difficulty has, however, been solved in part by a new type of turbine used in the French prototype tidal power plant now in operation at Rance, France.

The second method is called the two-pool system. It operates by admitting through filling gates water into a pool, the high pool, during the oncoming tide, and permitting it to flow continuously through a power house to a pool kept at a lower level. Thus continuous power is achieved. The amount of power produced varies, of course, in accordance with the difference in levels between the high and low pool. To keep the high pool at the highest possible level its gates are closed shortly after the maximum ocean level is reached. The low pool is kept at the lowest possible level by closing it off from the sea at high tide and permitting it to discharge at low tide the water it has received from the high pool. But since the levels of the two pools vary in accordance with the tidal cycle, an irregular amount of power is produced. This is particularly troublesome since the variation in output follows the gravitational pull of the moon as it passes overhead every 24 hours and 50 minutes, and so is out of phase with the 24-hour solar day and consequently with the normal pattern of daily use of electricity. For this reason some form of auxiliary power is required to supplement tidal power.

To construct a two-pool system successfully two conditions are required. There must be extensive basins capable of storing water during the tidal cycle and, as in all tidal power schemes, there must be a sufficient tidal range (i.e., the difference in water levels between high and low tide). The Quoddy Scheme meets these two demands in extremely favorable form. The first condition is present in the existence of two large natural basins, Passamaquoddy and Cobscook Bay. As to the second, the tidal ranges on the Bay of Fundy, of which Passamaquoddy and Cobscook Bays are arms, are among the highest in the world, reaching an extreme range at the head of the Bay of over 50 feet. The range of the tide at Passamaquoddy and Cobscook Bays varies from a minimum of 11.3 feet at neap tide to 25.7 feet at high tide, averaging 18.1 feet.

The idea of Quoddy originated with Dexter P. Cooper, the famed engineer, who began studying the possibility of harnessing the tides of Passamaquoddy from his home on Campobello in 1920. Cooper drew extensive plans for an international project using Passamaquoddy Bay in New Brunswick and Cobscook Bay in Maine and obtained authorization to construct the works from the Federal Power Commission and the Canadian, New Brunswick, and Maine legislatures. When these authorizations expired in 1929, Cooper, undaunted, turned to the possibility of several all-American schemes using Cobscook Bay as one or two pools and maintained an active interest in the project until his operations were taken over by the United States Government in 1935.

The United States Government began working on the project in that year for two reasons. An optimistic estimate of the cost of the project had been made by a special board set up to investigate the matter by the Administrator of Public Works, and the project provided a means of alleviating the serious unemployment situation in the area. Over $6,000,000 was expended on the project, but the work ended in 1937 when Congress failed to provide further funds.

Two years later a Senate resolution was passed calling for an examination of one-pool and two-pool schemes wholly within the United States, but the Federal Power Commission reported in 1941 that neither project could at that time compete successfully with power potentially available from Maine's rivers and with power produced by modern, efficient steam electric plants. But interest in an international project continued unabated, and as a result Canada and the United States in 1948 asked the International Joint Commission to review all previous plans and reports and to estimate the cost of carrying out a complete study to decide conclusively the engineering and economic feasibility of the project.

During the course of this investigation it was learned that the fisheries interests of New Brunswick were concerned with the effect of the project on the fisheries of the Bay of Fundy. This is hardly surprising. For these fisheries, especially the herring fisheries, are of major importance to the area and the Canadian Biological Board in 1926, and the International Passamaquoddy Fisheries Commission in 1934, had indicated that possible serious adverse effects to the fisheries might result from the project. Accordingly, the International Joint Commission in its report of 1950 recommended that the effect on the fisheries should be studied along with the engineering and economic aspects of the matter.

In 1956 the Commission was requested by both countries to investigate the engineering, fishing, and economic aspects of an international tidal power project in the area. To assist in the investigation the Commission set up the International Passamaquoddy Engineering Board and the International Passamaquoddy Fisheries Board. In its report to the Commission of October, 1959, the Engineering Board made it clear that a tidal power project could be built and operated in the area. It recommended as the most promising of the tidal schemes a two-pool project consisting of Passamaquoddy Bay as the high pool and Cobscook Bay as the low pool. The magnitude of the project can be visualized when one notes that Passamaquoddy Bay is 191, and Cobscook Bay, 41 square miles in area and that it would require nearly 7 miles of rock-filled dams, some portions of which would be in water 125 to 300 feet deep.

Because of the tidal variation only 95,000 kilowatts of the 345,000 kilowatts maximum capacity would be available at all times. The Board therefore studied the available sources of supply to supplement the tidal project and found that the most economic was the development of a hydroelectric development at Rankin Rapids on the St. John River in Maine, using all the available power at that site.

As regards the fisheries, the Fisheries Board reported that while some types of fish would be affected by the project there would be no reduction in the general abundance of the herring population, by far the most important fish, but it would affect the weirs inside the dams. The project provides for remedial measures such as fishways to ensure that it would have only a minor residual effect on the fisheries. It also provides for locks to permit navigation to and from the project area. Navigation conditions would in fact be improved in most of the region.

The engineering and fisheries aspects of the project, therefore, seem reasonably promising. Turning to the economic aspects, two questions required examination: whether there is a sufficient demand for power to warrant construction of the project; and whether it can be produced at competitive rates. As to the first, the Engineering Board concluded that the output of the tidal power project and the Rankin Rapids plant can be absorbed by the growing markets of Maine and New Brunswick. The sole remaining question, therefore, is whether the project can produce power in competition with traditional methods. This is determined by comparing the ratio of annual benefits to annual costs of the project with the same ratio for other methods of generating power. The annual costs include amortization of the initial investment, interest, and the annual cost of maintenance and operation. The initial investment is very large. The tidal project alone would cost $484,000,000 and with the Rankin Rapids Scheme $630,000,000, exclusive of interest. It follows that the rate of interest is a most important factor in considering the economic justification of the project. In the United States the Board assumed the project would be built by the federal authorities at an interest rate of 2½ per cent, and in Canada by the Government of New Brunswick at a rate of 4⅛ per cent. On this basis the Board, assuming an equal division of power output and first costs between Canada and the United States, came to the conclusion that the project, even when combined with the Rankin Rapids project, was not economically justified for Canada since it could produce power by other methods at a smaller annual cost. If built entirely by the United States at an interest rate of 2½ per cent, the tidal project combined with the Rankin Rapids project would be economically justified.

The International Joint Commission submitted its report on the project to the Canadian and American governments on April 10, 1961. It is in general agreement with the report of the Fisheries Board and the engineering aspects of the report of the Engineering Board. But it takes issue with the latter's economic conclusions. Only one major point will be mentioned here. It pointed out that the Engineering Board's report showed that the tidal project, when considered alone, was clearly uneconomic for the United States or Canada. It was only when combined with a development of all the power available at Rankin Rapids that power could be produced by the United States at a lower rate than it could be produced by other means. But this was simply adding the costs and benefits of the uneconomic tidal project to those of the economically feasible Rankin Rapids project, and this, as the Commission asserts, is not a valid representation of the economic worth of the tidal project. The report then examines the tidal project in combination with other auxiliary sources proposed by the Board and concludes, as was already evident from the Board's report, that none of these combinations is economically feasible.

From the foregoing, it seems unlikely that Quoddy will be undertaken for some time to come. This conclusion is fortified by the fact that not only may New Brunswick obtain cheaper power from the St. John River[18] or by the use of thermal plants; there are more promising tidal power possibilities at the head of the Bay of Fundy. But with increasing demands for power, Quoddy may well materialize eventually. If so, it will require the co-operation not only of the Canadian and American governments, but that of New Brunswick and Maine as well, and the chief instrument of co-operation may again be the International Joint Commission.

* * * * *

These have been some of the more important of the many boundary waters problems of the eastern side of the continent. Before concluding mention must be made of the day-to-day co-operation required for giving effect to treaty rights. This may be exemplified on the administrative and operational levels by the co-ordination of activities achieved by the St. Lawrence Seaway Authority of Canada and the St. Lawrence Seaway Development Corporation of the United States during the construction of the seaway. In the legislative field one has only to note the close resemblance between the Canadian and American statutes relating to tolls on the seaway and to the many concurrent provisions relating to navigation in boundary waters.

The co-operative attitude between Canada and the United States, so sedulously fostered by the International Joint Commission, will serve well in the solution of future boundary waters problems. Some

---

[18] For discussions of St. John River power development, see William F. Ryan, "Saint John River Power Development: Some International Law Problems," *U. of New Brunswick Law Jour.*, vol. 11 (1958), 20; Gerald F. Fitzgerald, "Legal Aspects of the Power Development of the Saint John River Basin," *U. of New Brunswick Law Jour.*, vol. 12 (1959), 7.

have already appeared on the horizon. Among these are the full development of the resources of the St. John and St. Croix rivers and later, perhaps, tidal power at Passamaquoddy. The more, but not far, distant future may possibly see the two countries again concerned with boundaries. As the resources of the continental shelf are exploited, it may become necessary to draw a line of demarcation between the jurisdictional areas of the United States and those of Canada.

3

International Water Problems in the West

The Columbia Basin Treaty Between Canada and the United States

Charles E. Martin

The negotiations between Canada and the United States over the Columbia River Systems, and the resulting treaty of 1961,[1] are merely a prolongation of an historic tendency of the two nations to settle their problems amicably, on a basis of mutuality and reciprocity, and through binational bodies adapted to deal with specialized problems, whatever the function. The agencies entrusted with the general oversight of such problems are:

1. The Canadian-American Permanent Joint Board on Defence.
2. The International (Halibut) Fisheries Commission.
3. The International Pacific Salmon Fisheries Commission.
4. The Joint United States–Canadian Committee on Trade and Economic Affairs.
5. The Canadian-American International Joint Commission.

Two observations should be made here. The first is that Canada and the United States have developed the unique and original device of the binational entities to deal with their mutual problems which require both a definition of relations and a settlement of conflicting positions. The second is that the Columbia River Treaty, and the entities which may be set up in pursuance of its provisions, have grown out of the investigations, recommendations, and negotiations carried on or made by the International Joint Commission.

[1] For text of treaty, see Sen. Ex. C, 87th Cong., 1st Sess. (1961); *Dept. of State Bulletin*, vol. 44 (1961), 234-243; Canada, *Parl. Deb.* (Commons), Sess. 1960-61, 1190-1197. The treaty is to come into effect upon exchange of ratifications.

I. The Columbia River Basin and the Treaty Area

Columbia River Basin statistics are almost as staggering as the problems they pose. The river originates in British Columbia, flowing a distance of 480 miles to the Washington border, and thence for 745 miles to the sea. Two of its principal tributaries—the Kootenay and the Pend Oreille rivers, "traverse" the territory of both countries. Several American rivers, notably the Snake and the Willamette, contribute to the Columbia volume on the American side. The "basin" (the area drained by the Columbia and its tributaries) is 259,000 square miles in extent, with 219,500 square miles lying on the American side and 39,500 miles located in Canada.

The province of British Columbia, and the states of Washington, Oregon, Idaho, and Montana, are concerned with, and affected by the provisions of the Treaty. The Treaty defines (Annex B, par. 7) the "Pacific Northwest Area," in measuring the "increase in dependable hydroelectric capacity and the increase in average annual hydroelectric energy, encompassing the 'loads' in the area," as "Oregon, Washington, Idaho, and Montana west of the Continental Divide," but excluding areas served on ratification date by two private power companies.

The Treaty title and its preamble refer respectively to the "cooperative development of the water resources of the Columbia River Basin," and to "the territory of the Columbia River Basin as a part of the territory of both countries," containing "water resources that are capable of contributing greatly to the economic growth and strength and to the general welfare of the two nations."

II. Applicable Legal Rules and Instruments

The legal rules and instruments which apply to the water resources of the Columbia River Basin, or parts of it, are of infinite variety. They originate from and operate on several different levels. They are, in summary, and without detailed enumeration:

1. *Provincial and state law* (laws of the province of British Columbia, and of the states of Washington, Oregon, Idaho, and Montana).

2. *Federal law* (the laws of Canada and the United States).
3. *International regulation.*
   a. *Treaty* (The Boundary Waters Treaty of 1909, which defined three classes of waters, and set up the International Joint Commission which is entrusted with a number of functions connected with the waters so defined).
   b. *International law.* While the law of international rivers is yet in a "twilight zone" of development, certain principles of possible legal settlement have been invoked, or rejected, as the case may be, by both Canada and the United States.

Since both international treaty and law have been appealed to in the controversy between Canada and the United States over the water resources of the Columbia Basin, brief reference will be made to each as a background of conflicting national interests against which the treaty negotiations, both exploratory and final, had to be conducted.

The Boundary Waters Treaty of 1909[2]

This treaty defined three classes of waters:

1. Boundary waters, defined in the preliminary Article, and regulated by Article III. This class of waters, together with the accompanying regulatory provisions, do not apply to the Columbia River Basin problems.

2. Waters on one side flowing through natural channels across the boundary or into boundary waters. By Article II, "exclusive jurisdiction and control over the use and diversion" of all such waters are reserved to the contracting parties and to the state and provincial governments on its own side of the line. Legal remedies are provided against injuries from each diversion identical with such redress as is provided within the territory of the diverting state. The diversions proposed by Canada were of the Kootenay into the Columbia, and of the Columbia into the Fraser.

3. Waters flowing from boundary waters or waters at a lower level than the boundary in rivers crossing the boundary. Dams or works which would raise the natural level on the other side without

[2] TS 548.

the authority the treaty requires are prevented by Article IV. The Libby Dam and Reservoir, urged by the United States, are under this Article.

Looking ahead for a moment, the Columbia River Basin Treaty, if effective, will postpone the proposed diversions under Article II of the 1909 Treaty for sixty years, and will authorize the construction of the Libby Dam and Reservoir.

The International Joint Commission

This important international agency, as already explained, is charged with the performance of a variety of functions. As regards boundary waters and waters flowing from them, the Commission exercises regulatory or judicial functions, with the authority of mandatory decision. In respect of waters crossing boundaries, or waters flowing into boundary waters, the Commission only explores and investigates. Accordingly, controversies between Canada and the United States regarding the waters of the Columbia, under Article II, over diversions having downstream effects, and calling for upstream storage, must be settled on the ministerial or head-of-government levels. Dams or works which would raise the natural level are subject to Commission regulation under Article IV.

Beginning with the Columbia River Reference of 1944, much work of an investigative character was assigned to the International Joint Commission, both during the intervening period of controversy, and during the steps taken by the two governments leading to the negotiation of the Columbia Basin Treaty.

The Law of International Traversing River Systems[3]

International law, as applied to the navigation and jurisdictional problems of boundary waters, is quite simple and fairly settled. Any doubtful questions can readily be settled, by treaty agreement or by arbitration.

In the case of the international traversing stream, rights of jurisdiction and diversion are quite unsettled, and are far from simple. The European river systems which have been regulated by treaty have dealt in the main with rights of navigation. Problems of diver-

[3] For survey and references, see *Legal Aspects of the Use of Systems of International Waters*, Sen. Doc. 118, 85th Cong., 2nd Sess. (1958).

sion have arisen in connection with certain great non-European river systems, such as the Nile, the Indus, and the Columbia and Rio Grande systems. The conflicting interests of the upstream and downstream states seem better resolved by treaty than by unilateral appeals to the several principles of law based on questions of sovereignty and jurisdiction under international law.

The principles of legal settlement which seem to apply most directly to the Columbia River problems are the following:

1. The doctrine of riparian rights, under which a downstream state would receive undiminished the natural flow of the river-course.

2. The territorial sovereignty theory, by which a state claims absolute sovereignty and exclusive jurisdiction and control over river waters and their uses within its borders.

3. The doctrine of appropriation for beneficial use, under which the appropriation first in time is first in right.

4. The doctrine of equitable apportionment, which provides that the benefits of river waters within an area or system be shared equitably between states exercising jurisdiction over the system or area.

Canada, in asserting her jurisdictional rights, rejected the doctrines of riparian rights and of prior appropriation. She rested her case solidly on the territorial sovereignty theory, which she claimed was expressly and unmistakably set forth in the 1909 Treaty. Under this authority, the right unilaterally to make the proposed diversions was fully justified, according to Canadian opinion. While not embracing the doctrine of equitable apportionment with any enthusiasm, if at all, Canada nevertheless claimed the right to make "reasonable" diversions, which, in the light of the alternatives open to Canada, were regarded as consistent with this principle.

The United States relied upon the doctrine of appropriation as applicable to the region. The proposed diversions would, it was urged, impair and injure rights already established due to downstream plant installations. New construction, both under way and already planned, would be adversely affected. These diversions, it was felt, would be incompatible with the doctrine of equitable apportionment, since the principle did not admit of unilateral determinations of what is reasonable. Slight appeal was made by the United States to the doctrine of riparian rights. To the Canadian charge of rigid American adherence to the theory of territorial sovereignty on former occasions, under the so-called Harmon Doctrine, United States opinion pointed to its recent treaties, the decisions of its courts in interstate cases, and especially the United States–Mexican treaty of 1944[4] as expressly embodying the doctrine of equitable apportionment.

III. Negotiation of the Treaty

Fancy and Friction or Facts and Friendship

The official legal debate, conducted mainly by the chairmen of the respective national sections of the International Joint Commission, found its way into unofficial channels, i.e., the law reviews of the law schools and the journals of bar associations and of international law societies. Negotiation solely on the conflicting national positions of legal rights would doubtless have led to inconclusive results. Reference to an international tribunal, with a resulting decision for one party and against the other, would have destroyed the basis as well as the spirit of the necessary co-operation for shared benefits through treaty arrangements, under the doctrine of equitable apportionment. It became clear that legal haggling had to yield to the investigations, and to some extent, the recommendations of teams of economists and engineers. National policy decisions and dependable international agreements could not be made without expert information and counsel.

The Period of Controversy and Misunderstanding

Joint action between Canada and the United States as regards Columbia River development was authorized under the Columbia River Reference of March 9, 1944. The two governments authorized the International Joint Commission to undertake studies which would be "in the public interest from the points of view of the two Governments . . . ," looking toward the prospect of the co-operative development of the water resources of the Columbia River Basin by the two nations.[5] From the beginning, there was no "meeting of the minds" of the two parties as to the precise meaning of the 1944 Reference, nor of the procedures which it authorized, whether expressly or by implication. Each government had a "case," which it pushed in every available way, and on every operating level.

[4] TS 994.
[5] *Dept. of State Bulletin*, vol. 10 (1945), 270-271.

In April, 1955, General McNaughton, Chairman of the Canadian Section of the Joint Commission, announced Canadian plans to utilize the water resources in the Canadian section of the basin, together with his proposal of three Canadian case studies which might lead to substantial diversions of "surplus" waters from the Kootenay into the Columbia, and from the Columbia into the Fraser. Such diversions, he declared, would not violate the Treaty of 1909 or injure any legally acquired United States right under the treaty. On October 4, 1955, Chairman Len Jordan of the United States Section, issued a general rejoinder.[6] He declared that the proposed diversions would impair existing plants, those under construction, and those already planned and publicly announced; denied that the suggested Canadian studies were within the "Columbia River Reference," and "in the public interest and from the points of view" of both governments; and challenged the accuracy of General McNaughton's predictions of the extent of "surplus" waters. He also referred to the damage such diversion would cause to the Fraser River Salmon Fisheries, as set forth in the report of the International Salmon Fisheries Commission of June 3, 1955[7]

A succession of events, both within and without the ambit of the Reference of 1944, seemed to drive the position of the two governments farther apart. Negotiations by the Joint Commission were for the time being reduced to a stalemate. The Libby Dam project in Montana, proposed by the United States, was rejected by the International Joint Commission. A movement started on the Canadian side to develop water power projects on the Peace River before attempting such development on the Columbia. In 1954 the International River Improvements Act was passed by the Canadian Parliament, which definitely impeded arrangements between provincial governments and foreign corporations for dam construction. Canada suddenly realized and strongly asserted the claims and advantages of her "economic nationalism." This was followed by a stubborn refusal by the United States to understand the causes underlying this new spirit, and by strong American resistance to its possible consequences.

Both Canada and the United States had to make some funda-

[6] For Mr. Jordan's statement, see *ibid.*, vol. 33 (1955), 981-985; this statement contains excerpts from General McNaughton's announcement of April, 1955.

[7] For text of report, see *ibid.*, 985-988.

mental decisions. Canada had already decided either to divert the waters in Canadian territory, or to realize substantial "downstream" benefits for "upstream storage." She must determine which of these alternatives would best serve her interests. And her demands on the United States must not be so extravagant that the "downstream benefit" policy would be a financial liability.

The United States, in order to avoid the possibility of future diversions and to take advantage of Canadian upstream storage providing a regulated downstream flow, had to accept the principle of sharing with Canada the downstream benefits which would be thus afforded.

A change in climate on the head of state and ministerial levels was soon reflected in the International Joint Commission. Canada elected joint Columbia Basin development rather than future diversion of waters. The United States accepted the alternative of paying for downstream benefits. What remained was to get the engineering teams into action, and after their report, to bring the negotiators together to draft a treaty.

The Investigations and Negotiations

To aid it in making valid and dependable recommendations to the two governments, the International Joint Commission set up the International Columbia River Engineering Board. Its studies indicated sites located in the Canadian section of the Columbia Basin where reservoirs could be built to the advantage of both Canada and the United States, and that better uses could be made of existing water resources, for the mutual benefit of both countries, both for the generation of power and for flood control. In March, 1959, the Engineering Board submitted an unusually significant report to the Joint Commission. It laid the foundations for a master plan for the development of Columbia River water resources in Canada. The report was based essentially on engineering and economic considerations, without regard to the fact or effect of the international boundary.

With the report in hand, the governments had to make some fundamental recommendations, and needed adequate information on which to base them. Accordingly, late in January, 1959, the two governments referred the following questions to the International Joint Commission for investigation and report:[8]

1. The benefits which will result from the co-operative use of storage of waters and electrical interconnection within the Columbia River system; and

2. The apportionment between the two countries of such benefits, more particularly in regard to electrical generation and flood control.

On December 29, 1959, the Commission's recommendations on these two questions were submitted to the two governments under the title: "Principles for Determining and Apportioning Benefits from Co-operative Storage of Waters and Electrical Inter-Connection Within the Columbia River System." An impressive array of principles under the headings of "General Principles," "Power Principles," and "Flood Control Principles" were set forth. By Power Principle No. 6, it was recommended that power benefits originating from upstream country storage having a downstream effect should be substantially equal between the two countries. By Flood Control Principle No. 4, the upstream country should be paid one-half of the benefits as measured in Flood Control Principle No. 3, i.e. one-half of the value of the damages prevented.

On February 11, 1960, the direct negotiations between the representatives of Canada and the United States got under way. The Chairman of the Canadian delegation was Mr. E. D. Fulton, Minister of Justice. The United States delegation included Mr. Elmer F. Bennett, Under Secretary of the Interior, Chairman; Mr. Ivan B. White, Deputy Assistant Secretary of State for European Affairs; and Lt. General Emerson C. Itschner, Chief of Engineers of the United States Army. The delegations held nine sessions varying from two to four days. Between sessions engineering and legal teams were constantly at work. It was, during the major part of 1960, a continuous process of consultation and negotiation. The technical data provided by the report of the International Columbia River Engineering Board and the recommended guidelines set up by the International Joint Commission formed the basis and even the substance of the negotiations.

In the earlier stages of the discussions, valuable leadership was provided on the American side by some members of Congress, especially the Senators from the four Northwestern states. A subcom-

[8] See *ibid.*, vol. 40 (1959), 243.

mittee of the Senate Committee on Interior and Insular Affairs, headed by Senator Richard Neuberger, was particularly helpful. Three members of the Senate Foreign Relations Committee from Northwestern states (Senators Mansfield, Morse, and Church) gave constant guidance and encouragement to the negotiations throughout the 1960 period of actual negotiations. Moreover, the United States–Canadian interparliamentary group discussed the several aspects of the Columbia Basin project.[9] The rigid separation of powers principle in the United States yielded in this case to close co-operation, within prudent limits, between the executive and legislative departments.

The details of the treaty must await our examination of its provisions. At this point mention should be made of a guiding principle faithfully observed by the negotiators, i.e., not to prejudge the necessary internal decisions each country must make in the process of treaty implementation. For one thing, the treaty does not specify the agencies to be set up as "operating entities" for the execution of the terms of the treaty. This was left open. For another, the Canadian delegation did not ask for agreements on such implementing decisions as would be properly within the jurisdiction of the Canadian Government.

On September 28, 1960, the two delegations submitted to their respective governments a joint progress report. The provisions of a possible agreement, both in general and special terms, were set forth. The negotiators recommended that the agreed principles should be reduced to treaty form. The report declared:

The United States and Canadian Delegations report that agreement has been reached between them on the basic terms which in their opinion should be included in an agreement for the cooperative development of the water resources of the Columbia River Basin that will operate to the mutual advantage of both countries.

On October 19, 1960, through an exchange of notes, the governments accepted the suggestions of the joint progress report as the basis for the treaty-drafting procedure.[10] The negotiators were urged to have the treaty ready for submission to the governments, if

[9] The Interparliamentary Group has continued its interest in Columbia Basin problems; see its report, Sen. Doc. 27, 87th Cong., 1st Sess. (1961), 5-6.

[10] See statement by President Eisenhower and White House announcement, *Dept. of State Bulletin*, vol. 43 (1960), 831-832.

possible, by the end of 1960. Prime Minister Diefenbaker promised that "public hearings would be held in accordance with the British Columbia Water Act before the recommendations for the construction of reservoirs in Canada were implemented." Such hearings, he declared, would give an opportunity for "discussion of details concerning the precise location of the storages and other related matters."

In the 1960 negotiations, the two delegations avoided purely selfish points of view, and did not advance inflexible positions of national interest. It was clear to them that many more advantages at much less cost would flow from joint development and control than from two competing and often conflicting operations, founded on the unilateral pursuit of rights based on claims of absolute sovereignty and exclusive jurisdiction.

Signature

The treaty was signed at Washington on January 17, 1961. An impressive ceremony included significant public statements by the two heads of governments.[11] For Canada, the instrument was signed by Prime Minister John S. Diefenbaker, Minister of Justice E. D. Fulton, and the Canadian Ambassador to the United States, A. D. P. Heeney. Signing for the United States were President Dwight Eisenhower, Secretary of State Christian A. Herter, and Under Secretary of the Interior Elmer F. Bennett.

IV. The Provisions of the Treaty

This treaty, with its many technical features, and with its involvement in complicated legal, financial, and engineering questions, cannot satisfactorily be reduced to summary form. These technical and complicated problems will increase with the treaty's implementation. All that can now be done is to indicate its more general features, with some reference to the general guide-lines by which technical questions will be decided. There can be no acceptable substitute for the text of the treaty. Consistent and continuing reference must be made to its governing articles. We must, nevertheless, undertake to set forth its principal features.[12]

[11] For an account of the signature ceremonies, see *ibid.*, vol. 44 (1961), 227-228.
[12] On the treaty's provision, see *Columbia River Treaty, Hearing before the Committee on Foreign Relations*, U.S. Senate, 87th Cong., 1st Sess. (1961).

Aims of the treaty. These are stated in the treaty preamble. In brief, they are to secure the joint development of the water resources of the Columbia River Basin, with the purpose of the enjoyment by the two countries and its peoples of the maximum benefits of hydro-electric power and flood control, as well as other advantages.

Dams in Canada. Canada agrees to build three dams for water storage in the Columbia Basin in Canada, within a period of nine years, with a storage capacity of 15.5 million acre-feet of water for increasing the Columbia River water flow. The dams will be located at Arrow Lakes, Duncan Lake (or alternate location), and Mica Creek. These dams are estimated to cost the Canadian Government a total of $345 million, the respective costs, in the order named above, being $72 million; $26 million; and $247 million.

Canadian storage operation. Canada assumes an obligation to operate the new storage so as to yield the maximum flood control and hydroelectric power benefits. Annexes "A" and "B" spell out respectively the principles of Canadian storage operation and the determination of downstream power benefits. Canada will operate the storage facilities under plans worked out and presented by the United States. Canada will also release water for power generation under mutually agreed plans, determined annually.

United States development. The United States will operate its existing hydroelectric facilities, and any additional ones constructed, in such a manner as will make the most effective use of the increased streamflow due to Canadian storage.

Canadian downstream power benefits. Canada is to receive one-half of the downstream power benefits, as determined by the treaty procedure outlined under Article VII and Annex "B." The treaty defines these "downstream power benefits" as "the difference in the hydroelectric power capable of being generated in the United States with and without the use of Canadian storage, determined in advance." Canada may, with American consent, dispose of any unused surplus of its power quota in the United States.

American compensation for flood control. For flood control benefits realized in the United States from Canadian storage, the United

States will pay Canada $64.4 million, spread over a nine-year period. Additional storage due to increased flood control demands will be provided by Canada, her compensation depending on the number of requests for such secondary service. Any loss to Canada of power resulting from additional flood control service will be paid by the United States in electric power.

Kootenay River development: the Libby Dam. The United States is granted an option, within a five-year period from the ratification date, of constructing a dam on the Kootenay River near Libby, Montana, for flood control and other purposes in the United States. Canada agrees to prepare and make available the land in Canada essential for flooding due to dam construction. Specifications are laid down for the maintenance of the water level (not exceeding 2,459 feet at the dam), and for the contingencies of possible United States' failure to exercise the option within the five-year period, and the termination of the treaty before the useful life of the dam. Orders of approval issued by the International Joint Commission regarding the levels of Kootenay Lake under the Boundary Waters Treaty of 1909 shall apply to the American operation of storage.

Water diversions. Neither country may, without the other's consent, evidenced by an exchange of notes, divert, for any other than a consumptive use, any water from its natural channel in a way that alters the flow of any water as it crosses the Canada–United States boundary. Canada has the right, after twenty years, to divert water, not to exceed one and one-half million acre-feet per year, from the Kootenay River into the headwaters of the Columbia River. Should the United States not build the Libby Dam, Canada may divert water from the Kootenay into the Columbia at an agreed maximum flow.

Implementation arrangements: entities within each country. Each country is authorized to designate such entity or entities as it may empower and obligate to formulate and carry out the operating arrangements necessary to implement the treaty. A formidable list of such powers and duties, among those indicated elsewhere in the treaty, are included under Article XIV, Section (2). Secretary of the Interior Udall declared before the Senate Foreign Relations Committee that, on the American side, flood control responsibilities would be assigned to the Army Corps of Engineers, and power responsibilities to the Bonneville Power Administration.

The Permanent Engineering Board. This joint board of four members, two from each country, is to be invested with a variety of expert and technical duties. The principal ones are the keeping of records and making inspections. The aim is to facilitate the settlement of differences between the operating entities set up by both countries. Its reports shall be assumed to be *prima facie* accurate save as rebutted by other evidence.

The settlement of differences. Differences which the two countries cannot resolve by negotiation may be referred by either to the International Joint Commission. Failing decision by that body, the dispute may be referred to a tribunal of arbitration, one arbitrator appointed by each country, and a third by the two countries jointly, who shall be chairman. Decisions of the Joint Commission and of duly constituted arbitral tribunals are binding on both parties. Alternative modes of settlement, including reference to the International Court of Justice, may be effected by an exchange of notes.

Contingent pre-treaty legal status. Nothing in the treaty, or any action under it, may abrogate or modify the obligations of either party under then existing international law regarding the use of the water resources of the Columbia River Basin, after its termination or abrogation. Upon treaty termination, the Boundary Waters Treaty, if in effect, shall apply to the Columbia River Basin, save where any continuing provision of the present treaty may conflict with it. Where both treaties (1909 and 1961) are terminated, Article II of the 1909 treaty shall apply to Columbia Basin waters. However, the effect of Article II may be terminated by either party after one year's written notice.

Liability for damages. Save the causes of war, strike, major calamity, act of God, uncontrollable force, or maintenance curtailment, each country is liable to compensate the other for losses of hydroelectric power due to breaches of the treaty. No liability may be established from acts not amounting to a treaty breach. Should

Canada fail to commence full operation of a storage dam, downstream power benefits due to the operation of such storage facility shall be forfeited for a period equal to that of the Canadian delay.

Implementing executive agreements. In several instances future treaty implementation is made to depend on an exchange of notes between the two governments. These relate in the main to financial, engineering, and technical decisions which will or may arise during the life of the treaty.

Life of the treaty. The treaty period will run for 60 years; with the exception of three Articles (XIII, XVII, and XIX) the treaty may be terminated by either party after being in force for sixty years, and after ten years' written notice. Such dams as may have a useful life exceeding the treaty period shall be operated for flood control purposes "until the end of the useful life of the dam."

v. Problems of Ratification and Other Questions

Action by the United States Senate

On January 17, 1961, the date of the treaty signature, President Eisenhower submitted the text of the treaty, together with an explanatory memorandum by Secretary of State Herter, to the United States Senate, with a view to receiving its advice and consent to ratification.

A public hearing was held by the Foreign Relations Committee on March 8, 1961.[13] Senators from the four Northwestern states, government officials concerned with the drafting and negotiation, and several private witnesses were heard in behalf of the treaty. No witnesses appeared against it.

Several inquiries were made at the beginning which resulted in explanations and clarifications acceptable to the Foreign Relations Committee. They were, in the main:

1. Conflict of federal power and non-federal power interests. Some non-federal power interests in Washington and Oregon sought a "co-ordination agreement" with federal power authorities which would assure the use of the Canadian storage with maximum efficiency and fairness to all parties. These interests, after the designation of federal

[13] See *Hearing* cited note 12, *supra.*

power representatives by the interested government agencies, to negotiate such an agreement, gave their support to the treaty.

2. Technical considerations. In the words of the Committee, "the treaty reflects a complex economic and engineering problem on which the judgment of experts must be given great consideration." The fair bargain struck between Canada and the United States hinged greatly on the thoroughness of the technical preparation for it.

3. Implementation procedures and the treaty. Arrangements for implementation through an exchange of notes raised the question of the integrity of the treaty as such. Senator Fulbright asked specifically regarding the meaning of Article XIV, Section (4) which declared: "The United States of America and Canada may by an exchange of notes empower or charge the entities with any other matter coming within the scope of the treaty." A memorandum from the Department of State explained that this language grants no authority to amend any substantive provision of the treaty in any way. It also explained that the operating entities are to function at the operating level, making technical determinations and performing day-to-day operations as required.[14]

On March 14, 1961, in executive session, the Committee voted unanimously to recommend to the Senate that advice and consent to ratification be given.

On March 16, 1961, the United States Senate gave its advice and consent to the Columbia River Treaty's ratification by a vote of 90 to 1. On a roll call vote, Senator Wallace F. Bennett of Utah cast the only dissenting vote.

Relations between British Columbia and the Dominion Government

In his commentary on the progress report of the negotiating Delegations to the two governments on October 19, 1960, Prime Minister Diefenbaker observed that the Government of British Columbia would be primarily responsible for the construction and operation of the facilities in Canada, while the Federal Government would assume responsibility for the "international aspects." Consultations between the federal and provincial ministers would, he said, soon be held on the implementation recommendations. With the Canadian costs known, the terms of sharing the costs between the provincial

---

[14] For text of memorandum, see *ibid.*, 42-43.

and federal governments could now be discussed. Federal funds advanced, he affirmed, would be recoverable on a self-liquidating basis. Public hearings under the British Columbia Water Act would soon be held.

On January 17, 1961, the Prime Minister, in explaining the terms of the treaty, observed that the timing of ratification, insofar as Canada was concerned, will depend partly on action by British Columbia. As regards Canadian costs, he declared:[15]

The government of Canada has made it clear to the government of British Columbia that it is prepared to join on an equal basis in the financing of the construction costs of the storage dams I have referred to. It has been made clear that we are prepared to do this on a basis that will call for repayment, not on a fixed schedule but as returns are earned through the sale of power. That offer is still open. My colleague the Minister of Finance has made it clear that he stands ready to meet the premier of British Columbia in order to discuss the offer at any time that may be mutually convenient.

The interests of the province of British Columbia were fully discussed by the Hon. Ray Williston, Minister of Lands and Forests, in an address delivered at Wenatchee, Washington, on April 7, 1961. All water resources within the province are administered under its "Water Act." All uses of water are governed by licenses. No physical steps toward construction of projects can be taken until license for use has been granted. Applications for licenses cannot be filed until all formal engineering studies have been made. Final treaty terms were to await these studies and the issue of the necessary licenses. The Provincial Government waived this understanding, permitting the continuation of negotiations on condition that Canadian ratification must await the completion of the engineering processes. British Columbia has designated the British Columbia Power Commission as its developing agency after ratification has taken place. The Commission has associated a private engineering firm with each of the proposed dams in Canada.

The functions and relations between the Dominion and provincial governments in Canada, in respect to this project, were significantly described by Mr. Williston as follows:

[15] For text of Mr. Diefenbaker's statement, see Canada, *Parl. Deb.* (Commons), Sess. 1960-61, 1200-1206; quoted passage at 1206.

The Federal Government is primarily interested to see that the terms of the treaty are carried out and that all negotiations are properly conducted between the countries concerned. The Provincial Government is responsible for the actual construction and operation of the works which are made necessary by the agreement. To this end an arrangement must be reached between the Canadian provincial and federal authorities as to what their individual responsibilities will be. This agreement must be finalized prior to the ratification of any treaty with the United States. Discussions are proceeding toward such an agreement at the present time and your speaker can assure this audience that he is confident that problems will be resolved in this regard before the licensing and engineering work has been completed.

Advantages to the United States

American advantages seem to appear, often expressly, in the terms of the treaty, and implicitly in all processes of interpretation and proposed implementation. However, Assistant Secretary White specified them as follows before the Senate Foreign Relations Committee:

1. The treaty will provide a very substantial block of additional hydroelectric power.

2. It can be acquired on such a basis as will maintain the rate structure for Federal power (presently $17.50 a kilowatt-year.)

3. The treaty will afford positive advantages to Canada, including the progressive reduction of power costs in British Columbia.

4. The treaty will afford flood relief in the Bonner's Ferry area in Idaho and in the lower Columbia Basin.

"Some related uncertainties"

Professor M. E. Marts of the University of Washington, in an article titled "A Long Step Forward on the Columbia: the Canadian–United States Agreement," appearing in the February, 1961, issue of *Water Power*, warned of some distressing "uncertainties" facing a realization of the treaty's objectives. He listed, among others, the following:

1. The problem of an agreement between the Federal Government at Ottawa and the British Columbia Provincial Government.

2. The absence of any specific obligation on the part of the United States to install additional machinery to make effective use of the

Canadian storage, while Canada is obligated to provide the full amount of storage within a specified period of time.

3. The effect of the Peace River proposal on the future market for Columbia River power in British Columbia.

4. The conflict between on-site power at Mica Creek and releases of Mica storage to meet the Canadian commitment to the United States.

5. The inclusion of the Libby dam, which may become an important concession by Canada and even a luxury to the United States.

6. The need for arrangements to recover downstream benefits from non-federal plants in the United States.

7. The equivocal position of the sponsors of potential projects in the United States until future power needs are met by this international development. In the meantime, the search for additional power in the Northwest must continue.

These "uncertainties" listed by Dr. Marts lie mainly in the areas of intra-Canadian relations, rival projects, market conditions, and relations with private and non-federal projects. They are based essentially on economic factors. These items show that neither the conclusion of the treaty, nor its ultimate ratification and entry into force will achieve the major objectives sought until such uncertainties are removed and many other problems are solved.

VI. CONCLUSION

On April 25, 1957, I laid before the 51st Annual Meeting of the American Society of International Law a set of eleven "principles and procedures" which I suggested should govern the future arrangements between Canada and the United States in respect of the development of the Columbia Basin water resources.[16] It happens by coincidence that all but one of these principles have been observed by the two governments in their negotiations and conclusion of the

---

[16] "The Diversion of Columbia River Waters," *Proc. Am. Soc. Int. Law,* 1957, 2-8; the "principles and procedures" appear at pages 7-8 as follows:

1. The United States should make clear its intent not to denounce the Treaty under Article XIV nor to invoke the principle of *rebus sic stantibus.* [Boundary Waters Treaty of 1909]

2. Canada should disclaim any interpretation implying such absolute sovereignty or exclusive jurisdiction as would mean a disregard for downstream rights.

3. The two governments should bring the rights and remedies under Article II in harmony with the following principle approved by the International Law Association August 31, 1956: "While each state has sovereign con-

Columbia River Treaty. The remaining one, it appears, may eventually be utilized in the process of treaty implementation.

The steps so far taken demonstrate the significant progress made since the original Columbia River Reference of 1944. The more important, and even the more difficult steps lie ahead. Accurate engineering procedures, sound financial measures, tactful diplomatic negotiations and wise legal decisions will be constantly required. New and unexpected situations will occur. The treaty is only the beginning of this challenging relationship.

The implementing entities under the treaty are envisaged as proceeding from the national authority of each government, unilaterally determined. The idea of a binational authority set up to act as a unit in behalf of both governments has not as yet made a deep im-

----

trol over the international rivers within its own boundaries, the state must exercise this control with due consideration for its effects upon other riparian states."

The right of each [nation] to appropriate waters lying on its side to beneficial uses, with due regard for the rights of each, should be definitely recognized.

4. Both parties should forswear unilateral action or independent procedure in all matters involving international rights and interests in the Basin.

5. Interstate and Interprovincial conflicts, and disputes between public and private power interests should impose no difficulties in settling the problems between the national governments.

6. The engineering teams of the two governments should seek, under the Columbia River Reference and through the International Joint Commission, a joint master plan for the development of their common streams which will afford an equitable solution for the problems of today and tomorrow.

7. All planning should be joint, and should be applied to the Columbia Basin as a whole, despite the international boundary which imposes an artificial barrier against a natural waterflow. Hydraulic and electrical integration of the two nation's interests in the Basin would mean joint use of the water, and joint apportionment of the power provided by it.

8. Negotiations should be undertaken looking to a special convention relating solely to Canadian–United States interests in the Columbia Basin. The Fisheries Conventions and Commissions offer ample precedent for this.

9. There should eventually be set up a bi-national (but not a supranational) authority or agency invested with the functions of investigation, planning and report, and with regulatory powers as well. Such a body should conduct all planning for basin development, authorize all joint uses of water, and apportion between Canada and the United States their respective shares of Columbia River power. Management essential to the joint undertaking should also be in its hands.

10. A formula should be determined, agreeable to both parties, which would evaluate the downstream benefits to the United States of upstream storage in Canada. The principle of "equitable apportionment" of benefits should govern the ratio of allocations between the two countries.

11. Reference of the problem to a global body such as the International Court of Justice is as unwise as it is unnecessary.

pression on the negotiating powers. The sheer magnitude of the project, together with its penetration into many areas where action is required and decisions must be made, may induce a friendlier approach to the suggestion. It would be an intriguing and, I believe, an effective device for handling a vital and colossal international problem where expert services and sound management should mean the most, and mere politics the least.

At the outset of this paper, I mentioned the unique and original methods by which Canada and the United States have managed to carry on their bilateral relations. Otherwise thorny and divisive problems have been reduced to a sound and mutually satisfactory status.

The utilization of the resources of one of the great river systems of the world by Canada and the United States, on the basis of mutuality and equality of benefits, is at this point the most impressive manifestation of this happy conditions of things. The sustained peaceful relations of the two countries has been carried by this means to far greater heights.

4

Perspective in the International Plane

John E. Read

Thinking in perspective, I am going to ask you to look at some problems which arise on the international plane. We are concerned with the behavior of nations—groups of human beings causing trouble as a result of internal indigestion such as population pressure, or external greed. In considering this problem of behavior, we are apt to transfer to it our thinking without regard for perspective. We apply to the Congo norms which have worked well in Oshkosh or Antigonish. What is even more irrational, we pass judgments—formed by our twentieth-century environment and way of life—upon Buluba tribesmen living in a Stone-Age world separated from us by many thousands of years. We warp our judgment by ignoring essential and relevant facts.

There are two factors which may give us perspective in forming judgments, and the first arises out of the common constitutional history of Canada and the United States. Both countries have taken, as the foundation of their political and legal institutions, the constitutional history of England as it was in the eighteenth century. They share the great constitutional principles which emerged from Magna Carta, the Habeas Corpus Act, and the Petition and Bill of Rights. They share the notion of the rule of law—that all men, great or small, and even governments, are subject to the law. They share these foundations and have developed them in parallel directions.

The supremely important matter of English history was neither the rise of democracy nor the brand of wine in which the Duke of Clarence was drowned in the fifteenth century. It was whether there should come into being, in England, sovereign power which could and would bring about justice, internal peace, and opportunity for Englishmen to live their lives; and whether that sovereign power should be institutionalized so as to be independent of the personal qualities of the ruling monarch.

It was nearly eight hundred years ago that, under Henry Plantagenet, sovereignty was established and embodied in permanent institutions, and the most important of these was national justice. The King's Courts were organized, with circuits covering the realm at regular intervals. The model of the Assize of Northampton has been closely followed throughout the common-law world.

As a result, the sovereign state emerged in England long before it came into being in Continental Europe; but it took five centuries to reach its goal. The problem was to achieve a position in which the great man and the yeoman, the Bishop and the Earl, the Baron and the Borough, and even the King and the Royal Government were subject to the law, and in which the judgment of the National Court was paramount. It was not until the Habeas Corpus Act of 1640 that the Star Chamber was abolished and the supremacy of the law embodied in the constitution.

Now, what have these dead bones got to do with the international plane in this year of grace, 1961? That is an unrhetorical question and it deserves an answer.

In the world today new nations are emerging from old empires and almost overwhelming an already tottering family of nations. These new states are different from one another, but they have a common pattern. There are some of their inhabitants who have had some contact with the modern way of life; but the experience of most has been confined to a tribal way of life more primitive than that, say, of the savage and pagan Anglo-Saxons. The primary need of all the new nations is to establish sovereignty in fact, in John Austin's sense of the word. They need national justice to bring tribal organizations under control. They need to establish a climate of law and order in which social and economic progress is possible.

On the other hand, political democracy has always been a later development. It was achieved in England in the last century, long after sovereignty had been established. It was achieved by the United States, two hundred years ago; but it was superimposed upon the rule of law. It was achieved in Canada a hundred and twenty years ago; but it followed and did not precede law and order.

There is a noticeable trend from democracy toward absolutism in the new nations. Some of them may end up in a form of dictatorship which a shrewd observer compares to the Tudor Monarchy. If that happens, we should not be unduly disturbed.

The second factor obscuring our judgment is disregard for time and circumstance. We overlook the fact that the notion of international law is a relatively new idea when regarded in historical perspective, and that the organized family of nations is only forty years old. But we also disregard the underlying circumstances; and, here, I want to refer to the notion of international law which prevailed at the turn of the century, and which still had adherents in my student days.

Historically, international law was coterminous with Christendom—it was the institutional expression, on the international plane, of Christian morality. Its only subjects were the nations of Christendom: they alone were bound by its rules: they alone could invoke its benefits. The sole source of its authority was the consent of like-minded nations, those nations that shared common moral standards derived from a common religious source.

But it was not only international law that was developed to govern the relations and serve the needs of a family of nations sharing a common religious and moral background. International justice emerged, and international organizations have been constituted: the League, the World Court, the I.L.O., the United Nations, and so many others that the alphabet is suffering from a nervous breakdown. All have been planned and founded upon the assumption that the members would share common standards of right and wrong—common notions of justice and injustice.

During the last fifty years that position has completely disappeared. Even in the sixteen years since the San Francisco Conference, it has fundamentally changed. Let us look at the change.

Fifty years ago, the family of nations included the nations of Christendom—Western civilization—plus a handful of others. This handful included Japan; and, in a lesser degree, the Sublime Porte; and, possibly but not certainly, China. The overwhelming majority— Christendom—represented the whole of the effective power of the world and gave dominant leadership on the ideological plane. Today, the family of nations includes a majority of countries, whether measured by counting heads or by population and power, which are beyond the limits of a badly shrunken Christendom and which do not share its moral principles.

Fifty years ago, Western civilization was on the march, with the objective of enabling the rest of the world, by peaceful means, to share its way of life. It had no apparent rival. Today, it is in retreat, almost in rout, and it is facing a resolute and determined, and so far successful rival.

In the present phase, we are crouching in the precarious shelter of a fluctuating balance of nuclear power, while the rival hosts are advancing on a world-wide front. In this Cold War, the contest is for men's minds: the front is neither East nor West; but ideological.

Propaganda made in Washington preaches freedom, meaning political democracy; and free enterprise, meaning the freedom of Madison Avenue to brainwash the children of the North American Continent in the interest of promoting the sale of Krispie Krunchie Caramel Treats. Political democracy and free enterprise may be pearls of great price to Americans and to Canadians: but they lack sales value to the Buluba tribesmen. They have behind them many centuries of tribal experience with plenty of political democracy and far too much free enterprise.

The Communist shop-window offers a much more attractive display; law and order and full bellies, with the loot of the imperial powers as loss leaders.

The West should change its emphasis and forget about its unsaleable stock and outbid the adversary. It can offer to the emerging nations programs which go beyond law and order and full bellies. It can offer justice, which is law and order plus. It can offer economic aid and "know how" and help, which ensure full bellies today and tomorrow. Above all, the West can offer human rights and fundamental freedoms, entirely lacking in the Red offer. The enrolling of the Peace Corps in the United States is the only imaginative step taken in the Cold War on the Western side.

In the present parlous state of the Western world there is need to advance on a wide front, with a dual objective—to prevent the onset of catastrophic nuclear war as an immediate objective, and to bring about the abridgment of the profound difference in moral values which is the heart of the East-West conflict, the long term objective. I intend to discuss one small aspect of such an advance; but, to maintain perspective, I shall outline a five point program of which it forms a part:

1. To build up and strengthen political and military co-operation in NATO to the point where the response to leadership is as effective as that of the Warsaw Pact Powers: in other words, to maintain the balance of power at all cost.
2. To build up and strengthen the United Nations, the only bulwark available in the present state of the world.
3. To build up the economies of all nations to the point where the gap between the "have" and the "have not" nations ceases to be an open sore.
4. To encourage all those factors which tend to lessen the moral gap between East and West, and which tend to eliminate those elements of the gospel according to Karl Marx which make coexistence difficult and good will impossible.
5. To establish the rule of law on the international plane.

The fifth point is primarily legal. But there is not enough time to survey the whole question, so I shall limit myself to one aspect: the way in which United States–Canadian experience might help in establishing the rule of law.

Here, I want again to recall the past. Law and national justice did not come into being as a conscious expression of sovereign power; instead, they emerged in the course of the evolution of the primitive society, and preceded the birth of the sovereign state. They were among the elements out of which sovereignty was fashioned.

I have already referred to the beginnings of national justice in England, and the way in which it led to the creation of sovereign power, and, in the course of time, to the rule of law. For centuries the new Royal Courts were in competition with rival systems of justice—ecclesiastical, feudal, and local—and it was the superiority of the Royal Courts, especially in the matter of proof—the jury system as against compurgation and ordeal—that led to their ultimate triumph. On the international plane the experience of the World Court in the last forty years has proved that it is a suitable instrument to serve the rule of law in international matters. But it is in competition with rival methods for the settlement of international disputes—force, diplomatic blackmail, and nuclear pressure—and there is need to bring it to the highest degree of efficiency in order to promote greater use of the Court to settle disputes and to build up a habit of resort to justice.

There is no possibility of agreement to establish compulsory jurisdiction. That was rejected in 1920, and again in 1945. Further, it is unlikely that any of the Communist states will submit to the Court's jurisdiction in a particular case. It is true that, by a slip of the pen, Albania submitted in the *Corfu Channel Case;* but it is unlikely that the pen will slip again. There is, however, one glimmer of hope on the Communist front. The President of the Court for the period 1961-1964 is Winiarski, a distinguished Polish jurist; and the Communist governments have faithfully observed the provisions of the Statute of the Court which ensure the independence of its members.

The project for bringing about a substantial measure of compulsory jurisdiction by means of Declarations under the Optional Clause made headway in the thirties; but it faltered badly through the technique of what is known in the United States as the Connally Amendment, a device which enabled a state making a Declaration to oust the jurisdiction of the Court at any moment before the actual delivery of judgment. This device was adopted by a number of countries, including Great Britain and France; but it has been abandoned by these two countries and there is a movement in the United States Senate to eliminate it from the United States Declaration. The Optional Clause is again in the ascendant; but there is no likelihood of its adoption by any of the Communist countries.

Their position, as regards both compulsory jurisdiction and the Optional Clause, reinforces the need for developing the highest degree of efficiency in the Court.

The World Court is an efficient tribunal for dealing with disputes which involve issues of international law, for interpreting treaties and other diplomatic documents, and for examining historical matters. But it is not as efficient in dealing with technical problems and issues of fact which depend upon testimony. Further, the Court is cumbersome and the average age of the judges is high. It could not deal effectively with issues which require local views and studies, or which need local testimony. It could not possibly have coped with the *I'm Alone* or *Trail Smelter Cases.*

It is here that I reach the central theme of Canada–United States treaty relations. A substantial part, in my view the most important part, of treaty relations between the two countries has been concerned with the settlement of disputes. The greatest name in the history of international justice is that of John Jay, and it was the treaty of 1794, which bears his name, that marked its birth. In the succeeding years, there was instance after instance in these mutual treaty relations of settlement of disputes on the basis of objective justice. I am thinking not only of the great arbitrations—*Fuca Strait, Behring Sea, Alaskan Boundary, North Atlantic Fisheries, I'm Alone,* and *Trail Smelter*— but also of the disposition of claims by commissions and the settlement of boundary waters problems by the International Joint Commission.

Looking at the problem as a whole, and considering both immediate and long-term interests, there can be no doubt that the results have been to the advantage of both countries. If there is any doubt as to the question of advantage, I suggest a comparison of this experience with the experience of France and Germany over the same period of time—one hundred and sixty-seven years.

Back in 1944/45, when the question of the re-establishment of the World Court was under consideration by groups of jurists organized by the American and Canadian Bar Associations, there was unanimous agreement that the Chambers of the World Court should be developed so as to incorporate lessons learned in the experience of the two countries in international arbitration. This view was taken into account by the Committee of Jurists in Washington when the Statute of the new Court was being drafted; but no effective provision has been made in the Rules of Procedure.

My suggestion is that the machinery of the International Court of Justice should be adjusted to provide for something comparable, on the international plane, to the system of itinerant justices established in England eight hundred years ago. Such a course would involve minor amendment to the Statute of the Court; but it would be non-controversial in character and unlikely to provoke a veto. The plan would be based on five principles:

1. It would offer to parties to a dispute the privilege of having it adjudicated by a Chamber of three or five judges. The Chamber would consist of three neutral and two national judges, or one neutral and two national members. The chairman would always be neutral. The neutral judge or judges would be chosen from the mem-

bers of the Court by the President in consultation with the agents. The national judges would automatically be assigned to the Chamber; but, if either or both parties had no judge on the Court, the provisions for *ad hoc* judges would apply. The judgment of the Chamber would be subject to appeal to the Court, unless the parties stipulated that it should be final.

2. The Court would provide administrative and secretarial help from the Registry, and would establish a set of simplified rules of procedure, which would govern proceedings unless changed or modified by the chairman, in consultation with the agents.

3. Normally, the Chamber would sit in both of the countries concerned, and arrangements for hearings would be made by the chairman, in consultation with the agents.

4. Provision would be made, in cases involving technical and scientific matters, to enable the parties to assign scientific or technical advisers to assist the Chamber.

5. Provision would be made for presenting oral testimony; and, where the issues affected private interests, to hear evidence and representations from such interests, subject to the concurrence of the agents.

The fourth and fifth suggested principles are based largely on the experience of the *Trail Smelter Arbitration*, which involved issues of international law of great importance and issues of fact which could be dealt with effectively only with the aid of competent scientific advisers. The third suggestion, regarding place of meeting, is based on the experience of the International Joint Commission, as well as the *I'm Alone* and *Trail Smelter Arbitrations*.

There are other suggestions of ways in which the World Court could be made more efficient, and I have made them on other occasions. But they are not germane to the subject of Canada–United States Treaty relations.

I do not propose to attempt a peroration; but I do want to bring home the significance of my suggestion. I believe that it is of vital importance that nations should resort to international justice in a broadening field of international relations. I do not suggest that all international differences are capable of solution by judicial methods;

but I do suggest that there is an ever-widening area within which they can be subject to the rule of law.

In the foreseeable future, there is no prospect of compulsory jurisdiction; and the only way of progress available in the world as it is depends on building up the habit of resorting to the Court. There is, in my view, an urgent need to make the Court more efficient and thus to induce nations to submit to its jurisdiction. There is a potentially effective lure. History has proved that it is far more profitable to lose an international law suit than to win a successful war.

5

Politics, Strategy, and the Commitments of a Middle Power

Theodore Ropp

This paper is primarily concerned with the defense relations of a small or middle power in a world in which an increase in the number of sovereign states and multilateral defense planning have become major features of international relations. Although some of these grants of sovereignty, e.g., to the Byelorussian Soviet Republic, may be specious, the non-Communist world's defense problems have surely been complicated by the fact that its great powers directly control a smaller proportion of its peoples than they did half a century ago. A world of more numerous and often less responsible lambs may not be a very stable one. The lambs may eventually force the lions to lie down, but even this process—*vide* the problems of the Congo or Portugese Africa—may have been rendered more difficult by the increased number of states that have declared their public concern with these questions. Many studies of multilateralization have concentrated on the great powers' efforts to utilize the resources of their smaller partners. This one is more concerned with the smaller than with the larger powers, more with Canada than with the United States, more with the historical factors which must be considered in Canadian-American defense planning than with the details of present policies, and more with the difficulties than with the advantages of multilateral defense planning through the treaty-making process.

Canadian-American joint defense planning began with the establishment of a Permanent Joint Board of Defence "to consider in the broad sense the defense of the north half of the Western Hemisphere," by the Ogdensburg Declaration of August 17-18, 1940.[1]

[1] The Canadian Government published the Declaration in its Treaty Series, 1940 CTS 14. It was published in the *Dept. of State Bulletin*, but not submitted to the United States Senate; see Stanley W. Dziuban, *Military Relations Between the United States and Canada, 1939-1945* (*United States Army in World War II*, Wash-

The Hyde Park Declaration of April 20, 1941 established the "general principle that in mobilizing the resources of this continent each country should provide the other with the defense articles which it is best able to produce ... and the production programs should be co-ordinated to this end."[2] The two countries began "limited" collaboration "for peacetime joint security" in the Joint Statement for Defense Collaboration of February 12, 1947, on the following principles:

1. Interchange of select individuals ... to increase the familiarity of each country's defense establishment with that of the other country.

2. General cooperation and exchange of observers in connection with exercises and with the development and tests of material of common interest.

3. [Gradual] encouragement of common designs and standards in arms, equipment, organization, methods of training and new developments. . . .

4. Mutual and reciprocal availability of military, naval and air facilities ... [and minimal formalities] for the transit ... of military aircraft and public vessels. . . .

5. . . . [no co-operative arrangement would impair] the control of either country over all activities in its territory.

6. . . . No treaty, executive agreement or contractual obligation has been entered into. . . . Either country may at any time discontinue collaboration on any or all of [these principles].[3]

Two years later both Canada and the United States signed the North Atlantic Treaty for the common defense of a much wider geographical area. While the 1940 *Permanent* Joint Board and the North Atlantic *Treaty* were new departures for both countries, Canada, through her membership in the British Empire and Com-

---

ington, 1959), 24, 28-29. The Declaration is listed in Dept. of State, *Treaties in Force* (1961).

  [2] 1941 CTS 14.

  [3] 1947 CTS 43. This Statement did not cover unified command, the principles of which had been outlined in the Joint Basic Defense Plan No. 2 of 1941. When such commands were established, the commander was "to coordinate the operations of the participating forces ... by the setting up of task forces, the assignment of tasks, the designation of objectives, and the exercise of ... coordinating control." He could not "control the administration and discipline of the forces of the nation of which he is not an officer, ... [nor] move naval forces of the other nation from the North Atlantic or the North Pacific Ocean, nor ... move land or air forces ... from the adjacent land areas, without authorization by the Chief of Staff concerned"; Stetson Conn and Byron Fairchild, *The Framework of Hemisphere Defense* (*United States Army in World War II*, Washington, 1960), 383.

monwealth, had been dealing with multilateral defense problems—
the interchange of personnel, co-ordinated weapons procurement and
development, mutual availability of bases, unified command, and the
assignment of functions to specified national contingents—since the
First Colonial Conference of 1887. During these years Canada's
population had increased from an eighth of that of the United Kingdom to more than a quarter. Although her population was not to
pass that of New York State for another five years, she had also
become an industrial power and was claiming "middle power" status.
Canada was now fully sovereign. From 1938 to 1960 her regular
forces were to grow fifteenfold and her armaments expenditures were
to increase even more in constant dollars, but without bringing her
any closer to that traditional attribute (or perennial illusion) of
national states, a fully independent military policy.[4]

In such a situation, what are some of the factors which determine
military policy? What light can the Commonwealth's experiences
with the problems of neutrality, bases, personnel interchange, co-
ordinated production and development, command, and the assignment of geographical areas or strategic functions throw on the even
more complex multilateral defense structures of the 1960's? These
factors vary from state to state, but at least four of them can be
considered in this context. First, certainly, are a nation's "historic
attitudes" on defense matters. The second factor is its strategic
situation and interests. These two factors may be applied, of course,
to the military-political problems of any state, large or small, but

[4] When the Mother Country was at war, an independent military policy raised
particularly acute problems. Laurier's 1912 formula—expressed somewhat differently
in 1900—was concerned only with Canadian action outside of Canada. "When
England is at war, we are at war; but it does not follow that because we are at war,
we are actually in the conflict. We can be in conflict only through ... the actual
invasion of our soil [surely including an attack on Halifax or Esquimault], or, the
action of the Parliament of Canada"; Canada, *Parl. Deb.* (Commons), Sess. 1912-
13, I (Dec. 12, 1912), col. 1034.

Prime Minister J. B. M. Hertzog's neutrality resolution of 1939 read: "The
existing relations between the Union of South Africa and the various belligerent
countries will, in so far as the Union is concerned, ... continue as if no war is being
waged: Upon the understanding, however, that the existing relations and obligations
between the Union and Great Britain or any other member of the British Commonwealth of Nations [with particular respect to the Simonstown naval base] ... shall
continue unimpaired and shall be maintained by the Union"; Union of South Africa,
House of Assembly Debates, vol. 36 (Sept. 4, 1939), 31.

A revision in 1938 of the Anglo-Irish Treaty with regard to former British bases
in the Irish Republic possibly prevented a situation arising in which a neutral state
was committed to the presence of a military base of a belligerent on its soil.

great powers have not always considered these factors in their dealings with the smaller members of their grand alliances. Third, small size by itself—the extreme case in the older Commonwealth is New Zealand, whose present population is less than two-fifths that of Ontario—complicates the difficulties of supporting those voluntary professional forces on which all of the older Commonwealth members are again relying.[5]   Fourth, certain other difficulties, as has been indicated earlier, seem to be inherent in any attempt at multilateral defense planning by treaty, and these difficulties tend to be compounded by the number of sovereign states involved and by the precise force commitments which were favored by American diplomats and defense planners in the nineteen fifties.   This paper makes no attempt to treat all four sets of factors equally, the first set obviously offering wider scope to an historian than the others, but consideration of these factors may indicate what can, or cannot, be expected to develop in Canadian-American defense relations.

I. Historic Attitudes

During the first half of the twentieth century the older Commonwealth states and the United States shared certain historic attitudes toward defense.   These attitudes were hardened in Canada, Australia, and New Zealand by the First World War, the first great war in which their peoples were really engaged, while the bitter internal political conflicts of this war tended to set the bounds of political action in the Second World War as well.   Their revolutionary postwar political commitments and the air and nuclear-age revolutions in military technology have, as yet, modified rather than revolutionized these traditional attitudes.   In sometimes surprising new guises, they still carry considerable weight in any political discussion of defense matters.

These historic attitudes may be listed as follows.   (1) Sea power—

[5] As will be noted later in this paper, a small new state cannot in peacetime commit as large a proportion of its manpower and income to defense as an older, larger state with a roughly equivalent standard of living.   The United Kingdom's wholly volunteer force planned for 1962 will represent about 1/138 of the population, to Canada's 1/145, New Zealand's 1/180, and Australia's 1/212.   These rough figures probably do not provide real support for the generalization above. And one can hazard the additional generalization that Australia has been spending more of her income on long-range economic development than has New Zealand.

the Royal Navy and/or the United States Navy—protected these states from invasion. While air power opened them for the first time to direct enemy attack, it also gave them a chance for direct retaliation and, in some ways, reinforced the mobility which sea power had traditionally given their comparatively small land forces. (2) Compulsory military service was politically more acceptable for home than for foreign service. (3) Volunteer professional forces were militarily more efficient and less "militaristic," i.e., less dangerous to civilian control of the armed forces and less likely to exalt power as the main end of political life. (4) Their geographical and even ideological isolation protected these states in a wicked world where others played "power politics" or, conversely, protected their own citizens from their own statesmen's efforts to join the game and thus involve them in expensive foreign "adventures." Isolationism also reflected the then new Commonwealth nations' desire for "real" sovereignty and their fear of involvement in great power or "imperialist" conflicts not of their own making or even against their national interests as they had come to interpret them. Isolationism was strong even in the Mother Islands because sea power had seemed to be able to isolate them from Europe's traditional Continental storm centers and because a sea power's resulting freedom of action was regarded as a prime asset of British diplomacy in upholding the balance of power. Some of these attitudes reappeared in the nineteen fifties when many Canadians (and Americans) became properly alarmed by the irresponsible bellicosity of numerous American military men, ideologues, diplomats, journalists, and politicians. In some respects, however, Canadians were simply transferring the onus of great power irresponsibility from British to American "imperialists," as certain sections of British opinion were transferring their fears of brinkmanship from a presumably aggressive France to the United States. These fears—some Canadians had been properly alarmed by British jingoism as far back as the South African War—have been compounded by the revolutions in military technology and compounded again by the smaller powers' inability to produce or to control the most apocalyptic of these new weapons.[6]

[6] See the volumes in *Canada in World Affairs* by B. S. Keirstead, *September 1951 to October 1953* (Toronto, 1960), 30-37; Donald C. Masters, *1953 to 1955* (Toronto, 1959), 9-32; and James Eayrs, *October 1955 to June 1957* (Toronto, 1959), 11-12. A feeling of utter helplessness is more damaging to informed public discussion than the greatest of conventional military or political dangers. Witness the

Though Canada had been the only self-governing British colony bounded by a possibly hostile great land power, we are chiefly concerned with the twentieth century, when Canada seemed to be protected by both Great Britain and the United States. In some quarters Canadians' resulting feeling of security may still reflect Sir Wilfrid Laurier's supposed remark to Lord Dundonald, the General Officer Commanding the Canadian Militia, in 1902, "You must not take the Militia seriously. . . . It will not be required for the defence of the country, as the Monroe doctrine protects us against enemy aggression."[7] In the 1930's the Quebec Nationalist, Henri Bourassa, and the C. C. F. leader, J. S. Woodsworth, thought that Canada could set an example of total disarmament. As the latter put it in 1936, in an illustration first used by Senator Raoul Dandurland, "If my house is located in the vicinity of fire-proof buildings, why should I not enjoy the low insurance rates?"[8] The Conservative Minister of Justice, Hugh Guthrie, a former Liberal who had split with Laurier in the 1917 conscription crisis, told the League Assembly in 1931 that, "The armaments of Canada are practically negligible. We maintain only such . . . forces as are necessary for the maintenance of law and order."[9]

The United Kingdom's pre-1914 efforts to utilize "the great military resources of the Empire for purposes of mutual defence"[10] cannot be detailed here, but many significant problems were at least

temerity with which Israeli and Afrikaner Nationalists are facing what would seem to be insuperable "old-fashioned" military and political problems. A sovereign state's "natural" desire for a free hand can be overcome only by the "clearest" and "most present" dangers. Karl von Clausewitz noted this long ago in his remarks about all pledges of "mutual assistance." "Even when both have a common and great interest, . . . the contracting parties usually only agree to furnish a small stipulated contingent [as will be noted later, when the treaty-making process is used, the desire for a good bargain often overrides more purely military considerations], in order to employ the rest of their military forces on the special ends to which policy might happen to lead them. . . . This was forced to give way . . . only . . . when the extremest danger drove men's minds into natural pathways (as *against* Bonaparte) and when boundless power compelled them to it (as *under* Bonaparte). . . . Nevertheless, it was no mere diplomatic tradition which reason could disregard, but [one] deeply rooted in . . . human nature"; *On War*, tr. O. J. Matthijis Jolles (New York, 1943), 594-595.

[7] Dundonald, *My Army Life* (London, 1926), 191.

[8] The Kelsey Club of Winnipeg, *Canadian Defence: What We Have to Defend* (Toronto, 1937), unpaged.

[9] Quoted by Woodsworth in Canada, *Parl. Deb.* (Commons), Sess. 1932, 2959.

[10] Sir H. T. Holland to the Governors of Colonies, July 23, 1887, in Maurice Ollivier, ed. and comp., *The Colonial and Imperial Conferences from 1887 to 1937* (3 vols.; Ottawa, 1954), I, 9.

obliquely considered. The United Kingdom pushed hard for colonial contributions to the Royal Navy, but "Dominion autonomy was given priority over purely naval considerations" because of the attitudes of Australia and Canada. Laurier's opponent and eventual successor, Sir Robert Borden, opposed regular cash contributions "from a constitutional and political standpoint. . . . I do not believe that it would endure, . . . it would be a source of friction. . . . Permanent co-operation in defence . . . can only be accomplished by the use of our own material, the employment of our own people, the development and utilization of our own skill and resourcefulness [the best argument for a share in arms production], and above all by impressing upon the people a sense of responsibility for their share in international affairs." Neither Laurier nor South African Prime Minister Louis Botha thought that a Dominion could remain neutral in an Imperial war. But cases, Laurier claimed, "must be determined by circumstances, upon which the Canadian Parliament . . . will have to decide." The moral commitments resulting from geographical or functional force assignments did not clearly appear in these discussions, although they were illustrated in the 1912 Anglo-French naval talks.[11]

The problems of precise peacetime force commitments did not really appear in these early discussions. The Dominions were neither emotionally nor legally fully sovereign, and the United Kingdom's negotiators were more interested in a voluntary show of Imperial solidarity than in large colonial military contingents. As the later Chief of the Imperial General Staff, W. G. Nicholson, put it at the 1909 Imperial Conference, "It is fully realized that in the hour of danger the ties of kinship and affection which bind the self-governing Dominions to the Empire will prompt them to rally with enthusiasm to its aid."[12] The ensuing Canadian naval debates do indicate, how-

[11] Gilbert Norman Tucker, *The Naval Service of Canada: Its Official History* (2 vols.; Ottawa, 1952), I, 104, 133-134. "The moral claims which France could make upon Britain if attacked by Germany, whatever we had stipulated to the contrary, were enormously extended" by the naval conversations; Winston Churchill, *The World Crisis* (one vol. ed.; New York, 1949), 69-70.

[12] Ollivier, *Colonial and Imperial Conferences*, II, 22. The possible impact of exact prior Dominion commitments in 1914 varied with the political situation in each Dominion at that time. A precise South African commitment, fully understood by responsible Afrikaner nationalist leaders, might have enabled the Union to plan an expedition to German Southwest Africa with more regard for Afrikaner sentiment. Precise commitments, as indicated below, might have set unduly low limits on Canadian participation in the coming war, but Australia was to be seriously divided by her politicians' overly enthusiastic wartime estimates of her possible contributions. Loyal New Zealand's great war minister, Sir James Allen, limited his promises to what his country could realistically be expected to bear in a protracted conflict.

ever, that any discussion of land contingents would have been even more acrimonious and might have tended to set low ceilings on Canadian participation. Clausewitz had remarked how great dangers and wartime passions tend to sweep limited peacetime commitments aside, but the Canadian partisans of limited participation would surely have argued that this prior "commercial transaction" had limited each partner's contribution "to the amount of risk he incurs or the advantage to be expected."[13] After the event, Canadian, American, Australian, and even British isolationists were to argue that neither the risks of non-participation in the First World War nor the advantages of participation had been as great as the all-out interventionists had then indicated. Since Canada actually enrolled 628,000 men in her armed forces and sent 425,000 of them overseas and since all of the Dominions, with the exception of South Africa, made a greater proportionate effort than was required of the United States, it is hard to imagine how prior peacetime commitments would have resulted in greater sacrifices or how the Dominions' participation in both wars can be regarded as other than enduring monuments to the principle of voluntary Imperial solidarity.

The 1909 Military Conference also recommended that, "without impairing the complete control of the Government of each Dominion over the forces raised within it, these forces should be standardized, the formation of units, the arrangements for transport, the patterns of weapons, etc., being as far as possible assimilated to those . . . for the British Army."[14] These principles have, of course, become major features of multilateral defense planning. But nobody was then aware of the enormous demands which a great war would make on industry, of the extent to which prosperity would become dependent on arms production,[15] or of the ways in which standardization

---

[13] *On War*, 595. Historical proof that prior peacetime commitments deter aggression must be carefully selective. Would a public British commitment to France have been more effective in preventing war than her historic Belgian commitment? The Germans had long since taken British intervention into account. Red China's solemn warning to the U.N. in 1951 was ignored because American military and political leaders were equally confident that their air power could detect and prevent and their air and ground forces could defeat massive Chinese intervention in the Korean peninsula.

[14] Ollivier, *Colonial and Imperial Conferences*, II, 8.

[15] After a vigorous exchange between the Secretary of State for War and the Canadian Minister of Militia over the Canadian Ross rifle at the 1902 Colonial Conference, nobody took up Australian Prime Minister Sir Edmund Barton's suggestion "That the respective Governments recognise the wisdom of establishing factories and works for providing arms, ammunition and equipment"; *ibid.*, I, 181.

of equipment and training and the demands of combat would upset the most carefully drawn agreements for Dominion control "over the military forces raised within it."[16]

Proposals for compulsory peacetime training which accompanied this reorganization of the Empire's land forces made little headway in Britain and Canada, where they became associated in the public mind with extreme conservatism, although they were never endorsed by either Conservative party. Compulsory training won considerable working-class support in Australia and New Zealand, which adopted such plans just before the war. The rather different South African scheme was based, in part, on the traditional commando system. Kitchener helped the Australians and New Zealanders develop their plans, perhaps as "the thin edge of the wedge" for such a plan at home, but officially because of Britain's interest in "homogenous military systems" for efficient mutual support "in the event of national danger."[17] None of these plans contemplated compulsion for overseas service, though Haig and J. E. B. Seeley, Haldane's successor at the War Office, warned Alexander Godley, then G. O. C. New Zealand Forces, in 1913 that "it would not be too long before I should be called upon to produce an expeditionary force from New Zealand for service in Europe."[18]

The Ross rifle scandal and the many related questions of procurement and supply are discussed later in this paper.

[16] Thus, during the Second World War Australian airmen found that, "despite goodwill on both sides, . . . military crises, . . . the constantly shifting emphasis of air operations, and the enormous geographical spread of conflict inevitably . . . overrode even inter-governmental agreements. . . . Commanders . . . paid scant respect to a man's nationality, but considered only whether he could do a particular job, . . . until Australians were serving in so many units . . . that for all practical purposes they were a part of a multi-national force"; John Herington, "Multi-National Forces: Some Problems for the Modern Historiographer" (MS paper for the Canberra meeting of A. N. Z. A. A. S. Jan., 1954), 10.

[17] The Australian and New Zealand plans were sparked by the "Yellow Peril"; the South African by the ever present Blacks; undated speech, "How Universal Service was Introduced into Australia," possibly by Kitchener's military secretary, Col. O. A. G. Fitzgerald; Kitchener to New Zealand Prime Minister Joseph Ward, March 2, 1910, Kitchener Papers (Public Record Office). This note was written a few days after the Mayor of Dunedin punched the Prime Minister in the jaw in a scuffle for a place in the great man's carriage; Philip Magnus, *Kitchener, Portrait of an Imperialist* (New York, 1959), 245. Kitchener's papers show him as little interested in the details of these schemes as he was in the new British Territorial Force, which he was to ignore in 1914. Magnus confirms Leopold Amery's view of Kitchener as "an improviser and a hustler" whose "ignorance and strong self-will often created unnecessary difficulties"; *My Political Life* (3 vols.; London, 1953-1955), I, 123-124.

[18] Godley, *Life of an Irish Soldier* (London, 1939), 148-149. Their proponents

On the eve of World War I, most soldiers thought that the next war would be short and that only the professional Expeditionary Force would reach France in time for the decision. Instead, the Empire was involved in total war and conscription for overseas service "became a test and a symbol" of a country's "prosecution of the war to the limit."[19] In Canada and Australia it became the most divisive issue since Confederation; in Canada and South Africa it also became a "test" of British racial supremacy in a binational state and of forced participation in "imperialist" wars. In Canada it was responsible for the 1917 Union Government of Conservatives and conscriptionist Liberals and for Union victory in a bitter wartime election. There were riots and passive resistance in French Canada. The resulting Conservative weakness in French districts was largely responsible for their exclusion from office for thirty of the thirty-six years after 1921, and the emotional connotations of " 'National Government and conscription' " was to make this "the central issue of Canadian politics to the very end" of the Second World War as well.[20]

The general belief that another war would not require large expeditionary forces and that the Dominions' major contribution would be economic (and profitable to some people) indirectly facilitated the Dominions' decision to stand by Britain in 1939. Hence, in 1939, as in 1914, there was no question of deliberate "interventionist" or "imperialist" deception. These ideas were implicit in Britain's own "limited liability" rearmament program of the late 1930's. Fortunately for Mackenzie King, these ideas were not to be challenged by events until after the Liberals had ousted the Union Nationale in Quebec in October, 1939, and had won the largest majority in

hoped that these plans would be "adaptable to the Mother Country." Those who got " 'a taste of the mill' themselves, will insist that others should follow"; G. F. F. Lascelles to Kitchener, July 23, 1912, Kitchener Papers.

[19] John W. Dafoe, *Laurier, A Study in Canadian Politics* (Toronto, 1922), 175.

[20] J. W. Pickersgill, *The Mackenzie King Record* (Toronto, 1960), I, 22. Conscription was adopted by the Asquith Coalition in Great Britain and the Reform-Liberal Coalition in New Zealand. It was defeated in two Australian referenda, one before and one after the formation of a coalition. The eventual domination of the conservatives in these coalitions left lasting political scars; Arthur B. Keith, *War Government of the Dominions* (Oxford, 1921). The South Pacific Dominions made proportionately larger manpower contributions than Canada, but the latter was the only Dominion to make a major industrial effort. Profiteering was almost as explosive an issue as conscription, and conscription of wealth became a necessary political slogan in the second war. There was no wartime coalition in South Africa, but Botha's South African party and the Unionists were tacit allies in the 1915 election.

Canadian history to that time in the Dominion elections of March, 1940.[21] The crisis in May, 1940, produced compulsion for home defense. And after Pearl Harbor, King sought release from his anticonscription pledges by plebiscite. A plebiscite, he explained, was not a referendum which would commit him to a specific policy. He interpreted the vote—64.2 per cent "Yes" in the Dominion, but 73.5 per cent "No" in Quebec—to mean "not necessarily conscription but conscription if necessary."[22] He survived a Cabinet crisis when this necessary point seemed to be reached late in 1944. Some home service men were sent to Europe, but Canada reverted to voluntary service for the Pacific and King narrowly won his last election in June, 1945, after Germany's surrender.[23]

French Canada has gone along with Canadian participation in NATO and in United Nations forces for Korea, the Middle East, and the Congo, although this last is no more striking than Irish participation. But the Progressive Conservative sweep of Quebec in the Dominion elections of 1958 and the Liberal capture of the provincial government in 1960 would seem to increase the caution with which either party would approach any proposal which might raise the conscription bogey, a bogey which may seem to be unduly magnified in this paper because those historic forces which produce "historic attitudes" have made it a "test and a symbol." One reason for this is the direct effect of conscription on individuals, an effect which can be observed in the emotions generated by the rather similar questions of compulsory education or compulsory arbitration of labor disputes. From time to time retired officers have proposed compulsory training, but its present abandonment in Australia, New Zealand, and Great Britain would seem to be an additional reason to rule

[21] The Liberals won 184 of the 245 seats. King wrote, "We really cleaned up, . . . and I thought often of what Sir Wilfrid said . . . when I told him of my intention to stand by him . . . against conscription—that I would have Quebec for the rest of my life"; Pickersgill, *King Record*, I, 75.

[22] *Ibid.*, 380. He hoped never to reach "the point where necessity for conscription for overseas would arise"; *ibid.*, 364.

[23] The Union Nationale had recovered Quebec, but "Quebec Saved our King" in 1945 by giving him 57 of his 130 seats. The United Kingdom adopted conscription in 1939 to warn Germany and bolster France, but did not apply it to either part of Ireland in either war. A coalition was formed in 1940. The United Australia–Country Party Coalition was beaten in the House of Representatives, but Labour eventually applied conscription to certain South Pacific areas. New Zealand Labour adopted conscription and was returned after two extensions. South Africa has never officially applied conscription. Smuts' United party followers formed a coalition with the Dominion and Labour parties and won an absolute majority in 1943, but various wartime discontents contributed to the narrow Nationalist victory of 1948.

it out in Canada. Compulsory training is now in effect only in South Africa, which has left the Commonwealth, has never officially drafted men for foreign service, and allowed Permanent Force members to opt for home service in the Second World War.[24] In Canada's case such an extreme national mobilization measure would be politically possible only in prolonged periods of acute international tension. It might be too late to be militarily useful, since short periods of training may be of little use in modern war.[25]

Professor James Eayrs thinks that Canada could have considered compulsion in 1955, when she shared "with Iceland the doubtful distinction of being the only member of the Atlantic Alliance not to have introduced compulsory military service."[26] This argument for a symbolic gesture ignores the great powers' customary indifference to such small-powers' gestures. During the First World War in particular the Dominions carefully watched British internal politics, but Dominion political trends were poorly reported in Britain. This is equally true of American-Canadian relations; only a few Americans know of Quebec's "historic attitude" toward conscription. The New Zealand and Australian governments made major anti-Communist gestures during the Berlin Blockade–Korean War era. New Zealand Labour carried conscription by referendum. The Australian conservatives' attempt to outlaw the Communist party was defeated by referendum in 1951. Neither effort caused much comment in the United Kingdom or the United States.[27]

[24] In spite of their opposition to conscription for "British" wars, the Nationalists' 1957 revision of the Defence Act may make it possible to use conscripts "for the defence of Southern Africa, Africa, and the Middle East Gateways to Africa"; *Exchanges of Letters on Defence Matters between the Governments of the Union of South Africa and the United Kingdom, June 1955*, United Kingdom, *Accounts and Papers*, 1955-1956, XLV, 2.

[25] This emotionally charged question is seldom discussed on its merits. Australia abandoned compulsory peacetime training as a waste of time and money, a view now held by many British professionals. The *Sydney Morning Herald*, June 30, 1958, reversed its former attitude by heading New Zealand's abandonment of compulsion "A Good Example." Many Australian regulars, it reported, thought that compulsion was "hamstringing the Army and contributing nothing to national security."

[26] *Canada in World Affairs, October 1955 to June 1957*, 14.

[27] Except in Australian–New Zealand relations, the Dominions are poorly informed of events in other Dominions. One Canadian, after South Africa's withdrawal from the Commonwealth, said to me that she had furnished only "a few English-speaking volunteers" anyway.

For the New Zealand referendum, see L. J. Watt, "The Referendum: Its Use and Abuse," M.A. Thesis, Victoria University, Wellington, 1956. This gesture did not save Labour, who abandoned compulsion after they returned to power in 1958. National criticism of this move does not seem to have been a factor in their victory

II. STRATEGIC SITUATION

The changes in Canada's strategic situation since Confederation hardly need further comment. She has moved from the position of hostage for British good behavior in North America, to a position in which she was probably "safer from conquest or coercion than any other land,"[28] into the dangerous "essential forefield of United States defence.... The latter depends so completely on Canadian co-operation, . . . access to ground installations on our territory, and the use of our air space that . . . the United States *must* achieve [our co-operation] . . . to be 'secure' . . . . Just because we cannot be neutral, . . . peace preservation, through deterrence of war and through . . . the quenching of any armed conflict that could grow into all-out war, must be another mainstay of Canadian national policy."[29] Canada's resulting responsibilities would seem to include: (1) participation in the air defense of North American heavy industry, a problem complicated by industrial concentration and dependence on the St. Lawrence–Great Lakes waterways, as well as the rudimentary character of civil defense preparations; (2) maintenance of mobile Arctic ground forces; (3) provision of naval defenses for the Arctic frontier, by forces oriented in the 1950's toward North Atlantic convoys, though one of sea power's advantages is the way in which ships may be redistributed functionally and geographically without fanfare; and (4) participation in international police operations.

Canadian participation in international police operations is facilitated by the fact that the other three functions of her armed forces can be represented as purely defensive, an odd reversal of the situation in which her primary contributions to her alliances were offensive. The quarter of the Canadian Army and the even larger proportion of her flying squadrons with NATO are historical relics. They represent a moral commitment which happens to be in line with Quebec's anti-Communist tradition. By comparison with her major Allies, however, Canada's moral position for international police operations—which may contribute to the policy objectives of her major Allies—is strengthened by the fact that she occupies no bases for

in 1960. For Australia, see Leicester Webb, *Communism and Democracy in Australia: A Survey of the 1951 Referendum* (Melbourne, 1954).

[28] Tucker, *Naval Service*, I, 15.

[29] John Gellner, *Problems of Canadian Defence* (Toronto, 1958), 1-2.

conventional "imperialist" operations. Her territory, however, does happen to lie between a major operational area for nuclear missile submarines and the major United States bases of SAC.

Since Canada's contributions can be represented as primarily defensive, a future government might find the home defense concepts of the 1930's politically attractive. They might possibly justify compulsory training, since a realistic civil defense program seems impossible without some measures of compulsion. Civil defense in the United Kingdom may be as hopeless as the 1957 White Paper implied, but neither Canada nor the United States has really faced this problem. In any case the first question raised in Professor B. S. Keirstead's study of Canadian defense for 1951-1953—"Was the disposition of the Canadian forces strategically sound?"[30]—cannot be answered without a new look at American and British policies. After their initial shock at the plain speaking of the 1957 White Paper, American policy makers have adopted many of its ideas. The United States is now attempting "to increase the survivability and therefore the effectiveness of our strategic deterrent forces, . . . [to] subject [them] to more deliberate command and control, . . . [and] to strengthen our non-nuclear limited war forces . . . to avoid situations in which we might be forced to use nuclear weapons because too narrow a range of non-nuclear weapons were available to us."[31]

For a variety of reasons a Canadian movement to contract out of the nuclear age or to free herself from American brinkmanship does not seem likely to have much political impact as long as her major allies are moving toward the control of tactical and strategical nuclear weapons and to increase their conventional forces.[32] Professor Keirstead's other questions—"Did Canada make a sufficient defense ef-

[30] *Canada in World Affairs, 1951-1953*, 132.

[31] Secretary of Defense Robert S. McNamara to the Associated Press, New York, April 24, 1961; *New York Times*, April 25, 1961, 29.

[32] Traditionally pacifist religious groups are not as strong in Canada as in the United States; the Catholic Church is stronger. These generally conservative pacifist religious groups are precariously allied with various intellectuals, the Friends bridging the gap between them.

The British movement has strong support in left wing Labour, but the ties which bound the separate Commonwealth Labour movements have weakened with the passing of many of the older leaders and the resulting "nationalization" of the various Labour parties. The Canadian C. C. F. and the Australian Labour party, for example, have put down provincial roots in opposite directions. The defeat of the last of these older Labour leaders may well result in the drifting of New Zealand's Labour party still farther from its traditional moorings. The movement of English-speaking South African Labour into the Nationalist camp was perhaps the decisive event of the 1948 election.

fort?" and "Were Canada's contributions to NATO, the Korean War, and North American defense adequate?"[33]—are almost impossible to answer. Statistics of comparative money or manpower contributions (including those in footnote 4 *supra*) are often specious and have little impact on public opinion. Not all such statistics are as naïve as those presented to the 1902 Colonial Conference, but Laurier's comments on Canada's indirect contributions to Imperial strength by developing her natural resources remain pertinent for the underdeveloped members of any alliance.[34] Clausewitz saw some of these political complexities. Their rediscovery after the simple certitudes of staff planning before 1914 has been a painful intellectual process.

III. THE PROBLEMS OF SMALL OR MIDDLE POWERS

Some of the special problems of a small or middle power have already been noted. The standardization of weapons and tactics was one of the major accomplishments of Imperial defense planners before the First World War. Canada, the only Dominion with a nascent arms industry, was the only dissenter. With bipartisan support from Canadian politicians and manufacturers, the government stuck by the Ross rifle, which failed in combat and seriously embarrassed the Borden Government.[35] The more general problems of a small power's participation in weapons research, development, and manu-

---

[33] *Canada in World Affairs, 1951-1953,* 132.

[34] "We have to create everything in Canada; and we have to take out of the Dominion Treasury sums of money for a class of services which is borne in the United Kingdom by . . . private capitalists"; Ollivier, *Colonial and Imperial Conferences,* I, 154, 165.

The War Office showed Canada spending 2s. per head for defense to the United Kingdom's 29/6 per annum. The Admiralty table, which included contributions offered at the Conference, showed the United Kingdom spending 15/2 per white inhabitant for naval defense, Natal 10/9 1/4d., Cape Colony 1/10 1/4d., Australia 1/ 3/4d., New Zealand 1/ 1/4d., Newfoundland 3 1/2d., and Canada o. This unintended argument for decimal coinage is in Canada, *Sessional Papers,* 1903, vol. 37, No. 12, 29a, 19.

[35] The rifle may have been insufficiently tested under combat conditions. Or the First Contingent may have been insufficiently trained in its use. Or British soldiers were overly contemptuous. Or the rumors of Canadians trading it for the Enfield may have been exaggerated by Sir Sam Hughes' numerous enemies. The resulting scandal, in any case, reinforces Hughes' sounder claims to consideration as the least successful of the Empire's defense ministers. Should their scientists do contract research or participate in projects in other countries? Security problems increase with the number of states participating, and Commonwealth countries have been disturbed by the possible permanent loss of trained scientists.

facturing cannot be considered here, but American policy makers are increasingly concerned with helping "the American economy absorb the impact of changes [in defense spending] without breaking stride." Such expenditures now involve a tenth of the United States gross national product and support about a tenth of the labor force.[36]

During and after the Second World War, profiteering, in a sense, became endemic rather than epidemic. Canada's economy, with its high dependence on foreign investment and serious unemployment problem, may well be more vulnerable to sudden shifts in defense spending than that of the United States. As Colonel Stacey has pointed out, the 1959 cancellation of the CF-105 Arrow, which threw 14,000 Canadians out of work in one day and may have affected some 30,000 workers, "demonstrated in a singularly dramatic fashion that henceforth Canada, willy-nilly, was apparently to be militarily dependent on the United States to an extent so far unknown."[37]   The peacetime armaments programs preceding the two World Wars throw little light on these problems. The differences in scale are too important. It can only be hoped that American defense planners remain fully aware of Canadian vulnerability. Any failure to take it into account might well have very serious effects on Canadian-American relations.

Tactical research and development may present fewer problems. Dominion contributions to the development of tactics and transport—perhaps because so few of their soldiers were regulars—constituted an interesting feature of both wars, but even tactical developments, broadly considered, can have political overtones. One of the major security problems of the West is the maintenance of order in southern and eastern Africa. South Africans have had much tactical and transport experience in this area. But American or British approval of the use of South African forces to suppress Communism—as defined in Pretoria, Lisbon, or Salisbury—would only complicate problems. Such approval might not be asked for. A request for South African aid by the governments of either of the Rhodesias or the Federation would raise constitutional issues. The Union's decision not to ask for readmission to the Commonwealth has not affected its defense commitments.[38]   South Africa's Nationalists, like the Israelis but

[36] McNamara, *New York Times*, April 25, 1961, 29.
[37] "Military Problems in Canadian-American Relations, 1960," MS, Seattle, 1960, 5.
[38] See note 24 *supra*. The close link between the Defence Forces and internal security goes back to the 1912 Defence Act.

for different reasons, may be counting on American anti-Communism and British Toryism to save them from internal or external difficulties engendered by their policies.

A great power commander whose forces include small power contingents may not always realize that even the regular units which the Dominions are now contributing—in marked contrast to the situation before the two World Wars—may not be quite comparable to great power units of equal strength and experience. By 1917, to take an extreme example, the New Zealand Division was one of the best in France. It was backed by the most efficient of the Dominions' replacement systems and the most united public opinion. But because of this the Division *was* New Zealand, the symbol of a tiny nation halfway around the globe. The British made repeated efforts to borrow from NZEF's replacement pool, which was often overfilled by convoy arrivals or unexpectedly light losses. General G. S. Richardson, the British officer commanding NZEF in the United Kingdom, and New Zealand's Defence Minister, Sir James Allen, maintained that the British authorities simply did not see how important it was to New Zealand that NZEF be kept at full strength. This does not mean that commanders may not take risks with such forces, but only that they should realize that this problem exists.[39]

Some examples of a great power's failure to consider the possible political consequences of proposals affecting small power contingents are familiar,[40] but one of the most interesting is little known outside of South Africa. On August 4, 1914, the Government offered to free British forces in the Union, some six or seven thousand men, for service elsewhere by replacing them with South Africans. In accepting this offer the British Government asked on August 7 that the

[39] MSS (War History Branch, Department of Internal Affairs, Wellington). This is an argument—see note 16 *supra*—for internationalizing such forces where possible. The loss of certain U. S. National Guard units in the Second World War resulted in other units being filled on a regional rather than a state basis. The South African Brigade in France never really recovered from the Delville Wood action in 1916, when it lost all but 5 of its 121 officers and all but 750 of its 3,032 men in a week. The loss of the Second South African Division at Tobruk in June, 1942, quite possibly had even more serious long-range consequences in South Africa.

[40] Australia's refusal to divert her returning veterans to Rangoon in 1942 may have been the only possible decision for a government facing invasion. The Canadians lost in Hong Kong in Churchill's exercise in brinkmanship were not numerous enough to create a major political crisis. King thought that an inquiry would be "a help to us as it will show where the onus really lies, how ready we were to meet a British request, and will put the blame . . . on those responsible for taking some men overseas who should not have gone"; Pickersgill, *King Record*, I, 352.

Union render a "great and urgent Imperial service" by occupying German Southwest Africa. "Other Dominions," the cable noted, "are acting in a similar way."[41] The Union Government called for volunteers. Some Active Citizen Force units already in camp were held in service. The new National party condemned the proposed expedition on August 26, but Parliament, meeting the day after the arrival of Lord Buxton, the new Governor General, approved it on September 9. The Rebellion—a much larger affair than the better known Irish Rebellion of 1916—began about a week later. The United Kingdom had given no thought to the possible consequences of its request, and Union Government was completely surprised.[42] Buxton summed up the results for Prime Minister H. H. Asquith on August 19, 1915, six weeks after the German surrender in Southwest Africa. Botha's "definite Imperial attitude" in calling "the Citizen Defence Force (commandeered them) for general protection, and for purposes of attack on the Germans ... jarred ... the feelings of the Dutch as a whole." The Rebellion had "consolidated ... and shown the unexpected strength, numbers, and bitterness of the anti-English ... Dutch," and exacerbated anti-Dutch feeling among the English. The Nationalists would not win the coming elections, but Buxton feared that they would leave Botha dependent on English support and create a *sauve qui peut* sentiment among lukewarm Dutch politicians.[43]

[41] *Correspondence on the Proposed Naval and Military Expedition against German South-West Africa; Cd.* 7873. United Kingdom, *Accounts and Papers,* 1914-1916, vol. 45, 437-440.

[42] The South African War had ended only twelve years before, but the Rebellion had many causes beside the pro-Germanism of some Afrikaner bitter-enders, the treason of Lt. Col. S. G. Maritz, and the ambiguous attitude of Commandant General C. F. Beyers. Pressure for action in a country still jumpy after the Rand riots and Hertzog's split with Botha, religious fanaticism, the killing of General J. H. de la Rey, rumors of commandeering based on a few cases in spite of official promises, and Smuts' failure to sense the mood of some of his former associates all played their parts. There were many indirect warnings. John H. Scott, for example, wrote John X. Merriman from Kokstad on September 1, that the proposed expedition was "utter madness." John X. Merriman Papers (South African Public Library, Cape Town), folder 338. On September 9 the *Cape Times* wrote that, but for the Defence Act, the Germans "would have been, ere this, far advanced into the heart of the Union." Three days later it reported "very few Germans ... within striking distance." The Germans raised 6,000 men from a European population of 15,000. The only military objectives were the two ports and the capital, Windhoek, with their radio facilities.

[43] H. H. Asquith Papers (Bodleian Library, Oxford), box 26. As in so many other cases, what happened is no more important than the Nationalist legends which grew up around the Rebellion. See G. D. Scholtz, *Die Rebellie, 1914-1915* (Jo-

iv. Multilateral Defense Agreements

The Commonwealth experience also throws some light on other multilateral defense agreements. Though the early negotiations between the Mother Country and her Dominions may exaggerate the utility of general commitments, the desire for a good "commercial transaction" may increase geometrically with the number of clauses and negotiating units. New technologies may now—though this was also the case before 1914 and 1939—make precise agreements obsolescent before they are ratified. The NATO goals set at Lisbon in 1952 had hardly been published before members were defaulting, but not before Canada's press and Parliament had acrimoniously debated the adequacy of her contribution.[44] The limits of West German rearmament were related to the Lisbon goals. Britain finally secured French permission for German rearmament by promising not to withdraw her four divisions and their tactical air support from "the mainland of Europe ... against the wishes of the majority of the High Contracting Parties ... [except in] an acute overseas emergency." A related American promise of March 10, 1955, was less detailed: "to continue to maintain in Europe ... such units ... as may be necessary to contribute [a] fair share of the forces needed for the joint defense of the North Atlantic area while a threat to that area exists, and [to] continue to deploy such forces in accordance with agreed North Atlantic strategy."[45] This was almost two years after the White House had announced that it was taking a "New Look" at defense expenditures and a little more than a year after the American thermonuclear tests which made the Lisbon goals obsolete. Other general questions are whether the dangers of public review of such commitments outweigh those of obsolescence and how aware the public of a smaller power should be of changes in the defense policies of

hannesburg, 1942). Students of French Canadian nationalism will be interested in F. A. van Jaarsveld, *Die Afrikaner en sy Geskiedenis* (Pretoria, 1959).

[44] Keirstead, *Canada in World Affairs, 1951-1953,* 138-144. The C. C. F. was charged with anti-Americanism and pro-Communism for what proved to be an accurate analysis of the Lisbon goals.

[45] *Protocol No. 2 on Forces of Western European Union. Documents Agreed on by the Conference of Ministers held in Paris, October 20-23, 1954; Cmd. 9304; Accounts and Papers,* 1953-1954, vol. 31, 961-1024. *United States Assurances to the Western European Union Countries; Cmd.* 9408; *Accounts and Papers,* 1954-1955, vol. 18, 393-396. CENTO, the successor to the ill-fated 1955 Baghdad Pact, is backed by a British treaty commitment and the moral commitment of an American "Observer Delegation" and participation in CENTO exercises.

the great powers to which it may be linked. The possibilities of upsetting a multilateral structure during such public reviews may increase with the number of states involved and the detailed nature of force or financial commitments.

Britain, rather than Canada or the United States, had to ask her allies for permission to reduce her ground forces in Germany, after the 1957 White Paper clearly revealed the disparities caused by technological revolution and British resources with the detailed force goals set at Lisbon and elsewhere. The reduction of the British Army of the Rhine was not, however, a return to an overseas "Blue Water" strategy but an attempt to recover the mobility which lay behind Britain's traditional insistence not to be committed in advance to a specific strategy by allowing so large a portion of her limited ground forces to be pinned next to an overwhelmingly superior ground enemy. Britain had lost her strategic freedom of choice in the decade before the White Paper; her many and increasingly detailed force obligations simply could not be met with the normal peacetime regular forces envisaged in that document. Larger conscript forces could not be properly trained and transported overseas or equipped with modern weapons without intolerable strains on her economy. Britain was still morally committed to many of the newly independent and even neutral Commonwealth states and was responsible for keeping order in her remaining colonies, while her ties with and moral commitments to the older Commonwealth states had been strengthened by two great wars. These states were still part of the single military system created before the First World War, even though its principles of weapons, tactical, and training standardization had been expanded to include the United States and NATO. Britain was also committed by interest and tradition to certain Middle Eastern states, in spite of, and in part because of, the nationalist revolutions sweeping that and other areas. "Many of these commitments [had] been integrated with the alliance systems of CENTO and SEATO into which Britain [had] entered concurrently with the United States," as her older commitments to the Low Countries and France had been integrated with NATO; "but they have an existence independent both of these alliances and of the cold war which brought the alliances into being. . . . The military necessities of the cold war have [merely] given them all a new significance."[46]

[46] Michael Howard, "Britain's Defenses: Commitments and Capabilities," *Foreign*

In such a situation simple answers will not do, any more, in fact, than has ever been the case. The simple ideological commitments often demanded by American public opinion and policy makers are dangerously naïve, but no more so than the detailed force commitments of British policy makers in the 1950's. There remain only those generalized statements of those "ties of kinship and affection" and national interest which have been the cement of the Empire, the Commonwealth, Canadian–United States relations, and Anglo-French-American relations throughout the twentieth century. Historians, fortunately, are not responsible for answering questions they may raise about the future, a fact not always understood by military men hoping to find certainty in the past or by those historians who, perhaps, have pandered more or less deliberately to this hope. As Edward S. Creasy put it, "When I speak of Cause and Effect, I speak of the general laws only, by which we perceive the sequence of human affairs to be usually regulated."[47]

Affairs, vol. 34 (1960), 81-91 at 83-84. Much of this paragraph is based on this brilliant summary.

[47] Preface to the first edition, 1851, of *The Fifteen Decisive Battles of the World* (Everyman ed.; London, 1943), xi.

6

Twenty-one Years of Canadian-American Military Co-operation, 1940-1961

C. P. Stacey

Considered in terms of the passage of time, at least, military co-operation between Canada and the United States "came of age" in the year 1961; for August of 1961 marked twenty-one years since Franklin Roosevelt and Mackenzie King issued the Ogdensburg Declaration and set up the Permanent Joint Board on Defence between the two countries. This may be a good moment, then, to review the record and try to discover how far these twenty-one years have brought military co-operation between the two North American countries.

I

The history of Canadian-American relations may be divided, very crudely, into four periods. The first is the period of conflict, ending with the Treaty of Ghent in 1814. It witnessed two Anglo-American wars, in both of which the United States launched unsuccessful invasions of Canada. The second is the period of threats and crises, ending with the Treaty of Washington in 1871. During this half-century war was a possibility at almost any time. Great territorial questions had to be settled between the two communities, and each community had to settle within itself great problems which invited foreign intervention—in the case of the United States, the slavery question, and in the case of Canada the governmental problem resulting from the North American colonies' relationship to the British Empire. But all this dangerous matter was in fact disposed of without resort to arms; and when the settlement of 1871 liquidated the Anglo-American disputes left behind by the American Civil War the way was open for the beginning of the third phase of the story, the period of increasingly amicable relations, which extends to the outbreak of the Second World War. Incidentally, it is only after 1871 that one can speak with any accuracy of an unfortified frontier.

This third period was not, it is true, entirely peaceful. It was a time of robust and aggressive imperialism and acute international rivalries. But Britain and the United States preferred to vent their energy on the lesser breeds rather than on each other—in the case of the British, on the Boers and the Sudanese, in the case of the Americans, on the Spaniards and the Filipinos. There were a few moments of tension. The Alaska boundary provided one, and another came out of President Cleveland's sudden truculent challenge to Britain over the Venezuela dispute. (That Christmas crisis of 1895 was the last time when Canada actually made large defensive preparations against American attack.) But in general the atmosphere was improving, if only because there were so few things left to fight about. The Canadian-American rivalries of the new age were economic rather than military. In the First World War the two sections of the English-speaking world fought as allies; and one of the few really good results of that war was a further civilizing of Anglo-American and Canadian-American relations. (One of my early memories is "Peace Year" at the Canadian National Exhibition; it was so denominated to commemorate the hundred years' peace between the Empire and the United States. "Peace Year," quaintly enough, was 1914.) Another thing the First World War did was to alter the international status of Canada. A symbol of the change was the opening of a Canadian legation in Washington in 1927. When the Second World War broke out Canada was conducting her own relations with the United States, and could no longer enjoy the privilege of blaming her diplomatic misfortunes upon the ignorance and stupidity of the British Foreign Office.[1]

The fourth period of Canadian-American relations is the period of common interests and co-operation—the period, indeed, of actual alliance—which begins in 1940. It is with this period that this paper deals.

[1] The present writer has developed some of these themes in the following: "The Myth of the Unguarded Frontier, 1815-1871," *Am. Hist. Rev.*, vol. 56 (1950),1; *The Undefended Border, The Myth and the Reality* (Canadian Historical Association, Historical Booklet No. 1, Ottawa, 1953); and *The Military Problems of Canada* (Toronto, 1940).

I do not propose to say a great deal about the forces that produced the sudden great rapprochement of 1940. But if we are to be realistic we must of course recognize the powerful influence exerted at the moment of the collapse of France by what Kipling once called "the ties of common funk." Canada and the United States came together, not because of love for each other, but because the menace of Nazism had reduced both to a state close to panic. The Canadian-American alliance is one of the minor monuments to Adolf Hitler. Indeed, a cynic might see it in a parallel to the involuntary alliance between two characters in *The Hunting of the Snark:*

> But the valley grew narrow and narrower still
> And the evening got darker and colder,
> Till (merely from nervousness, not from good will)
> They marched along shoulder to shoulder.

II

It might be forcibly argued that the results of the Ogdensburg meeting between Mr. Roosevelt and Mr. King have no place in a study of treaty relations between Canada and the United States, for no treaty was signed at Ogdensburg. The two statesmen simply issued a six-sentence press release which announced that they had "discussed the mutual problems of defense in relation to the safety of Canada and the United States" and had agreed to set up a Permanent Joint Board on Defence which was to begin studying those problems forthwith. Out of this remarkably informal beginning came the complex relationship which exists today.

Nobody in 1940 knew precisely where the Ogdensburg agreement would lead, although it was obvious that its implications might be very large. But almost no one was disposed to criticize. Canadians and Americans, awaiting in tense anxiety the result of the great battle then being fought in the air above England's southern counties, hailed the news from Ogdensburg like a victory. Observers in Ottawa, surveying the Canadian press during the week following the meeting, could not find a single adverse editorial reference; and this unprecedented chorus of praise was undoubtedly music in the ears of the Prime Minister. South of the border there was only a little less unanimity; such isolationist or partisan voices as were raised against the agreement served merely to emphasize how nearly universal was the support for it. What seems to have been the first important adverse comment in Canada did not appear for over a month; it was a letter from C. H. Cahan, an Opposition politician, who asserted that the Ogdensburg meeting had "created an impression, not only in Berlin but also in certain defeatist circles in this country, that the Government of Canada has become very pessimistic regarding the probable outcome of the Battle of Britain and is now hastily preparing its political and diplomatic defences against the day of wrath when Germany's conquest of Britain is completed."[2] But there seem to have been few to echo these sentiments. There are not many historical examples of an agreement between two nations commanding such nearly unanimous approval from the public on both sides.[3]

Mr. King had every reason for gratification, not least perhaps because the favorable reception accorded his arrangement with Roosevelt indicated a very considerable political advantage to him. (The one serious spot on the sun, from his point of view, was the fact that the British Prime Minister had received his account of Ogdensburg with decidedly modified rapture; but, fortunately, Mr. Churchill was not a Canadian voter.) Yet it is worth while to make the point that King was not so intoxicated by his meeting with the President as to lose sight of certain points of Canadian policy which he considered basic. He knew that the British Government was giving thought to selling or leasing to the United States bases in certain island colonies, including Newfoundland; but he made it quite clear to Roosevelt at Ogdensburg that "we would not wish to sell or lease any sites in Canada but would be ready to work out matters of facilities."[4] With respect to Newfoundland, it should be said that Mr. King was strongly seized of the importance of protecting Canada's permanent

[2] Letter of Sept. 24, 1940, Montreal *Gazette*, Sept. 25, 1940.

[3] On the Ogdensburg meeting and agreement, see, from the American side, Stanley W. Dziuban, *Military Relations between the United States and Canada, 1939-1945* (Washington, 1959), 13-30 (an account which contains a few errors of detail) and Nancy Harvison Hooker, ed., *The Moffat Papers* (Cambridge, Mass., 1956), 324-330. An account based on Canadian official records is C. P. Stacey, "The Canadian-American Permanent Joint Board on Defence, 1940-1945," *Int. Jour.*, vol. 9 (1954), 107. Mr. King's diary of the episode is quoted in J. W. Pickersgill, *The Mackenzie King Record*, I (Toronto, 1960), 129-139.

[4] Pickersgill, *op. cit.*, I, 135. All Canadian evidence supports this. The American Minister's record suggests that on the way back from Ogdensburg King indicated to him that bases could be obtained in Canada in much the same ways as in the islands (Hooker, *op. cit.*, 329; cf. Dziuban, *op. cit.*, 23); but Moffat must have misunderstood him.

interests there. He evidently felt that it was undesirable to place any obstacle in the way of the Anglo-American arrangement about Newfoundland; but it is relevant that the Canadian Air Minister, Mr. Power, left for St. John's on the same day on which Mr. King went to Ogdensburg, and while there he negotiated with the Newfoundland Government a comprehensive joint defense agreement under which the Newfoundland forces were placed under Canadian command and Canada assumed wide responsibilities for the security of the island.[5]

It is interesting also that in his subsequent confidential explanations in Ottawa King emphasized the limited nature of the new board's authority. It was, he said, a body whose business was to study and to recommend; decision and action were reserved to the governments. In a private interview with Opposition leaders in the House of Commons, he assured them, truly enough, that no "commitments" had been made. They were interested in the relationship of Britain to the new arrangements. King presumably did not tell them that there had been no consultation with London before he left for Ogdensburg (indeed, there had been small time for consultation); but he was in a position to say that a very full report had gone to Churchill. The fact that Churchill's reply had not been received at the time of the interview may have saved King some slight embarrassment.[6]

III

Thanks to various recent publications, official and unofficial, we now know a good deal about Canadian-American wartime co-operation after Ogdensburg, although the record is still incomplete, particularly on the Canadian side. And the story as we know it is on the whole pretty satisfactory. The two countries worked together for the defeat of Germany and Japan, not without misunderstandings, but without encountering difficulties so serious as to menace the goodwill subsisting between them or to constitute a material hindrance to the joint effort. No one should despair of relations between two communities whose leaders are capable of acts of statesmanship so con-

---

[5] C. P. Stacey, *Six Years of War* (Ottawa, 1955), 179.
[6] Pickersgill, *op. cit.*, I, 137-138.

structive and so imaginative as the Hyde Park Agreement of 1941, which, enunciating the principle that "each country should provide the other with the defence articles which it is best able to produce," solved almost at a blow Canada's intractable foreign exchange problem with the United States.

The success of the relationship on the military side certainly owed something to the Permanent Joint Board on Defence, which provided a ready and relatively informal channel for discussion possessing the advantages of "frankness, mutual confidence, and dispatch." The Board was most important before Pearl Harbor; after the United States entered the war more was done by direct military liaison.[7] But in all its aspects the relationship was deeply indebted to good understandings between individuals, and of these understandings the most important was of course that between Mr. Roosevelt and Mr. King. It would be easy to exaggerate the intimacy of the friendship between the two (and it was in King's political interest to exaggerate it); but we know enough now to leave no doubt that their personal association had significant consequences.

In spite of these various advantages, the wartime record leaves one with a strong impression of the innumerable difficulties presented by military co-operation between two independent nations, both proud to the point of conceit, one of which possesses a dozen times the population of the other and more than a dozen times the wealth. Canada, as what Canadians like to call a "middle power," was in a difficult position in the Grand Alliance. She made a considerable contribution to the joint effort, but was largely excluded from the councils which directed that effort. It was not altogether surprising that a British Government, especially perhaps one headed by Winston Churchill, should be willing in a time of war to set back the constitutional clock and claim, in effect, the right to speak for the Commonwealth as a whole. But the United States Government, and particularly it seems the military departments, was glad to accept this claim. Both the great English-speaking powers, it is evident, found the national status of the Dominions a nuisance. Without denying the force of the argument that military efficiency requires concentration of authority, one can still suggest that the disregard of Canadian interests was

[7] Stacey, "The Canadian-American Permanent Joint Board on Defence," *loc. cit.* An account of the Board's wartime operations by the first secretary of the Canadian Section is H. L. Keenleyside, "The Canada–United States Permanent Joint Board on Defence, 1940-1945," *Int. Jour.*, vol. 16 (1960-61), 50.

pushed to unnecessary lengths. A notable example was the prolonged refusal of the United States to accept a Canadian military mission in Washington.

Early in 1941 Anglo-American staff conversations were held to make tentative plans for joint military action in the event of the United States being drawn into the war. Canada and Australia were represented by officers who were kept outside the conference proper; the refusal to admit them even as genuine "observers" was apparently the result of American insistence.[8] The conference report recommended that Dominion military representation in Washington should be through the medium of the British military mission, of which the Dominion attachés would be members. The Canadian Government and Chiefs of Staff considered that, in view particularly of the special military relationship already established between Canada and the United States, this would be inadequate for Canadian purposes; the United States was accordingly asked to receive a Canadian military mission in Washington. The State Department, it would seem, was willing; but the War and Navy Departments were not. The argument was used that accepting a Canadian mission would afford an undesirable precedent which would lead to requests from other Dominions and from American republics. Even the intervention of the Prime Minister was unsuccessful in procuring a reversal of this attitude, which was persisted in for about a year. However, after the United States became a belligerent it changed, and in the summer of 1942 a Canadian Joint Staff was established in Washington—where, incidentally, it still remains.[9]

An American military writer has suggested that the United States attitude on the question of the military mission may have been influenced by another matter which was being discussed during these months in the Permanent Joint Board on Defence. Soon after the Board was established, its service members set to work on a joint defense plan to meet the situation that would arise if Britain were overrun or the Royal Navy lost control of the North Atlantic. The problem of command was not specifically dealt with until the spring of 1941, when the Canadian service members accepted a draft plan which, *in these desperate circumstances*, would have vested the "stra-

[8] Dziuban, *op. cit.*, 57.
[9] *Ibid.*, 71-76. Mr. King's interest in the staff mission in Washington is one matter which does not seem to be noticed in Mr. Pickersgill's book based on his diary.

tegic direction" of the two countries' land and air forces in the Chief of Staff of the United States Army, subject to prior consultation with the Canadian Chief of Staff concerned. At this same period, however, the two groups of service members were already working on another defense plan to meet the improved aspect which the war now presented—a plan under which, in the event of the United States entering the war, the two countries would co-operate with the other Allies not so much in the defense of North America as in offensive action to defeat the Axis. The United States was, naturally enough, very anxious that Canada should accept American "strategic direction" of her forces under this plan too. But neither the Canadian Chiefs of Staff nor their political superiors considered it desirable to make a concession which would have placed Canadian forces in Canada under U.S. command at a time when North America was not seriously menaced. At one stage the controversy became heated, and Colonel Dziuban is inclined to think that American officers withheld approval of the mission proposal in the hope of using it as a lever to change the Canadian attitude on command.[10] But the Canadians remained adamant, and after Pearl Harbor, when Canadian co-operation seemed more important to the U.S. services than it had before, the Americans reluctantly accepted the Canadian viewpoint. The relevant passage in the final version of the joint defense plan ran, "Coordination of the military effort of the United States and Canada shall be effected by mutual cooperation, and by assigning to the forces of each nation tasks for whose execution such forces shall be primarily responsible."[11]

A passage in the American official history serves to indicate what very serious possibilities of trouble had lain behind this controversy. The defense plan referred to had provided that a unified command might be established when mutually agreed upon; but it added that this would not extend to authorizing a commander "to control the administration and discipline of the forces of the nation of which he is not an officer, nor to issue any instructions to such forces beyond those necessary for effective coordination. . . ." This was the basic principle upon which Allied co-operation in the field was carried on so successfully in the course of the war, but some American officers in 1941 failed to appreciate its importance. The U.S. historians write,

[10] Dziuban, *op. cit.*, 74.
[11] Stacey, "The Canadian-American Permanent Joint Board on Defence," *loc. cit.*; Dziuban, *op. cit.*, 110-116; Stetson Conn and Byron Fairchild, *The Framework of Hemisphere Defense* (Washington, 1960), 344-383.

"Apart from the near impossibility of the two forces ever agreeing as to which should exercise unity of command, the great defect according to American staff planners was that unity of command, as defined in Joint Basic Defense Plan No. 2, did not confer authority over administration and discipline. Without this authority, there was, they contended, only the semblance of command."[12] If wind of these ideas had reached the Canadians concerned, it is not surprising that they were cautious about accepting American command. The storm that would have been raised in Canada by the suggestion that an American commander might claim the right to convene courts-martial to try Canadians, or to confirm the sentences of such courts-martial, can perhaps be imagined.

For the problem of representation of the "middle powers" in international organizations Mackenzie King had produced by 1943 what he considered a satisfactory solution, in "the functional principle of representation": "Representation should be determined on a functional basis which will admit to full membership those countries, large or small, which have the greatest contribution to make to the particular object in question."[13] Canada achieved some success along these lines, being admitted to two of the four Anglo-American non-military Combined Boards—the Combined Production and Resources Board and the Combined Food Board.[14] She never sought membership on the Combined Chiefs of Staff and admitted, although with no great enthusiasm, that the strategic direction of the war was the responsibility of Churchill, Roosevelt, and their own military advisers. She did seek membership on the Combined Munitions Assignment Board, on the basis of her very considerable contribution in munitions production, but her application was rejected. King obtained from Roosevelt a promise that membership would be accorded, but Harry Hopkins seems to have talked the President out of it. King recorded that Hopkins did not understand the Canadian position and did not want to understand it.[15]

[12] Conn and Fairchild, op. cit., 383.

[13] Speech in Canadian House of Commons, July 9, 1943, Parl. Deb. (Commons), Sess. 1943, 4558. See C. C. Lingard and R. G. Trotter, Canada in World Affairs, September 1941 to May 1944 (Toronto, 1950), 249-250. The speech actually referred to postwar organization, but pretty clearly derived from current experience in the direction of the war.

[14] See S. M. Rosen, The Combined Boards of the Second World War (New York, 1951).

[15] Pickersgill, op. cit., I, 410-411, 416.

In these major issues Britain was often a party to the controversy along with the United States. Throughout the war, however, Canada was constantly involved in secondary problems which affected only Canada and the U.S. Many of these arose out of American enterprises being conducted on Canadian soil; and the Canadian Government was constantly disturbed by the tendency of Americans engaged in these projects to forget international formalities and act as though they were in their own country. When in the spring of 1943 the government appointed a Special Commissioner for Defence Projects in North-West Canada[16] it was very largely with a view to curbing these tendencies in a tactful manner; and this measure seems to have been effective in this respect while in fact at the same time producing better understanding with the Americans on the ground.

IV

When one turns to consider Canadian policy after the Second World War, one is forcibly struck at once by the revolutionary contrast with the years before 1939. In those days Canada's policy was basically isolationist; the government's watchword was "no commitments"—no commitments to Britain or the Commonwealth, no commitments to anybody in advance of an actual crisis which would compel decisions to be made. There was no return to these ideas after 1945, though their influence was still traceable as long as Mr. King remained Prime Minister. After his retirement in 1948, the country found itself fully committed to policies of "collective defence"— and the influence of two world wars was reflected in the fact that there was virtually no public criticism of the change. Canada's attitude towards the United Nations contained no suggestion of the reservations that had been evident from the beginning in her view of the League of Nations a generation earlier; and her new Prime Minister, Louis St. Laurent, was one of the founding fathers of the North Atlantic Treaty Organization.

Canada, moreover, now maintained far larger defense forces than ever before in peacetime. A tendency to reduction in military expenditure apparent in 1947/48 was soon reversed under the influence of the Cold War, and the outbreak of hostilities in Korea in 1950

[16] Dziuban, *op. cit.*, 137-138.

produced a greatly expanded program. In terms of Canadian policy, the sending of considerable forces to fight in Korea was perhaps a less radical departure than the decision to station Canadian units in Europe in a time of peace. Since 1951 an army brigade group and an air division have been serving there under NATO.

After 1945, North American strategic conditions were utterly different from those that had produced the Canadian-American rapprochement of 1940. Nazi Germany was a thing of the past; but if there was no longer an actual enemy in the field there was an obvious potential enemy, Soviet Russia, looming up across the Arctic rather than across the Atlantic. In these circumstances the joint Canadian-American military program was maintained; but it changed front to the north, and with the passage of time its form also changed materially. As early as 1946 American generals were expressing alarm about the exposed state of the "Arctic frontier," and there were reports of pressure on Canada. Mr. King subsequently denied "emphatically" that the United States Government had asked for bases in the north, which led a *New York Times* reporter to observe that this was very true, but what the United States had actually suggested was that it should build the bases and that they should be staffed largely by Canadians. Doubtless with a view to clearing the air, a joint statement was issued by the two governments on February 12, 1947. "In the interest of efficiency and economy," it said, "each Government has decided that its national defense establishment shall, to the extent authorized by law, continue to collaborate for peacetime joint security purposes." It went on to observe that the collaboration would "necessarily be limited," and defined the principles on which it would be based. One of these was "Mutual and reciprocal availability of military, naval and air facilities in each country"; another was, "As an underlying principle all cooperative arrangements will be without impairment of the control of either country over all activities in its territory." The announcement stated further:

No treaty, executive agreement or contractual obligation has been entered into. Each country will determine the extent of its practical collaboration in respect of each and all of the foregoing principles. Either country may at any time discontinue collaboration on any or all of them. Neither country will take any action inconsistent with the Charter of the United Nations. . . .[17]

[17] Text of announcement, report of Mr. King's statement in Canadian House

This extremely cautious statement has upon it the mark of Mackenzie King. King's opponents used to accuse him of being unduly partial to the United States, and the portions of his diary that have been published certainly seem to indicate in him a tendency, which may have been atavistic, to put a more friendly construction on American actions than on those of the United Kingdom. Nevertheless, we know that on at least two occasions during the war King went on record in the Cabinet War Committee as apprehending, and proposing to guard against, American efforts to control postwar developments in Canada, and particularly in the north.[18] The last months of his administration did witness increased American activity in the Canadian north, but it was limited to the establishment of weather stations as a joint enterprise of the two countries. The first two such stations were operating by the autumn of 1947.[19]

For some years after 1945 the predominant opinion was that, in spite of the advent of the atomic bomb, another world war, if it happened, would have much in common with the last one; that it would be fought primarily in Europe and would have only a secondary North American aspect. The Canadian Minister of National Defence in 1948 expressed the view "that in the immediate future any attack on North America would be diversionary, designed to panic the people of this continent into putting a disproportionate amount of effort into passive local defence."[20] Revolutionary technological developments were to change all this. The years 1952-54 brought the hydrogen bomb (first in the United States, soon afterwards in Russia) and the public realization of this weapon's awful capabilities. The U.S.S.R. was known to have plenty of long-range bombers capable of delivering it in North America; but the menace grew as it became apparent that the Russians had made great progress with intercontinental missiles, something no one could doubt after the first *sputnik* was put up in 1957.

The prolonged Korean crisis of 1950-53 was something of a turning-point in Canadian-American military relations. In the course

of Commons Feb. 12, 1947, *Parl. Deb.* (Commons), Sess. 1942, 345-348; see also news story by James Reston reviewing recent events, *New York Times*, Feb. 13, 1947. On the 1946 reports, see F. H. Soward, *Canada in World Affairs: From Normandy to Paris, 1944-1946* (Toronto, 1950), 269-277.

[18] Pickersgill, *op. cit.*, I, 436, 644.

[19] Statement by Mr. C. D. Howe, *Globe and Mail* (Toronto), Oct. 22, 1947.

[20] Mr. Brooke Claxton in Canadian House of Commons, June 24, 1948, *Parl. Deb.* (Commons), Sess. 1948, 5784.

of it, indeed, the Canadian Army seems to have come close to being completely Americanized. Late in 1950 the Department of National Defence announced that the Army was to adopt armament and vehicles of the United States type, in order to facilitate industrial mobilization on a basis of North-American-made equipment. It was widely suggested that this might lead to a major reorganization of the Army on American lines and might mean that in future crises it would be found operating in conjunction with American forces rather than with the British Army with which it had so many traditional ties. It must be said, in mere honesty, that such a development would have been very unpopular in the Canadian Army. It did not, in fact, take place. A great deal of U.S. equipment was adopted, and more has been adopted since; but the equipment changeover was not absolute, and the organizational changes never transpired. The Canadian brigade group that went to Germany joined the British Army of the Rhine; the one that went to Korea served in the Commonwealth Division, and these arrangements worked satisfactorily.[21]

The anxious years of the Korean emergency saw the beginning of increased activity in the Canadian north. In 1949 Parliament had been told that though it was impracticable in Canada to construct a radar warning system as dense and effective as those in Britain or Germany during the last war, "an early warning system to cover certain vital approaches and areas is being developed." By 1952 the Minister of National Defence was saying that while "the most real danger" was in Europe, there was "much more real danger to Canada . . . than . . . in previous periods," and he mentioned in general terms joint air defense arrangements with the United States based on "radar stations with the necessary communications to enable the effective operation of fighter squadrons." By the end of 1954 all the heavy radar stations in the Pinetree system were installed and operating. This system, lying north of the most thickly settled areas of Canada, was built and operated partly by Canada and partly by the United States, the latter taking the larger share. By this time also the Mid-Canada Line, an all-Canadian enterprise, was being sited farther north, as was the great American-financed project across the Arctic, the Distant Early Warning or DEW Line, which was in operation by 1957.[22]

[21] C. P. Stacey, "Canadian Military Policy, 1928-1953," in 25 *Years of Canadian Foreign Policy* (Toronto, Canadian Broadcasting Corporation, n.d.).
[22] *Canada's Defence Programme, 1949-50. Issued under authority of Hon. Brooke*

V

The construction of the radar lines, and particularly the great DEW Line operation, did not escape criticism in Canada. Voices were raised to express anxiety lest Canadian sovereignty in the north should be impaired. On the whole, however, the public was not much disturbed. It was in the next period that really serious public criticism began to be heard for the first time since military co-operation began in 1940.

In the summer of 1957 the Liberal domination of Canadian politics ended after twenty-two years, and Mr. John Diefenbaker formed a Conservative administration. To the surprise of some people who had interpreted his election campaign as having anti-American overtones, one of the new cabinet's early actions was to accept the integration of Royal Canadian Air Force units into the North American Defense Command. Nine squadrons of the R.C.A.F. now passed under the command of an American general at Colorado Springs. NORAD has an "integrated" headquarters, which means in practice that the general has a Canadian Deputy and a certain number of Canadian staff officers. There is of course a very great gulf between a Commander and a Deputy. However, from a Canadian point of view and in one respect at least NORAD may be said to represent an improvement over those remote integrated headquarters, composed of Americans and Englishmen, under which large Canadian forces served in Italy and Northwest Europe in 1943-45.

In 1941, in the midst of a world war, the Canadian Government had refused to place Canadian forces in Canada under American command. The new government had now taken this action in a time of peace. Circumstances, of course, had changed. It was evident now that if another war came, it would probably come with stunning suddenness; in that case there would be no time to improvise command arrangements before the first blows were struck, and under the conditions of nuclear warfare those blows might be so appallingly damaging as to be decisive. Nevertheless, NORAD encountered severe criticism in Canada, and the critics, ranging from undergraduates to retired generals, have become more vocal with the passage of time.

Claxton, Minister of National Defence (Ottawa, 1949), 12-13; speech by Mr. Claxton in Canadian House of Commons, April 3, 1952, *Parl. Deb.* (Commons), Sess. 1952, 1079-1089; Department of National Defence *Report for the Fiscal Year 1954-55* (Ottawa, 1956), 65; *Canada's Defence Programme, 1955-56* (Ottawa, 1955), 6.

The fundamental function of NORAD is to defend the bases of the U.S. Strategic Air Command, the backbone of the Western nuclear deterrent upon which, in today's unpleasant world, our security depends. That such defense should be a bilateral rather than a NATO function may seem strange, and this limitation has had something to do with NORAD's relative unpopularity; but the control of SAC itself is strictly *unilateral*, and the United States pretty clearly has no intention of allowing it to become anything else. Perhaps Canada is lucky to have, if not a foot, at least a toe in the U.S. door through NORAD; and perhaps she should think twice before withdrawing it.[23]

It was on the economic front of the defense effort that Canadian public opinion received its greatest shock. In February, 1959, the government canceled the contract for producing the CF-105 Arrow, the Canadian-built interceptor fighter which had already been successfully test-flown. The Arrow's place in the defense of Canada was to be taken, in part at least, by the American Bomarc surface-to-air missile, while the American F-104G fighter was to replace the obsolete Sabre in the Canadian air division in Europe. The government explained that the threat of the manned bomber had diminished; by 1962, when the CF-105 would have come into service, "the main threat is expected to consist of long-range missiles."[24] But the enormous cost of producing the plane for Canada alone was certainly a very powerful factor; and the Canadian Government failed in attempts to sell it to its allies, including the United States. The cancellation of the contract instantly threw fourteen thousand people out of work, and newspaper reports said that the final number affected might be as many as thirty thousand.

This dramatic affair made it painfully clear to the Canadian public that in the future Canada, whether she liked it or not, was likely to be militarily dependent on the United States to an extent unknown in the past. The situation was bluntly stated by her Deputy Minister of Defence Production in September, 1960: "Unfortunately, as weapons become increasingly complex and costly, the independent development of major military weapon systems by Canada no longer

[23] For an informed discussion of this and other Canadian defense problems today, see General Charles Foulkes, *Canadian Defence Policy in a Nuclear Age* ("Behind the Headlines" pamphlet, Toronto, 1961).

[24] Hon. G. R. Pearkes, V. C., *Defence 1959* (Ottawa, 1959), 10.

seems possible."[25]   The question instantly arises, What is to become of the important defense industries of Canada created during and after the Second World War?   They are important to Canada and to the alliance.   The answer developed by Canada with American assistance has been the Production Sharing Programme, which may be roughly described as a Cold War version of the 1941 Hyde Park Agreement.   The object is to give Canadian industry a chance to compete for defense business in the United States.   The U.S. Government has been helpful.   "The Buy American Act provisions have been waived.   Duty free entry certificates may be obtained.   Security clearances are being expedited."[26]   On its side the Canadian Government has been assisting Canadian firms to the extent of financing tooling and other pre-production costs to enable them to compete with U.S. companies which have recovered such costs under earlier contracts.   The program has had a fair amount of success, and Canadian firms have obtained a respectable number of American orders for items which they can produce competitively.   It is to be hoped that it will be possible from now on to maintain an equitable flow of defense contracts in both directions across the border.   If this cannot be done, then Canadian-American relations are bound to suffer accordingly.

An agreement made in June, 1961, was important in both the economic and the military spheres.   Canada received from the United States sixty-six F-101B Voodoo fighters, to equip the Canadian NORAD squadrons.   In exchange, she took over the full operation and financing of sixteen stations in the Pinetree radar system which had formerly been U.S. responsibilities.   At the same time, it was agreed that the United States would pay three-fourths of the cost of producing in Canada $200,000,000 worth of F-104 G Starfighters for NATO powers in Europe—a project estimated to employ seven thousand Canadian workers for about three years, and thus an important contribution to keeping the Canadian aircraft industry in health.[27]   The Canadian Government now conceded that the manned bomber was a greater continuing threat than it had been disposed to admit in 1959.   Nevertheless, the Canadian strength in NORAD

[25] Speech by Mr. D. A. Golden, Toronto, Sept. 3, 1960.
[26] *Ibid.*
[27] *Globe and Mail* (Toronto), June 13, 1961.   The immediate criticism in the U.S. Congress which greeted this announcement was evidence of the importance of the obstacles which nationalist and protectionist sentiment is likely to put in the way of production sharing arrangements.

has been reduced from nine squadrons to five, and that of the air division in Europe from twelve squadrons to eight; the R.C.A.F.'s fighter force is thus greatly diminished.

VI

At the end of this brief and inadequate historical survey, I should presumably make some attempt at describing the present attitude of Canadians towards the military relationship which has grown up with the United States. I do so with diffidence, well knowing how unwise it is for any individual to take it on himself to interpret public opinion in a democratic state.

During the past few months we have heard quite a bit about neutralism in Canada. Canada certainly has some neutralists—I know one myself. Indeed, a book has been written—not by a Canadian, but by a former Canadian—recommending "an impregnable neutralism" as the policy for Canada in today's world.[28] But it would be a mistake, I think, to take these manifestations too seriously. I suspect that they are not much more important than the neutralism which appeared to be flourishing (under other names) in Canada before the Second World War, but whose essential insignificance appeared in 1939. There are many people who would like to think that Canada could escape embroilment in a third world war, but most of them, I believe, realize that such escape would be impracticable if the great powers actually were so criminally stupid as to go to war. Nevertheless, these neutralist declarations may be straws in the wind. Somes aspects of the Canadian defense arrangements with the United States appear to be disturbing a fair number of Canadians who are not neutralists (and, I should perhaps add, certainly not Communists). These people feel, I think, that the element of genuine co-operation in North American defense is becoming more and more negligible. They feel that Canada is in danger of becoming a mere satellite of the United States. They would like to see their country regain some freedom of action. But, the world being what it is, they find it difficult to say how this is to be accomplished.

Within the past year or two these issues have, for the first time, become involved in party politics. The neutralist prescription has

[28] James M. Minifie, *Peacemaker or Powder-Monkey* (Toronto, 1960).

commanded a degree of support only out on the left. In 1960 the convention of the Cooperative Commonwealth Federation, Canada's socialist party, went on record in favor of withdrawing not only from NORAD but also from NATO. The C.C.F. has now been merged in the New Democratic party, which held its founding convention in the summer of 1961. The proceedings suggested that the N.D.P. may be somewhat less radical in foreign policy matters than its predecessor, for the convention agreed that it might be appropriate to stay in NATO, provided NATO did not become a nuclear power in its own right; but it called for withdrawal from NORAD without bothering to discuss the arguments in the case.[29]

Failing a surprising reversal, the New Democratic party is in no immediate danger of having to form a government and put its doctrines into effect. More important politically is the attitude of the Liberal party, the official Opposition, which might be put back into power by the next general election or the one after that. The Liberals produced a new program at a national rally held in January, 1961. It dealt significantly, if not very impressively, with the question of NORAD, proposing that Canada should withdraw, not from NORAD as a whole, but from her interceptor role in it, limiting herself to the task of early warning. At the same time the Liberals grasped the nettle of nuclear weapons for Canadian forces, which the present government had refrained for over two years from coming to grips with. They adopted the policy of opposing the acquisition, manufacture, or use of such weapons "either under separate Canadian control or under joint U.S.–Canadian control."[30] They were apparently prepared, however, to compromise with this principle to the extent of permitting the use of nuclear weapons by Canadian forces serving abroad.

The Conservative Government, it is hardly necessary to say, stands by NORAD, since NORAD is its own child. And NORAD is not to be sloughed off quite like an old shoe, in any case; unlike earlier Canadian-American arrangements we have mentioned, it was the subject of a firm written agreement signed in 1958, which is to run for ten years or for a shorter period if agreed upon by both countries. (Its terms may be "reviewed"—not "revoked," as be-

[29] *Globe and Mail* (Toronto), Aug. 4, 1961; Ramsay Cook, "Moderation Wins Down the Line in N.D.P.," *Saturday Night*, Toronto, Sept. 2, 1961.
[30] *Globe and Mail* (Toronto), Jan. 12, 1961.

lieved by Mr. Minifie—upon request of either country at any time.)[31] Nevertheless, I have said enough to indicate that NORAD is the special target of the Canadian critics; and since the command's utility, in the coming age of intercontinental missiles and missile-firing nuclear submarines, is at least doubtful, it is conceivable, though hardly probable, that it will not live out its allotted span.

Part of the background of the Canadian uneasiness which I have been describing is the fact that Canadians, while certainly generally sympathetic to the United States in the present world crisis, do not all have unlimited confidence in American policy. They are in fact rather less inclined to run a high temperature over the Russian menace than Americans are. Canada's idea of a world policy was thus defined by a member of the Government in 1960: "an unremitting search for the lessening of international tensions and... means of bringing about permanent disarmament." Many Americans, I suspect, would consider this mere simple-mindedness. On the other hand, many Canadians would agree with the editor of a Canadian national magazine who wrote recently, à propos of the causes of "an undeniable decline of confidence" in the United States, "The answer can be summed up in one word—brinkmanship."[32] Anyone who remembers the sigh of relief that went up across Canada ten years ago, when President Truman finally decided to dismiss General MacArthur, will know exactly what the editor means. One could cite more recent cases.

This all adds up to the fact that Canada is in a dilemma. She is sympathetic to Uncle Sam's international aims (whatever reservations she may occasionally have about his methods); and in all the circumstances the military alliance between the two was probably inevitable. But today she finds that alliance tending to become more and more constricting at a time when Canada herself is in a more and more independent mood. The dilemma is made none the easier in practice by the reflection that it results in part from the military and economic facts of the present-day world, which are rendering real independence for small nations an increasingly elusive thing. It is made sharper by the recurring Canadian feeling that the senior partner's policy is sometimes ill-considered and reckless, and takes

---

[31] *Winnipeg Free Press*, May 19, 1958; for text of agreement, see 1958 CTS 9.
[32] *Statements on Defence Policy and its Implementation made by the Hon. G. R. Pearkes, V.C.... before the Special Committee on Defence Expenditures, June 1960* (Ottawa, 1960), 3; *Maclean's*, Jan. 28, 1961.

too little account of the vastness of the interests that are at stake. Canada has a great deal of interest in peace, and much less interest in American prestige or in the scoring of propaganda points in the Cold War. Yet there is little that she can do about all this. Her influence is considerable in London, but much less important in Washington.

*   *   *   *   *

What are the lessons, for Canada, of the twenty-one years' experience we have surveyed? Here, for what it may be worth, is one person's interpretation. Canada had better look after her own interests as well as she can, for nobody else is going to do this for her. She had better face the fact that she will always have to work hard to make her interests and her problems even partially understood by her neighbors; Americans in general are as little interested in Canadian-American relations as Harry Hopkins was, and they will forget she even exists unless she keeps on reminding them. She should use what small influence she may have with the U.S. Government to remind *it*, when opportunities arise, that the interests of other people besides Americans are involved in the consequences of American policy, and to strive to restrain it from making those excursions to the brink that keep giving other people heart-failure. She will find, I believe, that her influence with the United States is greater if she keeps her military co-operation within carefully restricted limits; she should be an ally and a candid friend, not a satellite. (It does not follow, however, that she should make a practice of batting her friends in the snoot; she may need friends some day.) She must be prepared to go on maintaining respectable armed forces of her own; and my personal opinion is that well-equipped and well-trained conventional forces are her best resource, for the moment, from the points of view both of security and influence. Such forces, ready to take the field in any local conflict on behalf of the Western Alliance, or in any police action on behalf of the United Nations, would be invaluable in any secondary crisis, which fortunately seems much more likely than a third world war.

You will have noted that these prescriptions are couched in general terms. The task of reducing them to practical measures of detail I am delighted to leave to the statesmen.   After all, that is what we pay them for.[33]

[33] This paper covers the twenty-one year period ending in August, 1961, but note may be taken here of some recent relevant developments.   On January 12, 1963, Mr. L. B. Pearson, leader of the Canadian Liberal party, made a new statement of Liberal policy on the question of nuclear weapons.   He advocated that nuclear warheads should be accepted for "those defensive tactical weapons which cannot be used effectively without them."   This applied to forces both at home and abroad.   Mr. Pearson also appealed for a non-partisan approach to defense problems, and suggested a comprehensive re-examination of Canadian defense policies.   The nuclear issue had been raised on January 3, by General Norstad, who stated that Canada had committed herself to accepting nuclear weapons for her NATO forces.   The United States became more directly involved when the State Department issued a press release in effect contradicting remarks made by Mr. Diefenbaker on the subject.   On February 4, Douglas S. Harkness, Minister of the National Defence, resigned because of the Prime Minister's reluctance to accept nuclear weapons.   Next day Mr. Diefenbaker's minority government was defeated in the House of Commons. In the election campaign that followed Mr. Pearson maintained the position he had taken on January 12, and in the election of April 8, the Liberals obtained the largest group in the Commons, only three seats short of a majority.   Mr. Diefenbaker resigned, and on April 22, Mr. Pearson became Prime Minister.   It was indicated that his government would immediately proceed to negotiate an agreement with the United States on nuclear weapons.

7

General Aspects of Canadian-United States Treaty Relations

Their Import for the Conduct of Relations Between Nations on the Basis of Respect for Law and Mutual Interests

Green H. Hackworth

This topic, as will readily appear, presents a twofold aspect—one relating to the treaty relations between Canada and the United States; the other envisioning the possible import of those relations vis-à-vis relations between other nations. In considering the first of these two phases it would perhaps be a bit superficial to look at the treaty structure in the abstract and thence proceed to the second phase, i.e., whether there is here presented an example that could and should be followed, *ipso facto*, by other states. A clear appreciation of the purport of the relationship between Canada and the United States requires more than this. It requires that this relationship be examined in the light of antecedents, that is to say, in the light of the historical background of the two countries. For it is only in the light of that background that we may have a proper perspective for understanding and evaluating that which has developed, and of visualizing its possible import in other situations of a similar or dissimilar character.

I. BACKGROUND AND ANTECEDENTS

It should be said at the outset that the historical background of Canada–United States treaty relations is, in many respects, unique. Canada, as a member of the British Commonwealth, and the United States, as a former British colony, have always had much in common— a common language, a similar culture, a comparable system of jurisprudence, an orderly administration of justice, and so on. These common attributes make for a form of cohesion between the two peoples—a sort of kinship, so to speak—and hence an easier approach to common problems. The treaty relations between the two countries owe their existence, in large measure, to this favorable atmosphere.

For a period of nigh onto one hundred and fifty years the relations between the United States and Canada, as between the United States and the United Kingdom, have been on the whole serene and peaceful. The common boundary between Canada and the United States of more than three thousand miles has remained unmarred by military installations.

This background and this dedication to common ideals and purposes have served to keep intact and to strengthen the bonds of good neighbors in a family of nations, some members of which have not always been so well disposed. It is this common heritage which has led the two countries to a wealth of treaties, conventions, and other agreements that have given to their relations a large measure of reciprocal goodwill.

These relationships have as a counterpart the relations between the United States and the United Kingdom, which through a process of peaceful settlement and co-operative endeavors have done much to develop and enrich the law of nations. Not since the Treaty of Ghent have differences between the United States and Great Britain failed of peaceful solution, either by agreement or by arbitration.

The examples of peaceful adjustment between the United States and Canada have extended over a like period and are no less noteworthy—they speak in the same voice. No difference has arisen that has not yielded to amicable solution; no instance has arisen in which one tried to outmaneuver the other; no hard bargains have been sought and no sharp practices have fettered the sense of fairness that has prevailed. The principle of reasonableness and of friendly co-operation has been the guiding star. It is with this premise in mind that the treaty relations between Canada and the United States may best be considered and understood.

II. THE STRUCTURE OF TREATY RELATIONS

In speaking of "treaties" I assume that we are using the term in its broad or generic sense, that is to say, as including all agreements having a binding international character, such as conventions, protocols, declarations, agreements and arrangements by exchange of notes, commonly referred to as executive agreements. I also assume that we have in mind not only agreements between the two countries directly but also those between the United States and Great Britain which pertain to Canada.

On the basis of these two postulates the present treaty structure between Canada and the United States, including supplements, extensions, and amendments, comprises no less than 180 in number— some executed in whole or in part, such as boundary adjustments or pecuniary claims settlements, and a vast number executory in character.[1] This latter group covers a variety of subjects: atomic energy, aviation, boundary waters, customs, defense, economics, extradition, finance, fisheries, health and sanitation, highways, maritime matters, migratory birds, military affairs, naval vessels, navigation, postal arrangements, hydroelectric power, tenure and disposition of property, smuggling, taxation, telecommunications, trade and commerce, and others. Certain of these agreements have served and continue to serve as particularly effective instruments of peaceful adjustment between the two countries.

Boundary Waters

Foremost in treaty relations between Canada and the United States is the Boundary Waters Treaty of 1909, providing for an equitable use of the waters that wash the shores of our two countries, including those that flow into and out of boundary waters, and rivers that cross the common boundary. This treaty had its origin in the Rivers and Harbors Act of Congress, approved June 13, 1902, calling upon the President to invite the Government of Great Britain to join in the formation of an international commission to investigate and report on the "conditions and uses" of the waters adjacent to the boundary line between the United States and Canada, including all the waters of the lakes and rivers whose natural outlet is by the River Saint Lawrence to the Atlantic Ocean, and to make recommendations for improvements and regulations as shall best subserve the interest of navigation in said waters.[2] Suffice it to say that such an

---

[1] See *Treaties in Force, A List of Treaties and Other International Agreements of the United States in Force on January 1, 1961*, Dept. of State Pub. 7132.
[2] *32 Stat.* 373.

investigation and report were made and the Boundary Waters Treaty of 1909 followed some three years later. It constitutes a landmark in the regulation and use in the common interest of a natural resource of inestimable value to the two countries and their nationals.

The treaty is outstanding not only by reason of its provisions concerning use of the waters along the common frontier, but also by reason of its provisions with respect to the instrumentality—the International Joint Commission—through which its provisions were to be implemented. The predominant position of the Commission is revealed by the provision that, except for existing uses, obstructions and diversions theretofore permitted or thereafter provided for by special agreement between the parties, no further or other uses, or obstructions or diversions, of boundary waters on either side of the line affecting the natural level or flow of boundary waters on the other side of the line shall be made except by authority of the United States or the Dominion of Canada and with the approval of the International Joint Commission (Art. III), and the further provision giving the Commission authority to provide for protection and indemnity against injury of any interests on either side of the boundary (Art. VIII).

The treaty reserves to each of the High Contracting Parties on its own side of the boundary, subject to any existing treaty provisions, exclusive jurisdiction and control over the use and diversion of all waters on its own side of the line which in their natural channels would flow across the boundary or into boundary waters. This broad reservation of sovereign rights does not, however, give the parties carte blanche to use such waters as they may see fit; for it is subject to a condition that any interference with or diversion of such waters resulting in injury on the other side of the boundary shall give rise to the "same rights and entitle the injured parties to the same legal remedies as if such injury took place in the country where such diversion or interference occurs" (Art. II).

Here we have a recognition of, but a departure from, the doctrine stated by Attorney-General Harmon in his opinion of December 12, 1895.[3] But instead of providing for international reclamation, as might have been expected, national treatment is the criterion—a distinct compliment to the local jurisdiction.

A further restriction on this freedom of action by the national

[3] 21 *Ops. Atty. Gen.* 274; 1 Moore, *Digest* 654.

authorities in their own domain is reservation of the right of each of the parties to object to any interference with or diversion of waters on the other side of the boundary which would be productive of material injury to navigation on the opposite side.

This latter provision came into play in an oblique fashion in connection with the diversion from Lake Michigan by the Sanitary District of Chicago, on which the Supreme Court issued its decree of 1930.

Canada had no part in the litigation before the court, but the effects of the diversion on navigation had been the subject of discussions between the British Embassy, in behalf of Canada, and the Department of State in 1912-1913 and in 1923-1926, in connection with which Canada invoked international law, the Webster-Ashburton Treaty, and the Boundary Waters Treaty.[4]

A case of the temporary diversion of water from boundary waters with the approval of the I.J.C. is that of the St. Lawrence River Power Co., a subsidiary of the Aluminum Company of America, which, in 1918, was permitted to construct a submerged weir in the South Sault Channel of the St. Lawrence for the diversion of water to a power plant at Messina, New York.[5]

A case of the construction of a dam in a boundary water, but at a point where it ceased to mark the boundary, is that of the dam at Grand Falls on the St. John River, the effect of which was to inundate land in the State of Maine. Permission to construct the dam was given by the I.J.C. to the New Brunswick Electric Power Commission in 1925 and to the Commission's successor, the Saint John River Power Company, in 1926.[6]

Cases of the construction of dams in waters flowing across the boundary, at lower levels than the boundary, are those of Grand Coulee dam and reservoir on the Columbia,[7] and the raising of the height of a dam on the Skagit River to increase power production for the city of Seattle.[8] Each involved an elevation of water levels in Canada, and hence required approval of the Commission.

In giving its approval of works the Commission frequently makes

[4] *Wisconsin et al. v. Illinois et al.*, 281 U.S. 179, 201-202; 1 Hackworth, *Digest* 618-623.
[5] I.J.C., Docket No. 15.
[6] I.J.C., Dockets Nos. 19 and 22.
[7] I.J.C., Order, Dec. 15, 1941, Docket No. 44.
[8] I.J.C., Order, Jan. 27, 1942, Docket No. 46.

specific provision for indemnifying parties injured by such works. This it did in the last three cases referred to above.

Between April, 1912, and May, 1959, there were referred to the Commission some seventy-three applications for the approval of projects, or for investigation and report on projects. Some of these applications were made by private people or organizations, some by one or other of the two governments, and some by joint action of the governments. They have ranged in scope and magnitude from the establishment or repair of fishways and the creation of reservoirs for wildlife, to major navigation and power projects.

Joint Projects: Saint Lawrence and Columbia Rivers

The St. Lawrence Seaway and Power Projects and the Columbia River Basin Project are by far the most important of the joint undertakings, details of which are outside the compass of this statement. It is interesting to note, however, that rights of navigation have always played an important part in the treaty relations between the two countries. Navigation of the St. John River, of certain channels of the St. Lawrence, of the Detroit, and of channels and passages in the Great Lakes system date from the Webster-Ashburton Treaty of 1842. Navigation of the St. Lawrence from the boundary to and into the sea was declared to be forever free and open to citizens of the United States by the Treaty of Washington of 1871. Navigation ranks first after domestic and sanitary purposes in the uses specified in the Boundary Waters Treaty of 1909.

The history of the Saint Lawrence Seaway and Power Projects dates from 1895, when an act of Congress authorized the President to appoint a committee composed of three members to confer with a similar committee designated by Canada, to inquire into and report upon the possibility of constructing canals to permit oceangoing vessels to pass between the Great Lakes and the Atlantic Ocean, and the estimated cost of the construction.[9] Such committees were appointed and reported some two years later.[10]

Between that time and 1932, when a treaty was signed, numerous other surveys, investigations, and reports were made by national groups and joint boards, including the International Joint Commission, which meanwhile had been established. For the most part all

[9] 28 Stat. 950.
[10] H. Dec. 192, 54th Cong., 2nd Sess.; For. Rel., 1895, I, 705-707.

agreed on the feasibility and desirability of a seaway and power development. Various routes (the St. Lawrence, a Great Lakes–Hudson River project, and an all-American route) were considered but the St. Lawrence was the one most favored.[11]

The treaty came to a vote in the Senate on March 14, 1934, but failed to receive the necessary two-thirds majority by a vote of 49 for, to 43 against. Thereafter, for a considerable period of time, attention was directed toward possible revision of the treaty with emphasis on power development in the International Rapids Section. This was later accelerated by the war effort in Canada and by the defense effort in the United States.

In view of opposition by certain interests in the United States—the railways, coal interests, and certain seaports—and the possibility that a new treaty might well suffer the same fate as the earlier one, it was decided to embody the essential parts of the treaty in an executive agreement to be approved by the Congress, where a majority vote would suffice, and by the Parliament of Canada.[12] The agreement was signed at Ottawa on March 19, 1941, and was promptly submitted to the Congress by President Roosevelt. Numerous efforts were made by joint resolutions in both Houses of Congress to bring about approval but it was not until May 13, 1954, that Congress gave its consent.[13] The act of Congress created the St. Lawrence Seaway Development Corporation, with directions to construct in United States territory deep-water navigation works on the United States side of the International Rapids Section of the River, and to co-ordinate its activities with those of the St. Lawrence Seaway Authority of Canada, which had been created by an act of Parliament of December 21, 1951.[14]

It will thus be seen that the St. Lawrence projects were under consideration for almost sixty years before final steps were taken to consummate an agreement. Meanwhile Canada, apparently becoming restive under delays in Congress, indicated readiness to undertake construction of the Seaway from Lake Erie to Montreal as a Canadian project, subject only to satisfactory arrangement being made to ensure the development of power in the International Rapids Sec-

[11] Dept. of State Research Project No. 99 (1949), 9.
[12] Ibid., 34-36.
[13] 68 Stat. 92.
[14] Acts of Canada, 15-16 George VI, c. 24.

tion.[15] The Seaway was formally opened by President Eisenhower and Queen Elizabeth II at a ceremony held at Montreal June 26, 1959.

The cost of the combined projects was estimated by engineers at between $800 and $900 million.[16] The actual cost appears to have exceeded the estimates. The Seaway project, originally estimated at $300 million, actually cost approximately $470 million.[17] Construction costs of the Power projects, originally estimated at $300 million, were, as of June 30, 1961, exclusive of transmission line projects, as follows: The Hydro-Electric Power Commission of Ontario: $300,-894,772.10 (Canadian funds); Power Authority of the State of New York: $342,797,128.16 (U.S. funds).[18]

Lastly, in the boundary waters category (omitting for the sake of brevity the Conventions of 1925 and 1938 regarding Lake of the Woods and Rainy Lake, respectively, and the Treaty of 1950 concerning uses of the waters of the Niagara River), we have the treaty signed January 17, 1961, providing for co-operative development of the Columbia River Basin. The project was initiated in 1944, when the two governments called upon the International Joint Commission, under Article IX of the Boundary Waters Treaty, to investigate and report on whether and in what specific respects co-operative development of the water resources of the Columbia River Basin would be practicable and in the public interest from the point of view of the two governments.

The treaty is to run for a minimum period of sixty years, terminable at the end of that or a subsequent date in accordance with the provisions of Article XIX. In broad outlines it provides for construction in each country of facilities for the storage of large quantities of water in the interest of flood control, increased power production, irrigation, etc. The work calls for an estimated total outlay in the United States of more than $400 million. The United States will pay to Canada more than $60 million, representing flood control benefits accruing to the United States by reason of Canadian storage. In addition, Canada will be entitled to a portion of the in-

[15] TIAS 3053.

[16] Sen. Doc. 165, 83rd Cong., 2nd Sess., 23, 31, 32, 37; Dept. of State Research Project No. 99 (1949), 9, 53.

[17] See questions and answers on the St. Lawrence Seaway, Senate For. Rel. Committee Print, 86th Cong., 2nd Sess. (1960), 1, 3.

[18] Letter of Aug. 31, 1961, from Power Authority of the State of New York to the author.

creased power developed in the United States. It is estimated that each country will receive a large block of new power at low cost.

Differences arising under the treaty which cannot be settled by the parties shall be submitted to the I.J.C., or in certain contingencies to an *ad hoc* arbitral tribunal, with the possibility, as an alternative procedure, of reference to the International Court of Justice.[19]

These agreements, relating to a great natural resource, have a direct beneficial effect on the life, the health, and the general welfare of the inhabitants of the two countries in a variety of ways. They comprehend such questions as sanitation, navigation, power development, irrigation, reclamation, and flood control, all of which are vital to the economic well-being of the two states.

Fisheries

The two countries have been at pains to preserve and develop fisheries on a co-operative basis, as evidenced in particular by the Convention of 1930, and the amending Protocol of 1956, for the protection, preservation, and extension of the Sockeye Salmon of the Fraser River System; the Convention of 1953 for the preservation of the Halibut fishery of the Northern Pacific and Bering Sea; and the Convention of 1954 on the Great Lakes fisheries. In all of these fields the water resources of the two countries and adjacent waters have been and are being utilized in the common interest.

III. THE IMPORT OF THE TREATY STRUCTURE

This brings us to a more speculative feature of the subject, namely, the significance of these treaty relations vis-à-vis the conduct of relations between other nations on the basis of respect for law and mutual interests.

No one can dispute the fact that the relations between Canada and the United States constitute a worthy example for other nations; nor can one doubt that emulation of the example by others would lead to greater respect for law and mutual interests, just as has been done for the two North American countries. But one is led to wonder whether it is realistic to assume, or to suggest, that such treaties, per se, lead to respect for law and mutual interests, or whether this may

[19] Art. XVI; for text, see Sen. Ex. C, 87th Cong., 1st Sess. (1961). The treaty comes into force upon exchange of ratifications, Art. XX.

not be stating the proposition in the inverse order; whether it might not be more in keeping with the realities of the situation to say that respect for law and mutual interests would or should lead to more desirable relations between and among nations? It may well be, and probably is, true that the treaty relations between Canada and the United States have strengthened their respect for law and mutual interests, but might it not be said with reason that pre-existing mutual respect and trust were a forerunner of these relations? I am persuaded that the latter may be true. One could very well reason that had it not been for mutual respect for law and reciprocal rights the two nations would not have agreed to a limitation of naval armaments on the Great Lakes, or to free navigation of boundary waters, or to a partnership in other uses of these waters. Without the pre-existing respect the treaty relations would have been in the nature of an experiment—a trial balloon, so to speak. In my view the rationale of the situation is that there already existed mutual respect as neighbors—a respect born of the historical background of the two countries, and that this mutual respect gave birth to and stimulated the happy relations which followed.

Many are the examples of treaties containing statements of lofty purposes and solemn commitments of the contracting parties, which are honored by some of the parties only to the extent that they are found to be convenient. The two Hague Conventions for the Pacific Settlement of Disputes, the Covenant of the League of Nations, and the Kellogg-Briand Pact, were thought to be bulwarks for the maintenance of peace; yet the First World War followed the Hague Conventions, and the Second World War followed all of these.

We now have the Charter of the United Nations, which was designed to fill gaps in the Covenant and to place on a more firm foundation peaceful international relations; yet this monumental structure is at times sorely tried. The hopes entertained for the role to be played by the International Court of Justice have been realized only in part. Some states take their legal disputes to the Court; others decline to do so, or to be impleaded.

I should not, however, be understood as thinking that we are experiencing a retrocession in mutual trust and respect for law and international obligations, although at times this may seem to be the case. On the contrary, I think that some progress has been and is being made, despite periods of retrogression. If it seems to be a slow process we need only remember that all great advances move that way; and that the society of nations is a most complex organism, the component parts of which have varied interests and varied notions and methods of satisfying those interests. The many agreements extant, the current pronouncements of statesmen, of political scientists, of lawyers and other scholars, on a rule of law and a respectable public order, cannot but have their restraining influence on the trend of events. No nation, however large or small or however ambitious, relishes the stigma of a lawbreaker or a disturber of the peace. Enlightened public opinion must have its effect. This is exemplified by the present play for prestige, and by the efforts made to justify, or to shift responsibility for, acts of a disturbing character.

Examples of relations somewhat akin to those between Canada and the United States are to be found on the border between the United States and Mexico; they are making their appearance on the River Nile, under the agreement of 1959; on the Indus, under the agreement of 1960; and in Western Europe in the form of the Coal and Steel Community agreement of 1951, and the European Economic Community agreement of 1957. Whether the co-operative activities of the two North American countries have been or may be an incentive we do not know, but the example is there for the world to see, and it may not be too much to hope that steps which have been taken may gain momentum when their value shall have been realized to a greater degree. Certain it is that the good neighbor policy which Canada and the United States have demonstrated cannot be viewed with other than approbation.

Finally, I think that it is not too much to expect, or at least to hope, that the purpose expressed in the first Article of the Charter of the United Nations: "To develop friendly relations among nations based on respect for the principle of equal rights and self determination of peoples" may eventually bear fruit.

It should not be the concern of one nation what form of government, or what social or economic order is maintained by another nation within its own borders, if that be the desire of the people of that nation. Adoption of the principle of noninterference, vouchsafed by the Charter, if scrupulously observed by all nations, would go far toward bringing about a state of tranquillity. The burdens of the armaments race, and the threats of atomic bombs and missiles, are the antithesis of what was hoped for by the signatories of the Charter.

War, with all its devastating potentialities, is not the answer to the present state of distrust and unrest. In this nuclear age the chaos and anarchy which war would bring cannot be limited to the belligerents. The whole world has a stake in peaceful settlements, to which all members of the United Nations are committed.

In a word, that which is sorely needed by the troubled world of today is a more zealous respect for the precepts of law, for mutual and reciprocal rights and duties, such as is revealed by the relations between Canada and the United States.

8

Canadian-United States Commercial Relations and International Law

The Cuban Affair as a Case Study

Edward McWhinney

The expropriation by the Castro Government late in 1960 of assets and property in Cuba owned by United States nationals, and the United States Government's embargo, invoked at the same time, against trade with Cuba by United States companies or nationals, brought into the open some long developing differences between United States and Canadian trade and economic policies. Proposed Canadian trade with Cuba after the American embargo aroused a deep intensity of feeling on both sides of the border; of this there is no doubt. Yet there is also little doubt that, while the Cuban Affair represented a high-water mark in Canadian-American political differences, it was also symptomatic of rather more deep-seated differences going back over a considerable number of years. Hence, after the Cuban Affair has been explored in the context of general Canadian–United States trade relations, several of these other areas of policy differences will be examined.

I. CUBAN EXPROPRIATIONS AND CANADIAN TRADE

As a matter of traditional international law theories—as received in Anglo-American and Continental European doctrines and jurisprudence—the Castro-sponsored expropriation of United States-owned assets in Cuba was illegal. Granting, for present purposes, the special character of the Castro accession to power, that it was a genuine popular revolution with its own distinct social and economic ideological base, and not merely a palace revolt or coup d'état with a change only in the personality and not in the ideological character of the decision-making élite, the objections to the Castro action against United States-owned property, in terms of traditional legal theories, seemed nevertheless overwhelming. It is generally agreed, of course, that a governmental nationalization of foreign-owned property, when motivated by some bona fide social and economic purpose involving the use of the property nationalized—for example, the effectuation of some overriding program of social and economic change involving ownership or control of the means of production, distribution, and exchange, and affecting the government's own nationals as well as foreigners—raises rather novel and urgent problems of international law not always encountered in the earlier international law cases where such governmental actions were all too often purely capricious and arbitrary outlets of xenophobia. But in the Castro expropriations, there were other and independent grounds of legal objection. Apart from the question of the existence of an obligation at international law to compensate for any foreign property seized, on which there is not complete unanimity of authoritative juristic opinion, and the further question of the manner and nature and extent that such compensation must take, on which matter, again, there is some further variance of legal opinion, the patently "discriminatory," "anti-American," character of the Castro expropriations was clear. They in fact applied only to property owned by United States nationals, property of the same essential character and extent owned by other nationals being conspicuously exempted from the operation of the Castro expropriation measures. International law authorities are agreed that any such nakedly differential treatment, operating unequally against particular groups or individuals solely because of their nationality, vitiates any claim to a bona fide social or economic purpose for the expropriation measures and renders the whole proceedings illegal at international law.

Canadian-owned assets in Cuba were exempt from the application of the Castro expropriation measures. While no definitive survey has been made of the character and extent of such Canadian-owned assets in Cuba, it is known that Canadian interests in insurance and banking in particular were very large. Thus it has been estimated that Canadian life insurance companies were writing 70 per cent of all life insurance carried by Cubans, with a total of $400 million of insurance on the lives of Cubans being underwritten by Canadian companies, and further millions of dollars of general insurance coverage being handled by Canadian companies.[1] In addition, thirty-two branches of two Canadian chartered banks (twenty-four branches of the Royal Bank of Canada and eight branches of the Bank of Nova Scotia) were doing business in Cuba, with an estimated minimum $100 million worth of assets,[2] at the time of the Cuban governmental decrees of October 13, 1960, nationalizing Cuban banks and foreign banks operating in Cuba. At the time the Castro nationalization decrees were first announced, it was indicated by a spokesman for the Royal Bank of Canada that the Canadian banks were exempt from such nationalization because the Castro Government "did not want to offend the Canadian government."[3]

Just what the Castro Government meant by this seems demonstrated by the fact of the sudden and apparently unexpected arrival in Ottawa, in December, 1960, of a ten-man Cuban trade mission headed by the Cuban Minister of Economy, Regino Boti. Mr. Boti indicated, on his arrival in Ottawa that Cuba was particularly interested in buying from Canada a wide range of goods and materials, including especially automotive and tractor spare parts, raw materials for bottle manufacturing, caustic soda, replacement parts for sugar mills, special types of lubricants, and petroleum refinery equipment. Mr. Boti said, further, that the Cuban administration estimated that it could buy up to $150,000,000 worth of goods from Canada on a cash basis with convertible currency earned from its sales to other countries.[4] The Boti mission to Canada was promptly welcomed by Trade and Commerce Minister George Hees with a statement, as reported in the press, that the Cubans were wonderful customers and that he would be happy to sell $150,000,000 worth of Canadian goods to Cuba in the next year.[5] These reports of the activities of the Boti

[1] *Financial Post* (Toronto), July 16, 1960, 1.

[2] *Ibid.*

[3] *Globe and Mail* (Toronto), Overseas Edition, Dec. 14, 1960, 1.

[4] *Ibid.*

[5] Mr. Hees' statements in the House of Commons in Ottawa were, however, more guarded. On Dec. 7, 1960 (*Parl. Deb.* (Commons), Sess. 1960-61, 578) he said, in answer to a question from Mr. Argue, "We are always glad to hear of people who wish to trade with Canada. I have heard that this [Cuban] delegation is on the way, but I have heard nothing further." On Dec. 8, 1960 (*ibid.*, 611) in answer to Mr. Deschatelets, he said simply, "Mr. Speaker, as I have said in this house on a number of occasions, this government is anxious to increase its exports to all countries of the world."

On Dec. 16, 1960 (*ibid.*, 870), the following exchange took place in the House of Commons: Mr. McIlraith: "The minister, in speaking of the [Cuban] visit—and

mission in Canada and of its reception by the Canadian Government were understandably received with rather mixed feelings in the United States. Perhaps the extent of these feelings is best summed up in the interview given by an unidentified Washington official to the Toronto *Globe and Mail*. In commenting on what he described as a "reluctance by Canada to join with the United States in fighting the growth of communism in Cuba," the official added that Canada seemed to be "more interested in making a few bucks than in thwarting the Reds in the Caribbean."[6]

As noted earlier, while the Cuban Affair represented a high-water mark in Canadian-American political differences in recent years, it was also symptomatic of deep-rooted differences in political and economic policy, and even legal thinking, tracing back over a span of years. Treated in the more immediate Cuban context, many leaders in Canadian political and economic life felt that the American difficulties in Cuba had been to a very large extent created by blindness in American policy itself. As the Toronto *Globe and Mail* editorialized:

The U.S. has made two basic errors in dealing with Cuba. The first was to give aid and support, for years, to the former dictator of Cuba, Fulgencio Batista. By helping to sustain this unpleasant gentleman in power, the U.S. helped to prevent peaceful political evolution which might have made a violent revolution unnecessary.

The second profound error was to take a hysterical attitude toward the new dictator, Fidel Castro. No sooner had Dr. Castro made his first, almost casual, contacts with the Kremlin, than the U.S. decided that he was a dangerous Bolshevik, and built him up into a 10-foot tall bogeyman.

I think I quote him directly from the Toronto *Telegram* of December 10, is reported as having said this: 'They're wonderful customers. You can't do business with better businessmen anywhere.' What special ingredients made those businessmen better than any other of our trading customers?"

Mr. Hees: "As I think the hon. member will realise if he thinks deeply into the matter, I was not referring to the people as personages, I was referring to the kind of trade which they offered to Canada. The hon. member, I think, will agree with me that when people come here, with whom we have normal trading relations, and are willing to buy for cash goods produced by Canadians, in Canadian factories and on Canadian farms, that will provide jobs for Canadians, that will be a good thing. . . ."

Mr. Pickersgill: "Did I understand the Minister of Trade and Commerce to say that he was misrepresented by the Toronto *Telegram?*"

Mr. Hees: "No. Mr. Speaker. I never claim to be misquoted by any newspaperman. . . ."

[6] *Globe and Mail* (Toronto), Overseas Edition, Dec. 14, 1960, 11.

The U.S. now sees Dr. Castro, bomb in hand, under every political bed in Latin America.

A moment's reflection shows how ridiculous is this alarmist view. No one has yet shown that Dr. Castro is a genuine Communist; his background and behaviour suggest that he is really nothing more than an eccentric and irresponsible political adventurer, seeking support wherever he can find it.[7]

Of course, what this particular Canadian criticism amounts to, in effect, is the proposition that the Latin American division of the State Department failed completely (to borrow British Prime Minister Harold Macmillan's graphic phrase regarding contemporary Africa) to sense the "wind of change" in Latin America and continued to back tired military dictatorships long after it was apparent that their days were numbered since lacking in any real popular base of power. If this criticism may seem to Americans to come too smugly from Canadians insofar as the Canadian Government, up to the present, has declined to become a member of the Organization of American States,[8] on the score mainly, it is understood, that membership would embroil Canada in unpleasant internal disputes in Latin America, it must be remembered that similar criticisms were advanced by Canada in the past against British and French policies in the Middle East and Colonial Africa, most dramatically undoubtedly in the Suez Canal affair of 1956 when the Canadian Government was avowedly hostile to the British-French joint action against Egypt. A similar increased sensitiveness to the "wind of change" in world events was perhaps behind Prime Minister Diefenbaker's leadership, at the Commonwealth Prime Ministers' Conference of March, 1961, of the Common-

[7] Globe and Mail (Toronto), Overseas Edition, Dec. 28, 1960, 7.

[8] Canada is not a member of the Organization of American States, but does participate in certain of its specialized agencies and technical organizations; 12 External Affairs (Ottawa) 878, at 881 (Dec., 1960). Indications of a possible change in the official Canadian attitude of non-participation in OAS are to be found in such measures as the recent widespread extension of Canadian diplomatic representation in Latin America and in the further decision to accept an invitation of the council of the OAS to send a Canadian observer to the eleventh inter-American conference, held in Quito in May, 1961; see statement by the Minister for External Affairs, Mr. Green, to the House of Commons, Jan. 20, 1961, Parl. Deb. (Commons), Sess. 1960-61, 1255. Mr. Green had earlier stated, in the House of Commons, that he believed there was some value in "letting the Canadian people do a little thinking about the question of whether they want their nation to join the organisation of American states in order that we may see what the reaction of public opinion will be"; statement by Mr. Green, July 14, 1960, ibid., Sess. 1960, 6374-75; and see also statements by Mr. Green on March 16, 1960, ibid., 2128, and May 20, 1960, ibid., 4075-76.

wealth Afro-Asian bloc action that succeeded in forcing the Union of South Africa's withdrawal from further participation or membership in the Commonwealth, such collective action on the part of Canada and the Afro-Asian Prime Ministers being designed as a protest against the racially discriminatory policies in force in South Africa. This was Prime Minister Diefenbaker's Tory Radicalism projected into foreign affairs, and it is not surprising that it may have some attractiveness also, for the young policy-makers of Mr. Kennedy's "New Frontier" in Washington, for it reminds one strongly of earlier, more venturesome, more experimental, periods in American diplomacy.

More narrowly, in terms of strict international law doctrine, differences in Canadian and American attitudes to Cuba may stem from differences in the general legal traditions operating even within the context of the strictly common law world. American international law doctrine, much more than Canadian, which is more essentially English-derived, so often combines essentially pragmatist-based positions with strong doses of natural law thinking. The normative-type propositions, for example, found in what we might call "American" international law attitudes—the Stimson doctrine of the duty of non-recognition of international situations brought about by "illegal" use of force, invoked so often in connection with American thinking on such matters as the issue of recognition or non-recognition of Communist China, have no strict counterparts or parallels in the international law doctrine of the Commonwealth countries per se. Although Canada, like the United States, so far does not maintain diplomatic relations with Communist China, Canadian attitudes seem much more impatient of long-contained disharmony between the factual state of affairs—existence of Communist China as a viable political regime exercising effective *de facto* control over mainland China—and the legal situation of nonrecognition of Communist China by so many Western powers which generally follow American leadership in foreign affairs. In the same way, in relation to Cuba, once the Castro regime was effectively established as being in control of Cuba, the issue of the means actually used to gain power and the mode of treating political opponents (of Cuban nationality) once power was in fact attained, tended to become irrelevant, in Canadian eyes, in the practical conduct of relations with Cuba: Mr. Hees' widely quoted, or misquoted, comment that the Cubans were good businessmen is not so far removed in spirit from the philosophy behind the English-based "declaratory" theory of recognition of foreign régimes, which looks to the political stability and continuity of the regime in question and generally does not seek to impose any moral criteria to appraise its "fitness" for reception into the world community. The essentially laissez-faire, "economic man," roots of the declaratory theory of recognition are clear in any case: on this view, it merely complicates unnecessarily the conduct of international legal relations to condition the recognition of, or for that matter (and more immediately relevant in a strictly Cuban context), the continuance of legal relations with, a foreign regime on its meeting of certain postulated, a priori standards of political ideology.

In the end result, the Canadian-American imbroglio over Cuba seems to have ended as suddenly as it began. For one thing, Canadian-Cuban trade, after the Cuban-American break, never attained the optimistic figures predicted by the Cuban Economy Minister, and in fact both fell below Canadian-Cuban trade figures for the corresponding period of the preceding, politically normal, year, and was also even below the level of the then currently continuing American-Cuban trade in nonstrategic materials.[9] Secondly, Prime Minister Diefenbaker moved promptly, apparently without any prior request or representations from Washington,[10] to block legal loopholes to the transhipment or re-export, from Canada to Cuba, of United States-produced goods and materials;[11] and the Canadian Government also acted immediately to prevent export of strategic goods (including armaments and munitions) to Cuba, even goods of purely Canadian origin.[12] And the Minister for Trade and Commerce, Mr. Hees, now proceeded to retract, most handsomely, his earlier remarks on the qualities of the Castro Cubans as good businessmen.[13] There

[9] See *Report on Canada's Trade with Cuba*. A Statement by the Canadian-American Committee of the Private Planning Association of Canada and the National Planning Association, U.S.A., Feb. 6, 1961.

[10] Statement by the Prime Minister, Mr. Diefenbaker, Nov. 23, 1960, *Parl. Deb.* (Commons), Sess. 1960-61, 113.

[11] See statements in the House of Commons by the Prime Minister, Mr. Diefenbaker, Dec. 12, 1960, *ibid.*, 701; by the Acting Minister of Trade and Commerce, Mr. Gordon Churchill, on Dec. 15, 1960, *ibid.*, 820; by the Minister of Trade and Commerce, Mr. Hees, on Dec. 16, 1960, *ibid.*, 867.

[12] See especially statements in the House of Commons, Nov. 22, 1960 (Mr. Hees), *ibid.*, 68; Dec. 9, 1960 (Mr. Diefenbaker), *ibid.*, 651; and Dec. 12, 1960 (Mr. Diefenbaker), *ibid.*, 701.

[13] "Well, like Fiorello La Guardia, when I make a mistake, I really make a beaut," said Mr. Hees. "I want to straighten that out right now. I have no sym-

seems little doubt that, as the Canadian-American Committee reported:

The Cuban government and the Cuban press have tried to create the impression that trade with Canada will expand greatly and to exploit frictions in Canadian-American relations. This impression is false and this propaganda must be recognised for what it is.

Canada is not aggressively seeking to expand trade with Cuba but is only maintaining "normal trade relations" that have existed for many years.[14]

In fact, as the Canadian-American Committee went on to point out, various tangible, objective factors would obviously tend to limit expansion of Canadian exports to Cuba, whatever the actual intentions and desires of the Canadian and Cuban Governments respectively. Most decisive, perhaps, is the fact that, as the American Committee significantly commented, in view of the difficulties encountered by many foreign traders in receiving payment for shipments to Cuba, most businessmen were likely to be cautious in entering on trading arrangements with Cuba.[15]

II. AMERICAN ANTITRUST POLICY AND CANADIAN CONCERN

The Canadian-American differences over trade with Cuba, short-lived though they in fact may seem to have been, are paralleled by differences in other areas of commercial and economic policy. One particular area constituting a major source of irritation has been what Canada regards as extraterritorial application of United States antitrust laws. As the Minister of Justice, Mr. Fulton, noted in the House of Commons in Ottawa, there has been considerable concern in Canada with United States antitrust action against United States parent companies of Canadian subsidiaries in respect of the participation of those Canadian subsidiaries in other Canadian enterprises.[16] Mr. Fulton was referring to the United States antitrust action in connection with the Canadian Radio Patents Limited in which three companies in the United States were made the defendants in the

---

pathy with Mr. Castro or with his regime and I disapprove thoroughly of what he is doing to some of the religious groups in Cuba," he said. Interview by Mr. Hees, reported in the *Globe and Mail* (Toronto), Overseas Edition, Jan. 25, 1961, 6.

[14] *Report on Canada's Trade with Cuba*, document cited note 9 *supra*.

[15] *Ibid.*

[16] Statement by the Minister of Justice, Mr. Fulton, in House of Commons, Feb. 3, 1959, *Parl. Deb.* (Commons), Sess. 1959, 617-619.

legal actions in United States federal courts and a number of companies incorporated in Canada named as co-conspirators. As Mr. Fulton said:

The object of the action appears to be to force the Canadian companies to make important changes in commercial practice which we consider to be the concern of Canadian rather than United States law.

Mr. Fulton proposed a special meeting with the United States Attorney-General to discuss the problem of the effect in Canada of United States antitrust actions, and this meeting took place on January 29, 1959.[17] As Mr. Fulton stated at the time:

What we are concerned about is the possible effect of the decree asked for in the United States in so far as it may require directors of Canadian companies to take certain actions with respect to the operations of those companies in Canada, which actions would not be dictated by the requirements of Canadian law, or be in accord with Canadian business or commercial policy, but would be dictated by requirements of United States law and be in accord with United States policy. I made clear that in our view such a result could only be regarded as an infringement of Canadian sovereignty.

Mr. Fulton's concrete suggestion to Attorney-General Rogers was that in such cases the United States should raise the matter with the Canadian Government and not seek to alter the situation in Canada by means of "unilateral action in United States courts." In appealing for "restraint" by the United States Government in seeking from United States courts measures that interfere with matters of Canadian commerce within Canada, Mr. Fulton suggested that any other United States course could only be based on the

unacceptable proposition that foreign subsidiaries of United States parent companies are merely projections of United States trade and commerce and subject to United States policy in priority to the laws and commercial interests of the countries in which such subsidiaries are incorporated and carry on business.

Attorney-General Rogers' reply was both to deny any United States' intent to infringe Canadian sovereignty by the antitrust actions in the United States courts, and also to deny, as a question of fact, that any threat to Canadian sovereignty was involved: the United States position, essentially, was not that United States laws should

[17] *Ibid.*

supersede the laws of any other country but only that all persons in any way subject to the United States laws, including the antitrust laws, should live and act in accordance therewith.

As a practical matter, it is obvious, of course, that there is a wide divergence of Canadian and American views as to what constitutes an infringement of legal sovereignty. The product of the joint meeting of the two Attorneys-General was, in any case, a formula, known as the Fulton-Rogers Agreement, whereby it was agreed, as a matter of procedure, that in any similar situations in the future, discussions should be held by the two governments "at the appropriate stage" when it becomes apparent that interests in one of the two countries are likely to be affected by the enforcement of the antitrust laws of the other.

III. AMERICAN INVESTMENT AND CANADIAN REACTION

A straw in the same wind indicating stiffening Canadian commercial attitudes towards the United States is represented by Bill C-70. "An Act to provide for the Furnishing of Financial and other Statistics relating to the Affairs of Corporations and Labour Unions carrying on Activities within Canada," introduced in the House of Commons on February 17, 1961.[18]

The new bill was greeted with an editorial in the Toronto *Globe and Mail*, headed "Find Out the Facts": "Is Canada being made into an economic colony by foreign-controlled corporations? Are foreign-controlled labour unions having the same effect? ... The hard facts are not known."[19] At the same time, the *Financial Post* pointed out that whereas the Bank of Canada used to publish, each year, the comparative financial results of more than seven hundred Canadian companies by industries, based on published statements, the series had to be dropped because no details were made public by such very large and important Canadian subsidiaries of American firms as General Motors, Chrysler Corporation, Campbell Soups, Standard Brands, Swift Canadian, Procter and Gamble, Dow Chemical, Canadian International Paper Company, and Shell Oil Company of Canada.[20]

[18] House of Commons of Canada, Bill C-70. First reading, Feb. 17, 1961, *ibid.*, Sess. 1960-61, 2147. Assented to, April 18, 1962.
[19] *Globe and Mail* (Toronto), Overseas Edition, March 1, 1961, 7.
[20] *Financial Post* (Toronto), Feb. 25, 1961, 1.

The new bill, introduced by the Minister of Justice, Mr. Fulton, has the effect of requiring foreign-controlled corporations and international labor unions operating in Canada to give full and public accounting of themselves. The foreign-controlled corporations will have to make public financial statements showing their assets, liabilities, profits; the number of shares held by Canadians and by foreigners; the nationality of, and the amount of money paid to, directors and officers. International (that is, American) labor unions operating in Canada will have to report the amount received in dues every year, and the disposition made of the money; names and nationality of union officials, and the manner of their election; names of locals under trusteeship, and the reason for that arrangement.

As the *Globe and Mail* commented:

Not the slightest exception can be taken to any of these requirements. If a foreign-controlled corporation is taking too much money out of Canada relative to its investment, Canadians have a right to know about it. If a foreign-controlled corporation is giving Canadians too little opportunity to share in its ownership or in its administration, Canadians have a right to know about that too. . . .

The same applies to the American labor unions operating in Canada (the only country in the world, we believe, which has no indigenous labour movement). Many Canadians have the impression that the American labor unions take more money out of Canada than they put into it. . . . The legislation will also show to what extent the labour unions in Canada are Canadian, to what extent they are American, to what extent they practice democracy in their own affairs.[21]

This concern as to the degree of foreign—meaning here United States—control of Canadian industry and labour is sometimes, as with the debate over the alleged extraterritorial application of United States antitrust laws, conducted at a metaphysical level in terms of debate as to whether or not a threat is posed to "Canadian sovereignty." Canadian constitutional lawyers will recall here some of the emotionalism present in the erstwhile debates of the role of the Privy Council ("an alien tribunal") in the development of Canadian law, or the contemporary discussions on the need for "repatriating" the Canadian Constitution. In terms of economic realities, however, the current Canadian bogey of the threat of an American economic

[21] *Globe and Mail* (Toronto), Overseas Edition, Mar. 1, 1961, 7.

take-over in Canada more substantially is a reflection of the doubts and divisions over general economic policy in Canada today.

The forces of contemporary economic nationalism in Canada are well represented, at the theoretical level, in the person of the now resigned Governor of the Bank of Canada—the federal government-owned, central credit control institution—Mr. James E. Coyne. Mr. Coyne's program is dramatically illustrated by a public speech, made while he was still Governor of the Bank of Canada—"We Can Buy Canada Back . . . But Stop Selling Canada Out"—in which he declared, among other things:

Our net international indebtedness at the end of this year (1960) will be about $17 billion. At the end of 1949 it was less than $4 billion. The amount quadrupled during the fifties, and has increased again by $1.5 billion or more in 1960. Already, 60% of the dividends paid by all Canadian corporations go to non-resident shareholders.[22]

Mr. Coyne's main concern was as to Canada's great indebtedness to the United States, and his fear that this will continue to increase still further. As Mr. Coyne pointed out:

By the end of 1957, foreign companies and other foreign investors had a controlling interest in 56% of all manufacturing industry in Canada, and in some sectors of manufacturing industry in Canada, the degree of control was 40%, 80%, and even 98%. In petroleum and natural gas, also, some 76% of the industry was foreign controlled, and in mining and smelting 61%. Of these foreign investments in Canada, residents of the United States own 76% and control 80% to 90% by value of all foreign-controlled companies in Canada.

His gloomy prediction is that "The amount Canada must pay year after year by way of interest and dividends will go on increasing for some years yet, and could easily rise to a level of more than $1 billion a year." The essence of Mr. Coyne's prescription for Canada's economic well-being, for the future, is that "As a nation we must learn to live within our means, and increase our means by our own efforts."[23]

Mr. Coyne strongly advocated the application of strict monetary controls which would discourage importing from abroad and which would force Canadians to go alone and create their own capital in their own country. Among specific remedies suggested are greater

[22] Speech to the Canadian Club, Toronto, by James E. Coyne, Governor of the Bank of Canada, published in the *Financial Post* (Toronto) Nov. 19, 1960, 25.
[23] *Ibid.*

consumption by Canadians of Canadian-produced commodities, and growth of Canadian consumption industries, which will result in decline of commodity imports; and greater rate of saving by Canadians, encouraged by means of high rate of interest which is also to discourage borrowing and to encourage growth of capital to be re-invested in Canadian growth, to be employed in Canadian economic development. Since Mr. Coyne, as Governor at the time of the Bank of Canada, was in charge of the supply of money, his public remarks implied very strongly that he wished to continue pursuing a tight-money policy as the most effective means of freeing Canada from her close economic ties with the United States.

It must be pointed out that Mr. Coyne had by that time become a politically rather controversial figure, and his views may not always have had general public endorsement,[24] especially, for example, his tight-money policy which had been severely attacked in some university economics faculties within Canada.[25] Differences between Mr. Coyne and the Diefenbaker Government eventually impelled Mr. Coyne's resignation as Governor of the Bank of Canada after a Government-sponsored Parliamentary Bill to remove him from office had been defeated in the Senate, in July, 1961.[26]

[24] See for example, the editorial, "The Isolationist," published in the *Globe and Mail*, Overseas Edition, Mar. 22, 1961, 6:
"Mr. Coyne has taken advantage of his unique position of power [as Governor of the Bank of Canada] to tell the Economic Club, which represents a cross-section of United States finance, that the Canadian Government is making a very poor job of managing the national economy; that Canada requires a large measure of economic controls and that most of our present troubles are the fault of the United States, particularly of United States investors in Canada.
" 'The necessity or usefulness of increased foreign investment in Canada since the war is sometimes greatly over-estimated,' Mr. Coyne stated. In case this might not be fully understood by his New York hearers, he also warned that, 'there is always the danger when any person becomes heavily indebted to another that their relationship will sour.' This broad hint from the Governor of the Bank of Canada, that Americans ought to keep their money at home was preceded by an attack on United States trade policies, which, he said, combined with United States investment to make it inevitable that Canada should head into trouble.
"... Now that Mr. Coyne has carried the war into foreign parts, it is imperative that Mr. Fleming [the Minister of Finance] stand up and tell Mr. Coyne to shut up."
[25] See criticisms, for example, of Professors David E. Smith and David W. Slater, Queen's University, published in the *Financial Post* (Toronto), Feb. 25, 1961, 33-36; and see article by the same authors, "Economic Policy Proposals of the Governor of the Bank of Canada," *Queen's Quarterly*, vol. 68 (1960), 106-127.
[26] See Bill C-114, passed by the House of Commons on July 7, 1961, and providing as follows: "The office of Governor of the Bank of Canada shall be deemed to have become vacant immediately upon the coming into force of this Act." The bill was rejected in the Opposition-controlled Senate, which at the same time also resolved, formally, that the Governor of the Bank "did not misconduct himself in office." Mr. Coyne thereupon, accepting this Senate action as a vindication of his

Nevertheless, the marked economic nationalism represented in the Coyne proposals is paralleled by similar expressions of Canadian nationalistic sentiment in other, non-economic areas, for example, in relation to such major foreign policy questions as the recognition of Communist China;[27] the attitude to the emergent colonial societies in Asia and Africa; the issue of control of nuclear weapons and disarmament where strong Canadian criticism of American policies were often apparent in the last years of the Eisenhower administration. Official public law responses in terms, for example, of the Canadian Government's protest on the manner of application of United States antitrust laws, and also the Government's introduction of Bill C-70 in the House of Commons in Ottawa, become more readily understandable in the light of a pervading sentiment of what we might call breast-beating nationalism that seems to be represented even in some governmental circles; and for which a mild form of "Anti-Americanism" is perhaps the most logical, in the sense of most immediately available, outlet at the present time.

IV. THE CUBAN AFFAIR IN PERSPECTIVE

Nevertheless, in spite of the occasional fire and brimstone in Canadian utterances of this nature, it would be absurd to believe that they presage any Castro-like legal actions by Canada against American-owned or controlled assets in Canada. Rather, they represent not too much more than an understandable impatience from time to time at the occasional gaucheries and sometimes downright bad public relations of American economic policy-makers, both in the public and

---

own role in the dispute with the Government, submitted his resignation as Governor of the Bank.

[27] In May, 1961, it was announced that Canada and Communist China had concluded an agreement for the sale of $400 million worth of Canadian wheat to Communist China; and that Canada had requested the Peking Government to send a trade mission to Canada to prepare for the delivery of other goods from Canada. Although the original pressures in Canada for recognition of Communist China seem to have arisen independently from the demands of economic interest groups, this may have become a case now where, to paraphrase Bismarck, "Trade reinforces the Flag." In the then rather parlous economic conditions in Canada's Western Prairie Provinces, the successful conclusion of the wheat deal with Communist China may have been a godsend—not least perhaps to the Diefenbaker Government, which held a large number of seats in the Prairie Provinces in constituencies responsive to the agricultural vote. In the federal elections of April 8, 1963, the Diefenbaker Government, though losing disastrously in the industrial Eastern cities, maintained its electoral dominance of the Prairie Provinces.

also in the private sector, where they interact with or have impact on Canadian affairs. The Canadian and American economies are now so closely interrelated and, at least seen cold-bloodedly from the Canadian viewpoint, so interdependent, as to make talk of a Canadian-American Common Market and Customs Union more and more appealing in many quarters.[28] Even without the building of such formalized, politico-economic, intergovernmental associations, the essential character and structure and (if one can use the term) also the ideological substructure of Canadian and American industry, are such as to produce fairly uniform or common responses in similar problem situations.[29] I can illustrate this point best, in closing, by returning to the Cuban Affair. After the expropriation by the Castro Government of American-owned and controlled banking institutions and facilities in Cuba, without (as noted) any action at all being taken by Castro against Canadian-owned or controlled banks in Cuba, there was some interest in the prospects of the Canadian banks being able to succeed to the American business in Cuba. And yet, within a few weeks, it was announced that by agreement between the Canadian banks and the Castro Government, the Canadian banks had sold out all their assets to the Castro Government. Why? This question was put by letters from the present writer to the Presidents of each of the two Canadian banks, asking the reasons. The Bank of Nova Scotia replied: "It is the policy of the Bank to keep its customer bank relations confidential. Accordingly, we regret that we must decline to comment on our experience in Latin America."[30] The President of the Royal Bank of Canada, Mr. W. E. McLaughlin, replied, in some greater detail, and his letter indicates some of the problems—viewed simply, in strict commercial terms—involved in conducting private enterprise in a nationalized economy:

All the banks in Cuba—both Cuban and foreign—with the exception of the Royal Bank of Canada and The Bank of Nova Scotia were nation-

[28] See, for example, the plea by the former United States Secretary of Defense, Neil H. McElroy, for a Common Market between the United States and Canada, on the score that such economic integration would make possible a much better use of capital, labor, and raw materials for both countries; address by Neil H. McElroy to the Board of Trade of Metropolitan Toronto, published in the *Financial Post* (Toronto), Feb. 18, 1961, 9.

[29] As to the problem generally, see the interesting discussion by H. Ian Macdonald, *Canada's Foreign Economic Policy*, in the Behind the Headlines Series, vol. 20, no. 4 (Canadian Institute of International Affairs, Nov., 1960).

[30] Letter from F. W. Nicks, President of the Bank of Nova Scotia, to the present writer, under date Feb. 9, 1961.

alized during September and October of 1960. We were permitted to continue operating on the same basis as we had until that time. However, most of the important business in Cuba had been nationalized and the business of the nationalized companies was being conducted at one or other of the nationalized banks. We therefore were left with declining business and were unable to close any of our branches or dispense with any of our staff due to Cuban Government regulations.

We had discussions with officials of Banco Nacional de Cuba, outlining our situation, and they proposed to us that they purchase our assets at book value and assume our liabilities, leaving us free to remit our invested capital and accumulated profits to Canada. They also took over all our staff and premises, the latter being part of the assets purchased, and our branches continued to operate as before but under the ownership and control of Banco Nacional de Cuba. We understand that within the past week the names of all the former banks in Cuba have been dispensed with, and all now bear the name of Banco Nacional de Cuba with a number identifying the particular branch.[31]

It must be emphasized that throughout the whole Cuban Affair, the trading banks in Canada displayed a quite remarkable and commendable degree of self-restraint and modesty in all their public statements and actions. As for the rest of the Canadian business and trading community, whatever rosy expectations may have been held in various quarters as to the prospects of reaping a quick profit from American misfortunes in Cuba, the practical results for businessmen in both Canada and the United States very quickly turned out to be the same. One may confidently assert therefore that the whole Cuban Affair has not, in the long run, resulted in any dramatic, clear-cut, long-range differences in Canadian and United States foreign policy in action.[32]

[31] Letter from W. E. McLaughlin, President of the Royal Bank of Canada, to the present writer, under date Feb. 7, 1961.

[32] Canadian and American international lawyers are, as one by-product of the Cuban Affair, experiencing a marked increase of interest in that general area of international law relating to expropriation of foreign property, including specialized aspects like the "Act of State" doctrine and involving also the impact of the doctrine of "Sovereign Immunities." See, for example, the Sabbatino case, Banco Nacional de Cuba v. Sabbatino, 193 F. Supp. 375 (S.D.N.Y. 1961); 307 Fed. 2d 845 (2d Cir., 1962). And see the Bahia de Nipe cases, reported in 197 F. Supp. 710 (D.C.E.D. Va. 1961); affirmed 295 Fed. 2d 24 (4th Cir., 1961). And see also Flota Maritima Browning de Cuba S.A. v. Steamship "Canadian Conqueror" and Republic of Cuba, 34 D.L.R. (2d) 628 (1962).

It may be noted that the federal elections of April 8, 1963, were highlighted by an "anti-American" issue, revolving around Prime Minister Diefenbaker's refusal to allow atomic warheads on U.S. missiles located in Canada and Opposition Leader (now Prime Minister) Lester B. Pearson's assurance that the Liberal party, if elected, would permit warheads.

9

Metals, Oil, and Natural Gas

Some Problems of Canadian-American Co-operation

Wesley L. Gould

Canada and the United States, occupants of vast areas of the same continent, have a joint concern in hemisphere defense. Political problems other than those of their own direct relations press upon them from without and have a heavy bearing upon the manner in which they employ their industry and use their raw materials. But as major sharers of continentally distributed resources their most enduring relations lie in the day-to-day activities of transportation and communications, of mining and manufacturing, and of those other activities that sustain societies and form the base for world power and influence.

Exploitation of resources may be approached from a nationalistic viewpoint. Americans have sought to promote their own lead and zinc and uranium industries without particular concern for those same industries north of the border. Independent oil producers and bituminous coal interests have feared imports of Canadian oil. Canadians have been apprehensive over the proportions of their exports to and imports from the United States.[1] They are not comforted by the control of about two thirds of their mining and oil development by American capital[2] and have no liking for pressure upon the legislature from a foreign controlled lobby.[3] To a nationalistic point of

[1] In 1960 exports to the United States dropped, although total Canadian exports rose, particularly to Western Europe and Japan. The percentage to the United States dropped from 61.4 per cent in 1959 to 55.7 per cent in 1960; Dominion Bureau of Statistics, *Weekly Bulletin*, Feb. 10, 1961, March 17, 1961.

[2] Direct investments by foreign capital in foreign-controlled firms amounted in 1960 to $12.8 billion of a total of investments in long-term forms of $22.3 billion; 85 per cent of the 1960 inflow came from the United States, over 1/3 to petroleum and natural gas and nearly 1/3 to mining; *idem*. On fears of effects of United States subsidiaries upon the Canadian economy, see *New York Times*, Feb. 16, April 9, and July 10, 1958. See also John Lindeman and Donald Armstrong, *Policies and Practices of United States Subsidiaries in Canada* (Canadian-American Committee, 1961).

[3] See G. V. Ferguson, "Likely Trends in Canadian-American Political Relations," *Can. Jour. Econ. and Pol. Sci.*, vol. 22 (1956), 442.

view can be attributed the regulations restricting gas and oil exploration in the Yukon and Northwest Territories, lands under territorial
waters, and the continental shelf to Canadian citizens and to corporations listed on Canadian stock exchanges or of which Canadians are
beneficial owners of one half the issued shares.[4] To the same viewpoint may be ascribed the Canadian Government's own expenditures
to develop strategic materials.[5]

A continental approach might suggest the creation of some form
of customs union such as was outlined in *Life* magazine in 1948 and,
more recently, by Hector B. McKinnon when he retired in 1959 as
Chairman of the Canadian Tariff Board.[6] But anything so radical
would founder on national fears and aspirations, as may be gathered
from the Canadian reaction to *Life*'s suggestion, including the *Ottawa
Journal*'s opinion that the Canadian economy could not stand the
shock of unhampered competition with the United States.[7] The
writer was obviously thinking in terms of trying to retain two national
economies rather than trying to establish an integrated continental
economy. The more moderate idea of co-operation has had greater
appeal to Canadians eager to assert their national identity.

Intergovernmental attempts to amalgamate the continental view
and national interests include the Reciprocal Trade Agreements,
GATT commitments, and the Convention and Protocol respecting
Double Taxation, signed March 4, 1942, and subsequently modified.[8]
The last of these accorded benefits to the permanent establishments,
defined to include mines and oil wells of enterprises of one state located in the other. Other governmental undertakings, such as those
related to boundary waters, are so clearly a matter of joint concern
that extreme nationalistic positions, longer asserted with effect in the
United States than in Canada, have eventually given way before such
facts as the refusal of watersheds to follow the 49th parallel.

A broader view than the continental, yet combined with national
interest, was early reflected in undertakings to conserve the living

[4] *Canadian Weekly Bulletin*, April 27, 1960, 5. The restrictions were relaxed
in May, 1961, to allow foreign companies not qualifying for leases to act as silent
partners; *Globe and Mail* (Toronto), May 25, 1961.
[5] See remarks of Hon. C. D. Howe, Minister of Defense Production, Canada,
Parl. Deb. (Commons), 2nd Sess. 1951, 211-218.
[6] *Life*, March 15, 1948; *Montreal Star*, April 1, 22, and 23, 1959.
[7] *Ottawa Journal*, March 16, 1948. See also the *Windsor Daily Star*, March 16
and 17, 1948; *Globe and Mail* (Toronto), March 20, 1948; *Saskatoon Star Phoenix*,
March 27, 1948; *London Free Press*, March 31, 1948.
[8] 56 *Stat.* 1399; TIAS 2347, 3916.

resources of the sea. Effective conservation may well require regulations embodied in a bilateral or a multilateral treaty and applied in detail through the co-ordinating agency of an International Pacific Halibut Fishery Commission or, more recently, the Great Lakes Fisheries Commission established under the Great Lakes Fisheries Convention, signed on September 10, 1954.[9] As an example of the work done, the Great Lakes Fishery Commission undertook in 1958 the treatment of fifty-two United States and twenty Canadian streams flowing into Lake Superior with lampreycide and completed the initial series of treatment by December, 1960. Under contract with the Commission, the work was done by the staffs of the Fisheries Research Board of Canada and the United States Bureau of Commercial Fisheries.[10] Here is an example of what can be done when on both sides of the border conservation is recognized as attainable only through united action.

But where exploitation rather than conservation is the objective, together with the correlative ends of business profit and the employment of workers, the recognition of a need for united action is not so vivid. When undertaken, intergovernmental co-operation to stabilize economies or to assure adequate supplies of raw materials may take not the form of a treaty establishing an international co-ordinating commission but such forms as government contracts, staff liaison, and unilateral but mutually compatible determinations of national agencies. Moreover, continental resource development may be most effectively promoted not by governments and diplomats but by wholly owned subsidiaries or by a co-ordinator of pipelines for the Gulf Oil Corporation who serves as director of the Interprovincial Pipe Line Company. It must be remembered that even though geographically the more remote regions of Canada can be compared with Siberia, there is no North American Kremlin to order engineers and workers to the remote regions to build cities and exploit resources. Canadian and American values and institutions oppose this even on a purely national basis.

1. METALS

The development of Canadian metal resources has been affected by governmental action both unilateral and bilateral. Bilateral en-

[9] TIAS 3326.
[10] *Canadian Weekly Bulletin*, Dec. 21, 1960, 4.

couragement to Canadian industry appears in the Hyde Park Agreement announced on April 20, 1941.[11] The concepts of economic co-operation of the Hyde Park Agreement were extended in the immediate postwar period[12] and later underlay the efforts of the Joint Industrial Mobilization Planning Committee, established by an exchange of notes of April 12, 1949.[13] The Hyde Park concepts were further extended in the Statement of Principles for Economic Co-operation of October 26, 1950.[14] The objectives set forth included (1) the development of a co-ordinated program of requirements, production, and procurement, (2) co-ordinated controls over the distribution of scarce raw materials and supplies, (3) mutually consistent emergency controls imposed, whenever possible, after consultation, (4) exchanges of technical knowledge and productive skills, (5) removal as far as possible of barriers to goods essential for common defense, and (6) consultations concerning any resultant financial or exchange problems. A step to assure at least annual high level discussion was taken when the Agreement Relating to the Establishment of a Joint United States–Canadian Committee on Trade and Economic Affairs was signed on November 12, 1953.[15] This Committee is composed of the cabinet members in charge of foreign affairs, commerce, agriculture (or, for Canada as appropriate, the Minister of Fisheries), and the respective treasuries, and other cabinet officials as subsequently designated.

Production sharing for defense purposes has at times provided a stimulus to the Canadian economy, although it should be borne in mind that only a very small proportion of the cost of intricate modern instruments of war trickles down to the producers of raw materials. However, in 1955 there was a drop-off in United States defense purchasing in Canada, the main item remaining on the program being the purchase of aircraft. More recently an effort to give impetus to production sharing took the form of the decision in July, 1958, to establish a Ministerial Committee on Joint Defense.[16] At a meeting at Camp David in November, 1959, the Committee agreed upon an

---

[11] *Dept. of State Bulletin*, vol. 4 (1941), 494; 1941 CTS 14.
[12] TIAS 1752; 1948 CTS 1.
[13] TIAS 1889.
[14] TIAS 2136; 1950 CTS 15.
[15] TIAS 2922.
[16] TIAS 4098. See also *New York Times*, July 11, 1958. The Ministerial Committee is composed of the United States Secretaries of Defense, State, and the Treasury and the Canadian Ministers of Defense, External Affairs, and Finance.

immediate increase in Canadian participation in the production of weapons and other equipment and upon long-term co-ordination of requirements, development, production, and procurement.[17]

Nickel

Why nickel possesses so high a wartime priority would be apparent upon examining the history of its uses after the superiority of nickel steel over carbon steel as armor plate for battleships was demonstrated. The United States Department of Defense in 1954 characterized nickel as the metal that "comes closest to being a true 'war metal.'"[18] Stockpiling of nickel, as well as putting it to more immediate uses, was quite clearly an essential part of the military program. Significantly, annual nickel imports in the mid-1950's were above the annual average during the Second World War.[19]

After the refusal in 1947 by the United States Munitions Board of an offer to supply nickel over a ten-year period, in 1948 a contract was signed with Falconbridge Nickel Mines Limited for the delivery of 40 million pounds over a five-year period.[20] In 1950 two other Falconbridge proposals were rejected, the second on the eve of the attack on South Korea. In January, 1951, a contract signed with Falconbridge called for the delivery over ten years of 50 million pounds of nickel, the Defense Materials Procurement Agency making an advance of $6 million. A contract of March 30, 1953, provided for the delivery of 100 million pounds before June 30, 1960, plus copper and up to 2 million pounds of cobalt. Like the 1951 contract, this contract carried options for additional deliveries. Moreover, to compensate Falconbridge for the development of its reserves, the 1953 contract provided a 40-cent premium above the market price at the time of delivery.

The stockpile purchase contract, dated April 19, 1951, with Sherritt Gordon Mines Limited called for the delivery, under the exercise of all options, of 80 million pounds of nickel by the end of 1958.

[17] *New York Times*, Nov. 10, 1959. In 1959 production sharing brought Canadian manufacturers $51 million of prime contracts and $45.3 million of subcontracts, excluding contracts for construction, petroleum, maintenance, communications, and general services; *Globe and Mail* (Toronto), Jan. 29, 1960.

[18] Department of Defense, Office of Assistant Secretary of Defense (Supply and Logistics), *Annual Materials Conservation Report* (Washington, 1954), 4.

[19] P. W. Bidwell, *Raw Materials: A Study of American Policy* (New York, 1958), 138.

[20] On nickel contracts, see *ibid.*, 153-157.

For Sherritt Gordon this contract was extremely important, for it enabled the company to build a refinery at Ft. Saskatchewan, Alberta, and to undertake exploration in and to exploit the ore from deposits at Lynn Lake, Manitoba.[21]

Eight small contracts with the International Nickel Company of Canada Limited were entered into between 1946 and 1952. About 50 million pounds of nickel were to be delivered at the market price or less. In September, 1952, the United States agreed to purchase another 54 million pounds of nickel from INCO. Far more significant was the contract signed with INCO in May, 1953, for the purchase of both copper and nickel.[22] Deliveries amounting to 120 million pounds began in December, 1953, and continued for a period of five years. A premium of 25 cents over the market price provided an allowance for amortization of new equipment to process the lower-grade ores and to allow for higher production costs. This contract permitted the opening of low-grade deposits and the mining and processing of about 110 million tons of ore from two mines in the Subdury area.

The contracts with INCO, Falconbridge, and Sherritt Gordon stimulated exploration and led to important discoveries of new deposits of nickel ore in northwestern Ontario, in the Hudson Bay area, in the Yukon, and in Manitoba.[23] However, by the end of 1957 the United States had a surplus in its Defense Production Act inventories, as well as in the strategic stockpile. The problem had become that of disposing of the surplus and of gaining relief from contractual obligations to purchase nickel.

On August 25, 1959, the General Services Administration reached an agreement with INCO that canceled all remaining deliveries under the "market price" contract and provided for the diversion of the nickel produced from the high-cost marginal ores to the market. In order to make up the difference between the market price and the premium price GSA undertook to supply surplus nickel oxide sinter from the government-owned plant at Nicaro, Cuba. The Government was thus relieved of the obligation to add 26 million pounds to

[21] On Lynn Lake exploration and development, see Manitoba Department of Mines and Natural Resources (Mines Branch), *Annual Report for Period Ending March 31st, 1959*, 2, 3-4.
[22] Defense Materials Procurement Agency Release, June 1, 1953.
[23] On INCO's project in the Thompson district of Manitoba, see Manitoba Department of Mines and Natural Resources (Mines Branch), *Annual Report for Period Ending March 31st, 1959*, 1-3.

the stockpile and of an expense in cash of over $25 million.[24] Subsequently, the arrangement was amended to include 16 million pounds of nickel cathodes.[25]

Cancellation of nickel deliveries hardly came at the most opportune time. For large new supplies have become available, the most important being INCO's Thompson mine in Manitoba. This is the consequence of a failure in the years immediately following World War II to assure adequate supplies for both civilian and defense purposes. Hence, a rational policy was lacking when rearmament imposed a need for new supplies. When the Paley Commission in 1952 concluded that projected Free World demands to 1975 would be difficult to meet, procurement activity took a leap to an extreme, extending to the exploitation of high-cost marginal ores as well as to expanded exploration and investment in the development of new sources. The consequence of the cancellations of deliveries in an unforeseen condition of surplus could only emphasize to the Canadians their dependence upon the United States and its good will even in respect to a mineral of which, on this continent, Canada has the lion's share. With that share now known to be larger and with stockpiling halted, nickel producers undertook to recover markets that had been lost to other metals during the shortage and to find new uses for its products. But, with the United States lacking important reserves of nickel ore, Canadian nickel producers retain their advantage of not having to be concerned about policies designed to assist American producers—a matter of particular advantage to Sherritt Gordon which might have been left with a refinery and mines useful only as long as United States Government purchases continued. At the same time, American users of nickel gained the advantage of being able to deal with important Canadian producers other than INCO.

Copper

Copper shortages were felt in the United States in 1951 and 1952. Yet at that time it was deemed politically wise to allow the export of copper, but under short-supply restrictions authorized by the Export Control Act of 1949,[26] to copper-producing countries and to allies.

[24] GSA News Release, Aug. 25, 1959.
[25] Canadian Weekly Bulletin, July 27, 1960, 3.
[26] 63 Stat. 7.

But after a period in 1953-1954 of free exports of refined copper and copper scrap, controls were reimposed in October, 1953. In February, 1955, exports of copper refined from domestic ores were entirely forbidden.[27] Late in 1956 the Department of Commerce recognized the end of the short-supply period by raising quotas for copper scrap and restoring the open-end quota on refined copper produced from domestic ores. It might be observed that the restrictions constituted also an intervention by government to compensate brass mills and other American consumers for the injury resulting from the price policies of domestic copper producers who for some years, by keeping the New York price for refined copper under the London price,[28] made it profitable to ship scrap abroad.

During the copper shortage Congress in the Defense Production Act of 1950[29] approved government aid to expand domestic and foreign copper production. Projects initiated soon after the beginning of the Korean War aimed at the addition of 300,000 tons to United States productive capacity. A mobilization goal of 2.27 million tons' annual supply from all sources, set by the Office of Defense Mobilization in February, 1952, was realized in 1956, at which time the expansion program for the domestic industry was ended. But the shortages were such that copper originally intended for the defense stockpile had to be diverted to industry, so that even at the end of 1957 the minimum stockpiling objective had not been attained.[30]

Government purchase contracts in the period were aimed either at assuring a market for over 1.5 million tons over a ten-year period or at building the defense stockpile. The nickel purchase contract between the Defense Materials Procurement Agency and INCO, signed in May, 1953, included the purchase of 100 million pounds of copper over a five-year period.[31] The 1953 contract with Falconbridge called for delivery of 52 million pounds of refined copper by December 31, 1958. However, in respect to copper the main concern of the United States Government was not Canada but Chile, where such political objectives were involved as securing better treatment in regard to discriminatory taxes and exchange control administration for American corporations, particularly Anaconda and Kennecott,

[27] *Export Control*, 14th Quarterly Report of the Secretary of Commerce (Feb. 28, 1951), 2; *ibid.*, 31st Quarterly Report (July 1, 1955), 15.

[28] Bidwell, *op. cit.*, 124.

[29] 64 *Stat.* 798.

[30] Bidwell, *op. cit.*, 124-125.

[31] Defense Materials Procurement Agency Release, June 1, 1953.

preventing the Soviet Union from acquiring Chilean copper and extending its influence in Latin America, and assisting Chile's inflation-plagued economy.[32]

Lead and Zinc

While both production and profits of United States lead and zinc mines have been subject to considerable fluctuation, a depressed condition has prevailed in most years since the 1920's. Over 80 per cent of imported lead in recent years has been supplied by Australia, Mexico, Peru, Canada, and Yugoslavia. In 1946 Canada, Mexico, and Peru had accounted for 73 per cent of the United States imports, while in 1956 they supplied over 50 per cent. The same three countries supplied 80 per cent of the imports of zinc.

Competition between producers of lead and zinc in the two countries has presented persistent problems for both governments. Stimulation of Canadian production has hardly been an objective of United States policy. Even though labor costs per ton of crude ore are higher in Canada than in the United States, the higher value of the products per ton, plus recoverable content of silver, gold, and copper, as compared with that of the longer-exploited United States resources, puts American concerns at a disadvantage.[33] In 1954 the Tariff Commission recommended an increase in the tariff, but the President preferred to increase the purchases of domestic lead and zinc under the long-term stockpile program. In his letter to Chairman Millikin of the Senate Finance Committee and Chairman Reed of the House Ways and Means Committee the President stated that he was directing the Secretary of State to inform those states supplying lead and zinc that the objective was to help domestic producers and to obtain assurances that they would not take unfair advantage of the program.[34] A subsequent effort in 1957 to increase the tariff foundered in Congress. Instead, on October 1, 1958, on the basis of a Tariff Commission finding, the President established quantitative restrictions amounting to 80 per cent of the average of imports in 1953-57, excluding lead and zinc, including some from Canada, entering under

[32] See Bidwell, *op. cit.*, 111, 125-128.
[33] *Lead and Zinc Industries*, Report of the U.S. Tariff Commission on Senate Resolution of July 27, 1953; Sen. Doc. 119, 83rd Cong., 2nd Sess., 253-254.
[34] Canadian Metal Mining Association, *Submission to the United States Tariff Commission Presented on Behalf of the Lead and Zinc Producing Industry of Canada* (Nov., 1957), 19.

barter arrangements for the disposal of surplus wheat.[35] This, of course, has been productive of Canadian complaint, as has also a freight-rate structure which was acknowledged by the Interstate Commerce Commission to be discriminatory against certain Canadian lead and zinc producers.[36] The appearance is that of a continued tug-of-war over lead and zinc as Canadian and United States producers, competing for the same market, both suffer from declining prices.[37] Canadian worries increased when President Kennedy signed a bill, similar to one vetoed by President Eisenhower, providing subsidies after January 1, 1962, to small United States lead and zinc mines to help them compete against large domestic producers and against imports.[38] Whether a continental approach to the problem would alleviate the marketing and price difficulties is questionable considering the state of the industry. Hence, the division into two favor-seeking national groups is little more than an aggravation of a persistent problem, although hope that the problem is temporary lay behind the decision of Brunswick Mining and Smelting Corporation Limited to proceed in 1961 with a project to bring its huge copper-lead-zinc mine near Bathhurst, New Brunswick, into production and to have a new zinc refinery in operation in 1963.[39]

Fluorspar

There was for a time a minor encouragement by the United States of the production of fluorspar, essential for the steel and aluminum industries. A Canadian firm operating Newfoundland fluorspar mines obtained a loan from the Defense Materials Procurement Agency for the construction of a mill in Wilmington, Delaware. There concentrates were processed from Canadian ore for the stockpile. After the contract expired in 1957, mining operations were suspended as it was found that the Newfoundland fluorspar could

[35] Francis Masson and J. B. Whitely, *Barriers to Trade between Canada and the United States* (Canadian-American Committee, 1960), 73-74; Constant Southworth and W. W. Buchanan, *Changes in Trade Restrictions between Canada and the United States* (Canadian-American Committee, 1960), 38, 63; Canadian-American Committee, *Wheat Surpluses and the U.S. Barter Program* (1960), 6, 12.

[36] Canadian Metal Mining Association, *op. cit.*, 8; *Dept. of State Bulletin*, vol. 42 (1960), 366.

[37] Southworth and Buchanan, *op. cit.*, 52-53.

[38] *Globe and Mail* (Toronto), Oct. 7, 1961.

[39] *Globe and Mail* (Toronto), June 16, 1961.

not compete in Canadian markets.[40] It may be questioned whether this particular extension of aid to a producer was justified.

Uranium

Perhaps the most glamourized Canadian uranium mining center is Port Radium on Great Bear Lake, where, however, the reserves are now near exhaustion and operations were ended in 1960.[41] The Port Radium mine was first put into production by Eldorado Gold Mines Limited in 1933, and the first ounce of radium was produced in 1936. Production was stopped in 1940, but with the progress of research on the atomic bomb the company was quietly asked to resume operations and produce uranium. Soon afterward the facilities were purchased by the Canadian Government and operated by the present Eldorado Mining and Refining Limited.[42] In 1952, in accordance with an arrangement between Canada, the United States, and the United Kingdom, the government-owned Eldorado mine began producing on a large scale.

After the Second World War the Canadian Government's intensive campaign of exploration and prospecting led to the important Beaverlodge discovery in northern Saskatchewan. Private industry joined the hunt in 1948, and its effort resulted in the Blind River discovery in 1953. Contracts were negotiated by Eldorado for the delivery of U_3O_8 to the United States Atomic Energy Commission. The Commission entered into a separate contract with Eldorado for each contract that Eldorado negotiated with individual Canadian producers. In general, the contracts covered a full five-year period, with deliveries extending to March 31, 1962, except for a few mines for which the final date was March 31, 1963[43]

Co-operative arrangements to make Canadian uranium available resulted both from negotiations between a United States agency and a Canadian government corporation and from those conducted

[40] Masson and Whitely, op. cit., 75.

[41] New York Times, May 10, 1960; Canadian Weekly Bulletin, Aug. 17, 1960.

[42] Department of External Affairs, Information Division, Reference Papers, No. 78 (Aug., 1955), 5-6; W. D. G. Hunter, "The Development of the Canadian Uranium Industry: An Experiment in Public Enterprise," Can. Jour. Econ. and Pol. Sci., vol. 28 (1962), 329-352.

[43] S. W. Clarkson, Uranium in the Western World: A Study of the Short-Term Market Prospects for Canadian Uranium (mimeographed, Atomic Energy of Canada Limited, Ottawa, 1959), 2; J. W. Griffith, A Survey of the Uranium Industry in Canada, Department of Mines and Technical Surveys, Mineral Resources Division, Mineral Information Bulletin MR 34 (Ottawa, 1959), 2.

through channels producing international agreements as contrasted with contracts. Agreements concerning the uses of atomic energy stimulated the production of uranium, even though these only formalized that which was occurring under the pressures of technological and scientific advance and of international tensions. For example, the Agreement for Co-operation on Civil Uses of Atomic Energy, signed by Canada and the United States on June 15, 1955, and in force on July 21, 1955,[44] refers in Article VI to the development of Canadian uranium production "under arrangements and contracts now in effect" and adds: "These arrangements and contracts shall remain in full force and effect except as modified or revised by mutual agreement." Subsequently, the sentence turned out to mean that Canadian uranium producers were assured of a market in the United States only until American producers required that same market.

Problems of production and delivery of Canadian uranium have not concerned only the United States and Canada. The United Kingdom, needing Canadian uranium for its own atomic energy program, requested the Atomic Energy Commission in the spring of 1956 to release 5500 tons of U_3O_8, then under contract to AEC, to be delivered between July 1, 1958, and March 31, 1962. Having obtained an understanding as to the ability of Canada to deliver a minimum of 68,000 tons to the United States in 1955-62, the Commission formally advised Eldorado on May 11, 1956, of its decision to release the requested amount and received Eldorado's acceptance on May 30, 1956. In April, 1957, the Commission agreed to release another 5000 tons to the United Kingdom between March 31, 1962, and March 31, 1963, contingent upon the minimum 68,000-ton delivery.[45]

In May, 1958, the United States and Canada announced that the mines could sell surplus uranium stocks to such countries as West Germany and Switzerland with which bilateral agreements had been concluded to assure the use of uranium in peaceful projects. Otherwise, an export was limited to 2500 pounds. Other customers that negotiated agreements or contracts with Canada for uranium deliveries were Japan and Euratom, two agreements with the latter being signed on October 6, 1959.[46]

[44] TIAS 3304.

[45] Letter from Gen. A. R. Leudecke, General Manager, Atomic Energy Commission, to J. T. Ramey, Executive Director, Joint Congressional Committee on Atomic Energy, March 12, 1960, *Hearings before the Joint Committee on Atomic Energy*, 86th Cong., 2nd Sess. (1960), 290-291.

[46] *Canada Year Book, 1959*, 498; Clarkson, *op. cit.*, 2; Griffith, *op. cit.*, 87.

The Atomic Energy Commission's schedule of imports of U_3O_8 from Canada called for deliveries ranging from a low of 1590 short tons in the fiscal year ending June 30, 1956, to a high of 13,870 tons in fiscal 1960. Deliveries were scheduled to drop in the next three years as the contract termination dates of March 31, 1962, and March 31, 1963, were approached.[47] But AEC's parallel undertaking to stimulate uranium production in the United States had better results than anticipated. By mid-1957 it was clear that domestic reserves would continue to increase rapidly. In August, 1957, the Commission relieved Eldorado of its obligation to deliver the minimum of 68,000 tons, although Eldorado had made firm commitments to certain producers to extend contracts that would have expired before March 31, 1962.[48] AEC commitments to domestic producers called for the delivery of more U_3O_8 than was scheduled from Canada in fiscal 1956-63, and they extended to 1967. The United States was becoming the world's largest producer of U_3O_8 with an oversupply in the West, while AEC was assured of a sufficient supply to allow modification on November 24, 1958, of its post-1962 purchase program, thus limiting the market guarantee for domestic producers.[49]

On November 6, 1959, the Atomic Energy Commission announced that it would not exercise its options to purchase additional uranium concentrate after 1962, but had agreed to a stretch-out arrangement covering March 31, 1962–December 31, 1966. In an April, 1959, meeting with John A. McCone, AEC Chairman, Gordon Churchill, Canadian Minister of Trade and Commerce, had pressed for early exercise of the options, emphasizing that Canada's uranium industry had been developed at United States urging. Chairman McCone's position was that the combination of oversupply and commitments to domestic producers made it impossible to accede to Mr. Churchill's request. Negotiations which followed produced a single contract which consolidated the several previously existing between AEC and Eldorado. The stretch-out of deliveries was arranged both to accomplish AEC's intention to reduce uranium deliveries in fiscal 1960-62 and to allow the Canadian uranium industry time for readjustment, even though the deferred production had been counted upon by the producing companies to provide amortization payments

---

[47] Clarkson, *op. cit.*, 10; *The Financial Post* (Toronto), April 25, 1959.
[48] Letter of General Leudecke to J. T. Ramey, March 12, 1960, *loc. cit.*, note 44.
[49] *Hearings* cited, note 44, 259-261.

due in the pre-1962 period. To meet this situation, the Commission agreed to make an advance payment to Eldorado of $2.50 for each pound of uranium deferred, which Eldorado would turn over to producers. Moreover, the United Kingdom Atomic Energy Authority offered to make an additional payment of $15.50 per pound on any deferments into January 1, 1965—November 30, 1966, up to 16 million pounds of the amounts covered by their contracts.[50]

Despite the attempts to soften the blow, the Canadian uranium industry could not avoid the effects. While Canadian producers were now allowed to transfer uranium sales contracts between companies, new development was hindered by Eldorado's requirement that the uranium to be delivered must be from mining claims or properties specifically referred to in existing contracts. Nineteen fifty-nine could only be looked upon as the peak production year for some time to come. Employment in the industry dropped from 13,626 in August, 1959, to 11,792 in January, 1960, and was expected to be halved by the end of 1961.[51] Elliot Lake in Ontario, a model town built at a provincial investment of $19 million and a private investment of $45 million, was particularly hard hit after four years' existence. By the end of 1960 the population had dropped from 25,000 to 15,000, while the work force declined from 10,500 to 2900. The provincial government announced on July 3, 1960, a program of aid to the affected families by means of work projects, and on February 7, 1961, a four-year interest-free loan plan totaling $4 million.[52] Some mitigation was promised by the announcement in March, 1961, of a letter of intent of 1957 by which the United Kingdom Atomic Energy Authority made a firm commitment to purchase 24 million pounds, subject to negotiation over prices and delivery schedules. Renegotiation talks, leading toward a sharply reduced price, were held in 1961 and 1962.[53] Earlier, some hope for the more distant future could be found in the statement of Jesse Johnson, Director of the Raw Materials Division of AEC, that 1964 promises to be the breakthrough year for atomic power and 1970 the year for the industry to start

[50] AEC Release, Nov. 6, 1959, with attached announcement by the Canadian Government.

[51] *Canadian Weekly Bulletin*, Aug. 17, 1960, 3.

[52] *Globe and Mail* (Toronto), July 4, 1960; Feb. 8, 1961. See also *ibid.*, Feb. 16, 17, and 26, 1960; Sept. 29, 1960; Jan. 24, 1961; March 7, 1961; July 19, 1961.

[53] *Ibid.*, March 24, 1961; June 10, 1961; Aug. 17, 1961; Jan. 17, 20, 1962.

getting back on its feet.[54] Whatever the effects of the United Kingdom commitment or the accuracy of the Johnson prediction, the fate of Elliot Lake is a warning against again placing an industry's eggs in one basket where they can remain only until the policy of the market country concentrates on promoting the interests of its own producers. It is also a commentary on the consequences of a parallel but unco-ordinated all-out development.

Contractual arrangements served effectively to develop the Canadian uranium industry. But even when buttressed by the clause in the executive agreement of 1955 that contracts would be modified only by mutual consent, the optional features of the contracts left room for legal unilateral action. Whether the willingness to negotiate the stretch-out arrangement will lead to the Canadian uranium industry's establishing itself on a more firm basis than that of sales to the Atomic Energy Commission remains to be seen, for the problem is, of course, complicated by the international political situation.

II. OIL

With the exception of the Canol Project[55] of the Second World War, the development of Canada's petroleum resources has proceeded without the aid of treaties or executive agreements, even to the laying of pipelines across United States territory. Petroleum pipelines in the United States are adjuncts of refineries, but they are also common carriers within the meaning of the Interstate Commerce Act and, as such, are subject to regulation in order to safeguard against the loading of transportation costs. Regulatory authority over rates and operations within the United States rests with the Interstate Commerce Commission. Until November 2, 1959, Canadian oil pipelines were subject under the Pipe Lines Act to the jurisdiction of the Board of Transport Commissioners, which had jurisdiction over the location, construction, and operation of oil and gas pipelines and, in the case

[54] *Ibid.*, Jan. 27, 1961.

[55] For the agreements of 1942 and 1943 establishing the project, see EAS 386-389, 416. For about a year crude from Norman Wells on the Mackenzie River was transported to a United States Government refinery at Whitehorse, products, chiefly aviation fuel, being piped to Skagway and Fairbanks; costs were 60 per cent higher than finished products brought by boat or rail. J. R. White, "Oil and Canadian Geography," *Canadian Geographical Journal*, vol. 60 (1960), 147. Being subsequently regarded as of questionable defense value, the facilities were disposed of between 1945 and 1960; TIAS 1565, 1695-1697, 4631.

of companies declared to be common carriers of which, apparently, there were none, over traffic, tolls, tariffs, and accounting systems.[56] Since that date they have been subject to the jurisdiction of the National Energy Board[57] which, among other things, issues certificates of public convenience for the construction of oil and gas pipelines and for petroleum products pipelines, issues licenses for the transport across provincial boundaries by pipelines of crude oil, gas, and petroleum products, issues annual licenses for the importation of crude oil including that originating in Canada but transported in part through a pipeline located in part outside Canada, and grants licenses for the export or import of other forms of energy. Construction of an international oil pipeline, such as the Interprovincial Pipe Line, has required the approval of Canadian authorities for construction in Canada and under the Canadian portion of the St. Clair River, as well as licenses, permits, and other authorizations issued to an American subsidiary by both federal and state agencies. Included among the latter are authorizations to cross the Straits of Mackinac, the St. Clair River, other navigable waters, and state and federal lands. Thus, for example, the Lakehead Pipe Line Company, Inc., Interprovincial's American subsidiary, has been subject to the jurisdiction of the Michigan Public Service Commission in respect to construction, the issuance of securities, and other matters.

Three pipelines of the Canadian system cross United States territory.[58] One, the Montreal-Portland Pipe Line, brings crude oil into Canada and need not be discussed here. Longest is the Interprovincial Pipe Line, which brings Alberta crude from Redwater near Edmonton to Sarnia and Toronto by way of Gretna, Manitoba (near Neche, North Dakota), Superior, Wisconsin, the Straits of Mackinac, and under the St. Clair River. The line was completed to Superior in 1950, to Sarnia in 1953, and to Port Credit and Clarkson in the Toronto area in 1957. A parallel line between Edmonton and Superior was completed in 1958. En route it picks up crude gathered in eastern Saskatchewan by three pipeline companies which carry the crude to Cromer, Manitoba, where it enters Interprovincial. In 1958

[56] *Statutes of Canada*, 1952, c. 211.

[57] *Ibid.*, 1959, c. 46; amended, *ibid.*, 1960, c. 9.

[58] See *Reference Material on Canadian Oil and Gas*, prepared for the Ways and Means Committee of the Independent Petroleum Association of America (mimeographed, 1960), 9-12; E. M. Holbrook, "Oil from the Earth," (5th ed.; Imperial Oil Limited, 1957), reprinted from *Canadian Geographical Journal*, vol. 39 (1949), 21-22; Royal Commission on Energy, *First Report* (Ottawa, 1958), chaps. 2, 6-18.

upwards of 25 per cent of the crude oil carried by Interprovincial was from Saskatchewan, the fields being five hundred miles closer than those of Alberta to the refineries at Sarnia and Toronto.[59] Interprovincial, by reducing the dependence of Ontario upon the United States, along with the Trans Mountain Pipe Line, has been a significant factor in enabling Canada to make important savings of United States dollars.[60] Between the Redwater field and Sarnia, Interprovincial supplies crude oil to prairie refineries and to refineries in Minnesota, Wisconsin, and Michigan. A spur line runs from Clearbrook, Minnesota, to the Minneapolis-St. Paul area. Of the 1930 miles of pipelines between Redwater and Toronto, 971 miles are on United States territory, as well as the 256 miles of the spur line to St. Paul. No additional pipeline was needed to bring Canadian crude from the United States section to the Detroit-Toledo area, and since late 1960 it has been delivered to the Mobiloil refinery at Trenton, Michigan, and to Gulf and Standard Oil (Ohio) refineries at Toledo.[61] An application to bring Canadian oil to the Ashland Oil and Refining Co. and the Socony Mobil refineries in the Buffalo area via a ninety-mile spur line from Hamilton to Tonawanda led spokesmen for American independent oil producers to urge import restrictions.[62]

There have been high level discussions in Canada of a proposal to build a second pipeline eastward from Alberta to supply the Montreal refineries.[63] Impetus for such a project was provided by United States restrictions on imports of Canadian oil between July, 1957, and June, 1959. Such a pipeline would produce competition for Venezuelan and Middle Eastern oil, but, as the Royal Commission on Energy, which did not favor the project, pointed out, at the cost of

[59] R. Tyre, "Saskatchewan's Oil and Gas," *Canadian Geographical Journal,* vol. 56 (1958), 127-128.

[60] Deliveries in 1960 averaged 349,470 bbls. per day, with an average of 190,516 bbls. per day going to Ontario and 62,891 bbls. per day to the United States. On the added facilities to increase throughput for 1961, see National Energy Board, *Report to the Governor in Council,* June 6, 1960, 4-6.

[61] *Reference Material on Canadian Oil and Gas,* 17, 19; *Oil and Gas Journal,* vol. 59 (1961), 74. The Interprovincial Pipe Line Company, organized on the initiative of Imperial Oil Limited, was incorporated in 1949 by special act of the Canadian Parliament. Oil companies among the original shareholders were Imperial Oil Limited, holder in 1960 of 33.18 per cent of the shares, Canadian Gulf Oil Company, and Canadian Oil Companies Limited. The United States section is owned and operated by the Lakehead Pipe Line Company, Inc., a Delaware corporation that is a wholly owned subsidiary of Interprovincial.

[62] *Globe and Mail* (Toronto), May 12, 1961.

[63] *Winnipeg Free Press,* Dec. 12, 1959.

a reduced wellhead price.[64]   This issue has included the corollary question of whether to build north or, like Interprovincial, south of Lake Superior, the latter route being a bit longer but less expensive.

The Trans Mountain Pipe Line runs from the vicinity of Edmonton to Burnaby, British Columbia, in the Vancouver area.[65] A spur line that reaches the border near Sumas, Washington, was extended in 1954 to the Socony Mobil refinery at Ferndale, Washington, and in 1955 to Anacortes, Washington, where both Shell and Texaco refineries are located, the latter being connected to the system in 1958. When Trans Mountain was planned, it was thought that Canadian crude would move to California refineries, particularly in the San Francisco area, but the lower cost of foreign crudes kept Canadian oil from the California market.

The construction of oil pipelines across United States territory was not unaffected by governmental activity. Trans Mountain stands as a symbol of Washington's encouragement of exploration for and development of petroleum resources in Canada. Exceptional priorities were granted by the United States defense authorities during the Korean War to make available steel pipe, oil-well drilling machinery, and other equipment. The "voluntary" oil import quotas of 1954 were not applied to refinery areas that could be supplied most conveniently from western Canada.[66]

Despite the encouragement noted, American policy in 1957-59 followed a course that proved upsetting to Canadians. In the Puget Sound area Canadian crude oil competes with crude from Venezuela, the Middle East, British North Borneo, and, since May, 1961, Alaska.[67] Under the 1954 "voluntary" quotas recommended by the President's Cabinet Advisory Committee on Energy Supplies and

[64] Royal Commission on Energy, *Second Report* (Ottawa, 1959), chap. 5, 41-49.
[65] Average deliveries to all Canadian and United States points in 1960 were 113,143 bbls. per day. Trans Mountain Oil Pipe Line Company was formed in 1951. Subscribers included Canadian Gulf Oil Company, Imperial Oil Limited, Shell Oil Company of Canada Limited, Standard Oil Company of British Columbia Limited, Union Oil Company of California, and Richfield Oil Corporation. Trans Mountain operates the United States section through its wholly owned subsidiary, Trans Mountain Pipe Line Corporation.
[66] John Davis, *Oil and Canada–United States Relations* (Canadian-American Committee, 1959), vii, 27.
[67] In the first half of 1960 the Puget Sound refineries imported Canadian crude in an amount equivalent to 40 per cent of their refinery capacities; *Reference Material on Canadian Oil and Gas*, p. 17. Alaskan production in 1962 was expected to equal half the capacity of Puget Sound refineries; *Globe and Mail* (Toronto), May 26, 1961.

Resources Policy, both Venezuela and Canada enjoyed preferred positions. The Suez Canal blockage in 1956 produced a diversion of American and Venezuelan crude that was reflected in a rise in Canadian exports to the United States, the 1957 figure amounting to about one third of the Canadian output.[68] When in 1957 Middle Eastern oil again moved to its markets, restrictions upon importations into the United States were sought. The President's Special Committee concluded that restrictions on Western Hemisphere sources were needed,[69] and in July, 1957, the "voluntary" restrictions, established on a more formal and comprehensive basis, were applied to Canada for the first time. A 15 per cent voluntary reduction was extended to the Northwest by a presidential order of December 24, 1957. Even though the reduced import volume was in excess of Trans Mountain's schedule, deliveries to Washington refineries were reduced by 66.9 per cent, those to the Shell refinery at Anacortes being halted until after the United States had removed restrictions against Canadian crude.

In March, 1959, pursuant to a finding that petroleum products were being imported in quantities and under circumstances that threatened to impair national security, mandatory quotas were re-established. The theory behind the national security provision, first adopted in the Trade Agreement Extension Act of 1954 and broadened in the Acts of 1955 and 1959 as a substitute for outright restrictions sought both by the bituminous coal industry and by independent oil producers,[70] is that imports slow the search for new domestic oil fields necessary for wartime use.[71] The thesis that imports of a dwindling resource endanger national security[72] was not well received in Canada. Vociferous Canadian objections, calling attention to GATT, NATO,

[68] Grant L. Reuber, *The Growth and Changing Composition of Trade between Canada and the United States* (Canadian-American Committee, 1960), 67.

[69] *Report of the Special Committee to Investigate Crude Oil Imports,* Department of Commerce, July 29, 1957, 5.

[70] Bidwell, *op. cit.,* 316-317. Independent oil producers wanted imports limited to the 1954 ratio of 10 per cent of domestic production.

[71] See W. L. Thorp, "Trade Barriers and National Security," *Papers and Proc. of the Am. Econ. Assoc.,* vol. 50 (1960), 433-443. See also *Report on Energy Supplies and Resources Policy,* White House Press Release, Feb. 26, 1955.

[72] Cf. the circumstances of the Montana Power Company's importation of natural gas from Alberta in 1952, *infra,* p. 172, and Presiding Examiner Ivins' conclusion: "It is common knowledge that natural gas is a highly valuable resource available in limited exhaustible quantities in the United States. It seems self-evident that any reasonable augmentation of our limited domestic supplies is desirable unless clearly outweighed by damage to the public interest"; 14 F.P.C. 227 at 240.

and Canadian-American defense commitments,[73] bore testimony that the United States Government was less sensitive to Canadian feelings than to pressure from the domestic oil industry. However, in June, 1959, a formula was announced that virtually exempted overland shipments from the mandatory restrictions.[74] Canada and Mexico alone could benefit. But, with an increase in imports from Canada in 1961, particularly to the Midwest, restrictions were again suggested. Investigations by the Department of the Interior, the office of Civilian and Defense Mobilization, and the House Small Business Committee were undertaken, and Secretary of the Interior Stewart Udall called upon Canada to restrain the flow of oil to the United States east of the Rocky Mountains.[75]

III. NATURAL GAS

Until the Alberta discoveries in 1947 and after, which in 1959 accounted for 71 per cent of Canada's production of natural gas,[76] only small fields in Ontario and New Brunswick were exploited. Significant imports from the United States were not to be relied on, for the most demanding markets in the United States lay on or near the routes that would have to be followed and, to add to the uncertainty, American gas could be cut off by presidential order.

The first United States exports into southwestern Ontario in 1947 were limited to summer surplus gas. Canada has been a steady importer of natural gas since 1952, when about 6 billion cubic feet were imported. The volume reached a peak of almost 35 billion cubic feet in 1958, but has dropped since then.[77] Canada became a net

---

[73] E.g., *Royal Commission on Canada's Economic Prospects, Final Report* (Ottawa, 1957). The Canadian Government contended that the restrictions were contrary to GATT principles, to agreed principles of Canadian-American defense co-operation, and to understandings reached on economic matters by NATO members; Davis, *op. cit.*, 27-29. Lester Pearson, invoking NATO principles of economic co-operation, commented that "Oil in Alberta is as safe from hostile interference, and as available for United States use, as is oil in Oklahoma"; *Christian Science Monitor*, Jan. 10, 1958. Cf. Bidwell, *op. cit.*, 319, to the effect that it is difficult to stretch the GATT language allowing certain quantitative restrictions to cover oil imports.

[74] Davis, *op. cit.*, 10-12; Southworth and Buchanan, *op. cit.*, 37-38, 62-63.

[75] "Canadian Oil Policy May Face Showdown Soon," *Oil and Gas Journal*, vol. 59 (1961), 74-75; *Globe and Mail* (Toronto), May 12, June 19, Oct. 6 and 7, 1961.

[76] On the Alberta reserves, see Canadian Bank of Commerce, Reference Section, "Natural Gas Comes of Age," *Circular Letter*, No. 10, Oct. 14, 1960, 2, 3.

[77] *Reference Material on Canadian Oil and Gas*, 34.

exporter of gas after the completion in 1957 of the Trans-Canada Pipe Line and of the Westcoast Transmission Company's system. Trans-Canada, following a 2142-mile route north of Lake Superior, transports gas collected in the Alberta foothills from the Alberta-Saskatchewan border to Montreal and other eastern markets, as well as to terminals along the way.[78] The Westcoast Transmission Company's system brings gas from the Peace River area of British Columbia and Alberta to the state of Washington. Symptomatic of Canada's present export-import position is the Federal Power Commission's approval on July 25, 1960, of the abandonment of the transport of gas, carried on since 1953, to Niagara Gas Transmission Limited for transport to Toronto and delivery to the Consumers Gas Company, subject to Trans-Canada's capacity to provide. The border facilities were to be kept available for either import or export as emergencies on either the American or the Canadian system might require.[79]

Legislation—state, provincial, and national—has not served to make the export of natural gas in either direction any easy matter.[80] Exports have been permitted only after the authorities have satisfied themselves that local requirements are being met. Residential requirements, ordinarily given priority, introduce the complication of early saturation, for new customers sign up as rapidly as new transmission lines are built. Lines but a few years old have to be "looped" or paralleled by new lines. Hence, Alberta, empowered to grant or withhold permits to export from the province, has endeavored to insure the retention of gas in amounts and at prices intended to encourage the development of industries. Alberta reserves the right as an emergency measure to cut off all exports of natural gas for commercial or industrial purposes. No producing province need make available additional gas after the twenty- or twenty-five-year period of an original contract and license has expired. Moreover,

[78] On United States investment in Trans-Canada and in Westcoast Transmission, see Royal Commission on Energy, *First Report* (Ottawa, 1958), chap. 1, 25-33, chap. 4, 2-14. On political aspects, see H. G. J. Aitken, "The Changing Structure of the Canadian Economy with Particular Reference to the influence of the United States," in *The American Economic Impact on Canada* (Durham, N. C., 1959), 27-33.

[79] Docket Nos. 18,877 *et al.*, 24 F.P.C. 71, 78.

[80] See the statement by the Canadian-American Committee sponsored by the National Planning Association (U.S.A.), the Private Planning Association (U.S.A.), and the Private Planning Association of Canada, entitled *Wanted: A Working Environment More Conducive to Canadian-American Trade in Natural Gas* (Nov., 1959), especially pp. 4-6.

the National Energy Board in June, 1960, advised the Montana Power Company that, despite sympathetic treatment, it should "maintain and improve its sources of supply within the United States, as a precaution against the contingency of future circumstances in which it would not be in the Canadian public interest to approve applications for additional supplies of gas from Canada."[81] To render the duration of projects even more uncertain than does naturally available supply is hardly conducive to sizable investments in facilities solely dependent upon the exportation of gas. Canada's national export legislation authorizes the National Energy Board to issue permits of twenty years' or more duration. Should a permit not be extended, the particular export ceases at the expiration of the period specified. The Canadian Exportation of Power and Fluids and Importation of Gas Act (1955) limits the granting of export permits to gas that is surplus to Canadian needs. On the American side, the producing states have sought to retain control over amounts calculated to meet their future needs, while the Federal Power Commission has allowed only such exports to Canada as could be cut off at any time that a need developed in the United States.[82]

The first Canadian export of natural gas to the United States was that of 1952 to the Montana Power Company. The company's reserves were being depleted by the end of the Second World War, and an exploration program failed to disclose new reserves in Montana or adjacent areas in the United States. A supply was located in Alberta approximately eighteen miles north of the border. The reserves were eventually purchased by Montana Power's wholly owned subsidiary, Canadian-Montana Gas Company Limited.

The largest purchaser of Montana Power's gas is the Anaconda Copper Mining Company, which by 1952 was using approximately 10 billion cubic feet annually out of an estimated total annual consumption on Montana Power's system of 21 billion cubic feet. The threatened consequence was an exhaustion of Montana Power's reserves in 11.15 years. Under the circumstances, Montana Power had expressed its intention to terminate natural gas service to Anaconda.

Aside from the importance of Anaconda to the economy of Montana, the Korean War then in progress had emphasized the importance of Anaconda to national defense. Consequently, the United

[81] National Energy Board, *Report to the Governor in Council*, June 20, 1960, 12.
[82] John Davis, *op. cit.*, 8-9, 28.

States Department of Defense asked the Canadian Department of Defence to request a Special Act of the Alberta Legislature allowing a special permit to export gas for Anaconda's benefit, even though studies concerning Alberta's needs had not been concluded and no gas had been declared surplus to those needs. The result was the passage of the Gas Export Act (1951)[83] authorizing the provincial Petroleum and Natural Gas Conservation Board, with the approval of the Lieutenant-Governor, to permit the removal of gas up to 10 billion cubic feet annually or 40 million cubic feet daily for the exclusive benefit of Anaconda. The permit could be and, on June 11, 1951, was issued to the McColl-Frontenac Oil Company Limited and the Union Oil Company of California. The gas was to be gathered and transmitted to the border at a point near Whitlash, Montana, by the Canadian-Montana Pipe Line Company Limited, also a wholly owned subsidiary of Montana Power. The permit covered the five-year period from April 7, 1951, to April 7, 1956, even though the facilities to be constructed were to have a financial life of twenty-five years.[84]

Approval of the Federal Power Commission for the importation was sought under Section 3 of the Natural Gas Act of 1938, which provides that the Commission shall issue import orders "unless, after an opportunity for hearing, it finds that the proposed ... importation will not be consistent with the public interest."[85] Approval of the necessary construction was sought under the then pertinent Executive Order No. 8202 of July 12, 1939,[86] which directed the Federal Power Commission to receive all applications for permits to construct, operate, maintain, or connect at the borders the facilities required for the importation of natural gas. After securing the recommendations of the Secretaries of State and of War, the Commission was to submit each application to the President with a recommendation as to whether the permit should be granted and upon what terms and conditions. In its Opinion No. 223 (February 5, 1952) the Commission approved

[83] *Statutes of Alberta*, 1951, c. 36.

[84] See *The Montana Power Company*, Opinion No. 223 (Feb. 5, 1952), Docket Nos. G-1712, G-1717, 11 F.P.C. 1 at 2-7; Presiding Examiner's Decision (March 21, 1955), Docket Nos. G-2805, G-2806, 14 F.P.C. 227 at 231-232.

[85] 52 *Stat.* 821, 822; 15 U.S.C. 717b. On the meaning of this provision, see *Cia Mexicana de Gas*, 167 F. 2d 804, 806 (1948); *Pacific Power and Light Company v. Federal Power Commission*, 111 F. 2d 1014, 1016 (1940). See also the Presiding Examiner's decision of March 21, 1955, in the *Montana Power Company*, 14 F.P.C. 227 at 237-240.

[86] 4 *Fed. Reg.* 3243.

the importation subject, among other things, to precise conformity with the Alberta authorization and to the assessment against Anaconda alone, either directly or indirectly, of the costs of importation, including the costs of construction, operation, and maintenance of necessary and incidental facilities.[87]

Prior to the expiration date of April 7, 1956, the Montana Power Company sought an extension of the permit and also authorization to supplement and augment its over-all system requirements with Canadian gas for a period of twenty years. No new facilities were required except to extend the service to other Montana communities. Application for a Canadian federal export permit was still pending before the Minister of Trade and Commerce, but the Alberta Petroleum and Natural Gas Conservation Board had on May 14, 1954, granted a twenty-year permit for the exportation of maximums of 20 billion cubic feet annually and 100 million cubic feet daily. In order to remove the restrictions of the construction and operation permit of 1952, it was necessary to get a new permit, this time under Executive Order No. 10485, of September 3, 1953,[88] which allowed the Federal Power Commission itself to issue the order except in cases of disagreement among the Commission and the Secretaries of State and Defense, in which case the matter had to be submitted to the President. Subject to the filing of necessary authorizations from the Canadian Government, the Presiding Examiner, in a decision subsequently affirmed by the Commission, on March 21, 1955, authorized the importation until May 14, 1974, and in 1960 the National Energy Board extended the Canadian license to the same date. But the source proved inadequate and supplies from other Canadian fields also had to be authorized.[89]

An issue of interest to students of international law was raised by the competing fuel interveners, including the United Mine Workers. The competing fuel interests argued that the application should be denied "in the absence of some intergovernmental agreement assuring the continuity and adequacy of gas supply." Taking note of the longstanding good relations between the United States and Canada, of the absence of agreements concerning railways, telephone, telegraph,

[87] 11 F.P.C. 1, 10, 11.
[88] 18 *Fed. Reg.* 5397.
[89] 14 F.P.C. 227, 241-242; Docket Nos. G-17,350 *et al.*, 24; National Energy Board, *Report to the Governor in Council*, March 21, 1960, section 9; and June 20, 1960.

and express service, of the Hyde Park Declaration of 1941 revitalized in the Korean Emergency in the Statement of Principles of Economic Co-operation of 1950, and of preceding natural gas authorizations, the Presiding Examiner Ivins concluded: "In the light of this background of amity and comity between the United States and Canada these applications should be dealt with on their merits. This would seem to be a natural concomitant of due process."[90]

A twenty-year project of Westcoast Transmission Company Limited to export at a point near Sumas, Washington, up to 303,462 Mcf of natural gas per day from the Peace River area of British Columbia and Alberta for distribution by its wholly owned subsidiary, Westcoast Transmission Company, Incorporated, failed to obtain the approval of the Federal Power Commission. In its Opinion No. 271, issued June 18, 1954, the Commission approved Pacific Northwest Pipeline Corporation's service of the area with gas from United States fields. The Commission declined to allow the consumers concerned to become solely dependent upon a foreign source which could be cut off by unilateral action, although Chairman Jerome K. Kuykendall objected to taking final action against importations from Canada that might prove to be the soundest of projects.[91] Westcoast, faced with possible loss of funds spent in promotion, negotiated a gas purchase contract of December 11, 1954, whereby Pacific Northwest, which had earlier opposed Westcoast's application and then had demanded a 50 per cent interest in Westcoast as consideration for executing a contract, obtained an option to purchase 25 per cent of Westcoast's common shares outstanding after public offering. The option was later exercised by Pacific Northwest's wholly-owned subsidiary, Westcoast Investment Corporation.

In the following year the Pacific Northwest Pipeline Corporation made application for the importation and for the temporary exportation of a maximum of 12,000 Mcf daily for distribution in Vancouver and for a permit to export, after Westcoast Transmission had completed its construction in the fall of 1947, 12,600 Mcf daily for twenty years for use principally by the Consolidated Mining and Smelter Company of Canada Limited at Trail, British Columbia.

[90] 14 F.P.C. 227, 240. Nor did Niagara Mohawk's intervention on the same ground impress the National Energy Board, *Report to the Governor in Council*, March 21, 1960, section 10, 7.

[91] Docket No. G-1429, 13 F.P.C. 221, 235-236, with Chairman Kuykendall's dissent, 240-241. See also the denial of rehearing, 13 F.P.C. 1249, 1250-1251.

In its Opinion No. 289 of November 25, 1955, the Commission granted authorizations to import and to export and a certificate of public convenience authorizing the necessary construction.[92]   Later, British Columbian authorities requested Pacific Northwest to supply an additional 20,000 Mcf per day on an interruptible basis from November 1, 1956, to November 1, 1957, when Peace River gas was expected to be available.   In its Order of October 26, 1956, the Federal Power Commission authorized the additional temporary exportation.[93]   Peace River gas now flows into Pacific Northwest's system, now part of El Paso Natural Gas Company's system, deliveries in 1959 averaging 184,000 Mcf per day.

In 1956 a reversal of the position asserted in Opinion No. 271 occurred.   In the Examiner's decision of September 28, 1956, in the *Midwestern Gas Transmission Company Case* the suggestion was made that a treaty be entered into to assure a definite supply of gas at a reasonable price, but the Commission in its Order of November 15, 1956, took the position that a project depending wholly upon Canadian gas "could be found to be in the public interest, depending on the particular facts of a given case."[94]   Moreover, the Commission had already, in Opinion No. 296 of October 6, 1956, approved an importation from Mexico on the basis of "mutual faith, confidence, and respect."[95]

Six applications were made in 1959 for the importation of Canadian natural gas.   A few years earlier the then new Midwestern Gas Transmission Company, a wholly-owned subsidiary of the Tennessee Gas Transmission Company which also has a 17 per cent interest in the Trans-Canada Pipe Line, anticipated the completion of Trans-Canada and proposed to supply certain areas of Michigan, Minnesota, Wisconsin, and Illinois with both Canadian and United States gas.   Companies already serving the Middle West vigorously opposed the project and presented their own proposals.   In Opinion No. 316 of October 31, 1958, the Commission denied all applications and asked the companies to make new filings modified to conform to what the Commission thought to be in the public interest.   In regard to the importation, the Commission favored it as consistent with

[92] Docket Nos. G-8932 *et al.*, 14 F.P.C. 157, 181-182.

[93] Docket No. G-8932, 16 F.P.C. 1094.

[94] Docket Nos. G-9451 *et al.*, 16 F.P.C. 466, 484-485, and 486, 488.

[95] *Texas Eastern Transmission Corporation*, Docket Nos. G-2503 *et al.*, 16 F.P.C. 27, 36.

"policies of cooperation and joint endeavor" in defense and "general economic relationships" but did not find that Trans-Canada had demonstrated its ability to meet potential maximum Canadian demand.[96]

In 1959 Midwestern proposed to purchase 204 million cubic feet daily from Trans-Canada Pipe Lines Limited at the border near Emerson, Manitoba, and to build a pipeline system to Marshfield, Wisconsin. At Marshfield 158 million cubic feet daily would be sold to the Michigan-Wisconsin Pipe Line Company which applied for permission to transport it to Appleton, Wisconsin, for sale to the Michigan Gas and Electric Company for distribution in the Upper Peninsula except to the Cleveland Cliffs Iron Company. Midwestern Gas Transmission also proposed to sell to companies servicing consumers in North Dakota, Minnesota, and Wisconsin. On October 31, 1959, the Federal Power Commission approved the applications of Midwestern and Michigan-Wisconsin.[97] Subsequently, certain coal interests moved to reopen the Midwestern case on the ground that the contract between Midwestern and Trans-Canada covered a twenty-five-year period, while Trans-Canada's license, originally for twenty-five years, extended only to its original expiration date in 1971. This motion was denied by the Federal Power Commission.[98]

In 1960 and 1961 approvals were given for importations by the St. Lawrence Gas Company, Inc., a subsidiary of the Consumers Gas Company, an Ontario distributor,[99] by the Pacific Gas Transmission Company, the El Paso Natural Gas Company (successor by merger to Pacific Northwest Pipeline Corporation), and the Montana Power Company.[100] The first of these importations, accorded a 20-year life, was for the purpose of servicing the Ogdensburg-Massena area, while the other three, of twenty-five years' duration, were for delivery in California, Idaho, Montana, Oregon, and Washington. Presiding Examiner Howell Purdue twice approved the St. Lawrence Gas Company's request, the first approval occurring even though the

[96] Docket Nos. G-2306 et al., 20 F.P.C. 575, 584-585, 591-592. See H.G.J. Aitken, "The Midwestern Case: Canadian Gas and the Federal Power Commission," Can. Jour. of Econ. and Pol. Sci., vol. 25 (1959), 129-143.

[97] Opinion No. 331, 22 F.P.C. 775.

[98] Federal Power Commission, Docket Nos. G-18,313 et al., Release No. 10,975, G-5839, May 27, 1960.

[99] Federal Power Commission, Docket Nos. G-17,500 et al., Release No. 10,921, G-5807, April 8, 1960, Release No. 11,459, G-6181, May 12, 1961, and Release No. 11,589, G-6270, Aug. 8, 1961.

[100] Federal Power Commission, Docket Nos. G-17,350 et al., Release No. 11,078, G-5909, Aug. 5, 1960.

National Energy Board had refused an export license to the seller, Niagara Gas Transmission Limited, also a subsidiary of Consumers, on the ground that posted export price was too low and delivery too uncertain.[101] A revised application was subsequently approved on condition that the market be limited to St. Lawrence County, New York,[102] and this action was followed by the second approval by the Presiding Examiner and a subsequent approval by the Federal Power Commission itself in its Opinion No. 347 of August 8, 1961.

In contrast, an application by the Tennessee Gas Transmission Company, holder of one of the four largest interests in Trans-Canada, for a five-year importation, over facilities constructed under a 1953 export permit, of an interruptible 204 million cubic feet daily—interestingly, the same amount that Tennessee's subsidiary, Midwestern, had asked permission to import and that Tennessee at the same had sought to furnish Midwestern from its United States supplies—from Trans-Canada Pipe Line Limited was twice denied by Presiding Examiner Harry W. Frazee after the export had been approved by the National Energy Board. Grounds of disapproval included failure to show need in view of Tennessee's domestic supplies which the Examiner deemed adequate for the foreseeable future.[103] But the Federal Power Commission's unanimous Opinion No. 349 of December 14, 1961, approved the importation but of a much smaller amount than was sought.[104] Consideration of the adequacy of the domestic supplies available to an American concern was included in the reasoning of the National Energy Board when it approved Westcoast Transmission's export to El Paso. The Board found that making Canadian gas available would enable El Paso to divert other gas from the Pacific Northwest to southern California.[105]

The cases just referred to indicate the unsatisfactory situation that exists when independent authorities, not only national but also provincial, must co-ordinate. Conflicts of local interest and national interest and of differing national interests must be reconciled if resources,

---

[101] National Energy Board, *Report to the Governor in Council*, March 21, 1960, section 10, 12, section 12, 26.

[102] *Ibid.*, May 31, 1960, 20.

[103] Federal Power Commission, Docket Nos. G-20,388 *et al.*, Release No. 10,933, G-5814, April 22, 1960, Release No. 11,155, G-5966, Sept. 23, 1960, and Release No. 11,521, G-6219, June 20, 1961; National Energy Board, *Report to the Governor in Council*, March 21, 1960, section 5, 24-29, section 12, 11.

[104] Federal Power Commission, Release No. 11,764, G-6400, Dec. 14, 1961.

[105] National Energy Board, *Report*, March 21, 1960, section 8, 11.

distributed by nature throughout a continent, are to be used in the various settlements and enterprises that man has separated with national, state, and provincial borders. Within those borders the established laws and authorities are based not only upon particular interests but also upon different standards of value. Even if one eliminated the states and provinces and concentrated all authority over natural gas at Ottawa and Washington, the problem of different standards would remain.

The first duty of the Federal Power Commission as it performs the functions assigned to it by the Natural Gas Act of 1938 is to act in the public interest, which, under the influence of Granger concepts about railroads and utilities, has meant the consumers' interests. This very requirement led the Federal Power Commission to treat Canadian natural gas at first as a supplementary source of supply and to require assurance that the Pacific Northwest would have an American supply. More recent decisions, including the National Energy Board's expression of concern for the proper utilization of El Paso's United States supplies, seem to reflect the continental view that here is a resource exploitable and usable by interests on both sides of the border. The continental view is also evident in both the distribution schemes and the commercial organizational schemes whereby, for example, the St. Lawrence Gas Company of Ogdensburg is a subsidiary of the Consumers Gas Company of Ontario while the Canadian-Montana Pipe Line Company is a subsidiary of the Montana Power Company. However, on the basis of Pacific Northwest's tactics in obtaining an interest in Westcoast Transmission, it is possible to conclude that certain manifestations of a continental view spring from an acquisitive tendency. Moreover, these are not the arrangements required to provide guarantees against unilateral stoppage of the international flow of gas for local or national reasons. On the other hand, prohibitions of exports, as in the 1961 rejection by the Alberta Oil and Gas Conservation Board of a proposal for large-scale movement of natural gas liquids to the United States, have been interpreted as including a recognition of a need to avoid dislocation of United States production.[106]

Different standards apply in rate-making. In the United States the interest of the consumer takes precedence, even though the exploitation of natural gas requires an investment in an exhaustible resource.

[106] *Globe and Mail* (Toronto), July 18, 1961.

However, in its Opinion No. 338 of February 29, 1960, in the *Phillips Petroleum Company Case* the Federal Power Commission held that ridiculous results would obtain if cost were the only basis and held that regulation should be based upon a determination of fair prices, based on reasonable financial requirements of the industry rather than on the utility rate base and expenses of each company.[107]

The Canadian Exportation of Power and Fluids and Importation of Gas Act (1955) reads: "The price charged by a licencee for power or gas exported by him shall not be lower than the price at which power or gas, respectively, is supplied by him or his suppliers and under similar conditions of sale for consumption in Canada."[108] Canadian consumers are thus protected against the payment of higher rates than foreign purchasers of Canadian gas. Otherwise, the price is a matter of negotiation between the producers and the transporting and marketing utilities. The protective feature of the legislation served to allow the National Energy Board to deny the first application of Niagara Gas Transmission to export to the St. Lawrence Gas Company on grounds including the lowness of the posted export price. An additional source of discrepancy between Canadian and United States prices has been the concern of Canadian regulation with retail, not wholesale, prices.[109]

Differences in standards traceable to legislation are rather delicate matters to handle through the diplomatic process. They certainly are not to be dealt with by means of the pressure politics in which domestic interest groups can engage. Even an administration sympathetic to the suggestions of an embassy must tread carefully for domestic political reasons. In so far as such quasi-judicial bodies as the Federal Power Commission and the National Energy Board are concerned, it would be a most serious breach of propriety on the part of a domestic politician, let alone the Energy Counsellor at a foreign embassy, to make any suggestion that even remotely constituted an interference with freedom of decision. Without an overriding law of an international nature, differing principles embodied in national legislation endure unless domestic pressures induce legislators to bring diverse statutes to a common meeting ground. Nevertheless, the quasi-judicial regulatory agencies can seek workable rulings in

[107] Federal Power Commission, Docket Nos. G-1148 *et al.*, Release No. 11,158, G-5968, Sept. 28, 1960.
[108] *Statutes of Canada*, 1955, c. 14.
[109] Davis, *op. cit.*, 2, 24-26.

particular cases through the knowledge that each possesses of what its foreign counterpart is doing. As a means of expediting decisions the Borden Commission suggested that arrangements be made with the United States whereby, when an import or export license were to be sought, a Federal Power Commissioner would sit with the National Energy Board and an Energy Board member with the Federal Power Commission, each as an *ad hoc* observer without vote.[110] The recommendation was not implemented, but whether this was due to differences in basic concepts and procedures, to constitutional and legal differences, or to reluctance to surrender a morsel of executive authority even by inference is uncertain. Failure to implement has not meant the discouragement of close liaison. Standards of a technical nature, as well as accounting methods, can be rendered uniform through staff action. In such cases, with such objectives in mind, embassy specialists have had a role to play in aid of staff liaison, and informal arrangements appear to have worked rather well. Moreover, on February 17, 1960, the Joint Committee on Trade and Economic Affairs issued a communiqué calling for close co-operation between the National Energy Board and the Federal Power Commission and for the two governments to keep each other closely informed of developments bearing on transborder movements of petroleum and natural gas.[111]

IV. CONCLUSION

What has been said in the preceding sections suggests a need for continental management of resources. To a certain degree this has been accomplished by private enterprise by means of ownership and control of subsidiaries across the border. However, from the point of view of the Canadian this sort of continental management often appears to deal with the issue of conservation versus utilization by conserving Canadian and utilizing United States resources. On the other hand, independent oil producers in the United States regard themselves as threatened by an opposite development whereby it would be the Canadian resources that would be utilized. Hence the public authorities find themselves inescapably cast as overseers of

[110] Royal Commission on Energy, *First Report* (Ottawa, 1958), recommendation 29 and chap. 3, 14-15.

[111] *Dept. of State Bulletin*, vol. 42 (1960), 366.

resource utilization on a continental basis. But it is as national authorities employing national instruments of government that they must perform this function. In respect to the resources here considered, there is no International Joint Commission to assist, although it is conceivable that the Commission might become involved were the future exploitation of oil and natural gas reserves under Lakes Erie, Huron, and St. Clair to result in water and beach pollution.[112]

It has been suggested that a natural gas treaty might be a desirable alternative to the adoption of similar industrial practices and regulatory techniques by cautious performance.[113] If the objective were a truly continental approach to the gathering, transmission, and marketing of natural gas, such a treaty might perhaps embrace Mexico as well as Canada and the United States. Restricting the scope to natural gas would not, of course, alleviate difficulties such as those presently faced by the Canadian uranium industry. But it would have an effect upon oil, for the two are found together and regulation affecting the one has its impact upon the other. Particularly is this true where price and the impact of conservation measures, presently imposed by states and provinces, upon price are concerned.

A question that most certainly would have to be considered in respect to a natural gas treaty would be the desirability of impinging upon the authority of states and provinces, assuming that it could be done, particularly in Canada, where treaties are not self-executing and where, as long as Privy Council rulings remain the law, provincial legislation is required in respect to matters within the powers of the provinces.[114] The impediments erected by British Columbia to implementation and even ratification of the Columbia River Treaty suggest that a treaty might not serve to alleviate concern over the power of a province unilaterally to cut off a source of fuel. Aside from this particular aspect of effectiveness, it may also be asked whether a treaty might not serve as an instrument to establish not only common standards for conservation but also common standards for use. This, too, would involve an intrusion into an area of local rather than regional

---

[112] Ontario Committee on Oil and Gas Resources, *Report*, Part I (Toronto, 1961), 11-13.

[113] E.g., Davis, *op. cit.*, 30.

[114] *Re Arrow River and Tributaries Slide and Boom Co.*, [1932] 2 D.L.R. 250, 260-261; *Reference re Weekly Rest in Industrial Undertakings Act*, [1937] A.C. 326 at 347-348; *Francis v. The Queen*, [1957] 4 D.L.R. 760; *The Attorney-General of Canada v. The Attorney-General of Ontario*, [1937] A.C. 326. See also David R. Deener, "Treaty Powers in a Federal Parliamentary System: The Case of Canada," *Proc. Am. Soc. Int. Law*, 1959, 288-293.

authority. It certainly may be seriously questioned whether state public utilities commissions properly give priority to home consumption of gas instead of to consumption by industry, particularly by defense industries. While the priority of treaties over state legislation in the United States is provided for in the Constitution, the political reaction to such an intrusion upon state powers might better be avoided.

National agencies might be regarded as somewhat more easily subjected to a treaty regime. Despite the fact that the Federal Power Commission in 1959 rescinded its own prescribed plan of regulation that conformed to the International Joint Commission's plan and, to avoid conflicts should the International Joint Commission amend its plan, replaced it with an order to the Power Authority of the State of New York to comply with the IJC requirements in regulating the outflows of Lake Ontario and the St. Lawrence River,[115] it is to be doubted that there is a desire to surrender any existing powers to an international commission. Failure to implement the Borden Commission's recommendation for observers to sit with the Federal Power Commission and with the National Energy Board when each hears applications for export and import licenses is suggestive. Yet it is not impossible that the enunciation of certain rules and guiding principles to be applied by national agencies would prove acceptable. Perhaps common technical standards could be prescribed by treaty. In this connection it should be noted that the Canadian-American Television Agreement of 1952[116] dealing with the allocation of channels within 250 miles of the border has depended upon an informal frequency-co-ordination procedure initiated in 1951 in harmony with which, in its most recent form of a working arrangement between the Federal Communications Commission and the Canadian Department of Transport, the latter body promulgated new rules, effective April 1, 1961, designed to meet public demands for expanded television coverage.[117] In respect to common standards pertinent to natural gas transmission, the effectiveness of current liaison might render formal agreement superfluous or at least basically declaratory. In respect to price, an agreement could prove useful to alleviate American fears that Canadian legislation would permit a gouging of American consumers de-

[115] Project No. 2000, Release No. 10,552, Aug. 3, 1959.
[116] TIAS 2594.
[117] Federal Communications Commission, 26th Annual Report for the Fiscal Year 1960 (Washington, 1960), 148-149; Canadian Weekly Bulletin, April 12, 1961, 4.

pendent upon Canadian sources. As for supply, conceivably a definition of what is surplus to Canadian needs might be attempted, but it also may be argued, as also in respect to price, that experience in the exportation and importation of natural gas has been too brief to permit a treaty definition of "surplus" that would not be out of harmony with tomorrow's situation. The same may be said about a definition of what is an adequate domestic supply which entered Presiding Examiner Frazee's decision rejecting the Tennessee Gas Transmission Company's application after the exportation had been approved by the National Energy Board. For the projection of today's definition into tomorrow's circumstances is quite a different matter from the assignment of the power either of definition or of determination in the particular case to an agency, national or international, which can alter its definition or determination as it encounters new circumstances.

Whether or not a treaty concerning just natural gas or also oil and metals is negotiated, it can hardly be said that such an instrument would of itself be the basis of international public activity in the management of resources on a continental basis. Certainly the 1955 Agreement on Civil Uses of Atomic Energy hardly assured Canadian uranium producers of a continuing market. More vital than a treaty is the record of Canadian-American unity which Presiding Examiner Ivins in the *Montana Power Company Case* (1955) found to be sufficient grounds for allowing both importations and exportations of natural gas. To this must be added the capacity of persons in authority to learn from the experiences of Elliot Lake and of the period of oil restrictions, now asked for again, while also looking sympathetically upon nationalistic outbursts and threatened business interests. Treaty or no treaty, any evolution of continental management of resources rests upon these foundations.

10

Canada-United States Treaty Relations

Trends and Future Problems

Maxwell Cohen

My task is to seek out the trends in the treaty relations of Canada and the United States and to speculate about the future of these relations, about the problems inherent in, or emerging from, these relations. Let me begin by suggesting that a discussion of Canadian–United States treaty relations can not be limited to the technical forms of these agreements or even to the particular substance of individual undertakings; rather this dialogue can be meaningful only if we see the question of treaty relations in the context of the total political, economic, and social complex that marks the sharing of the North American continent by the two countries.

To some extent, therefore, the theme of Canada–United States treaty relations faces a dilemma. It cannot avoid the lawyer's technical problems. Yet if it were to concentrate too much on the technical aspects of treaties it would lose sight of the essential substantive issues of which the treaties are in general a formal reflection. If, however, it pays too much attention to the issues of substance, it may touch too lightly on those juridical matters which while on one level may seem to be questions of form, nevertheless, on other levels, are often symptomatic of deeper issues. For myself I shall try, first, to present something of a portrait of the evolution of treaty relations as part of the general story of Canadian-American dealings over the past century and a half; second, to search out whatever special juridical experience in those relations that seems worth marking because of its uniqueness; and, finally, to ask whether lessons of form and the realities of substance point to new areas of treaty relations that lie over the common horizon.

Let me begin by suggesting certain technical difficulties in the gathering of information in this field. The plain truth is that there has yet to be published in Canada a satisfactory collection of the bilateral and multilateral agreements that continue to be binding upon Canada. Bear in mind that the *Canada Treaty Series* begins only in 1928. The principal sources for information on United States–Canadian treaties, agreements, exchange of notes, and so on, therefore are to be found in the various treaty collections published in the United States, in the *British Foreign and State Papers* and other British collections, and in the League of Nations and United Nations treaty series. I am not unmindful of other sources such as de Martens and possibly some German sources, but these likely are not complete. More important is the fact that the precise character of the treaties entered into by the United Kingdom multilaterally, on behalf of the entire imperial system, has never been analyzed fully either in the United Kingdom or Canada in order to determine what may be said to be inherited as a matter of state succession by an independent Canada—whatever may be the date decided on for marking this juridical independence.

While the Department of External Affairs may have its own departmental index of treaties, no published version of this index is available and the Department has been naturally cautious about providing access to its files. Moreover, neither the Government of Canada nor the Government of the United Kingdom has actually determined among themselves the status of many of these eighteenth and nineteenth century agreements insofar as they may be considered obligations binding upon Canada today. This is particularly relevant to the vast array of commercial treaties and often involving "most favored nation" status which the United Kingdom entered into on behalf of the imperial family in this period. Some of the difficulties of the lack of precise knowledge in this field were implicit in the valuable paper recently presented to the Association of Canadian Law Teachers by Professor Lawford of Queen's University dealing with treaties and right of transit on the St. Lawrence River.[1]

Nevertheless, it is possible to make certain rough assumptions about these inherited treaty obligations and the absence of precision does not affect very much the general validity of a rather broad analysis

---

[1] Hugh Lawford, "Treaties and Rights of Transit on the St. Lawrence," *Can. Bar Rev.*, vol. 39 (1961), 577.

of United States–Canadian treaty relations—particularly those of the pre-1919 period.

Within these limitations, therefore, I should like to suggest that a certain pattern emerges in a total view of Canadian treaty relations—a pattern discernible over a period of time and also discernible with respect to matters of substance.

In my view it is possible to say that roughly there appear to have been five periods of development in the relations of Canada to the United States which reflect themselves in the particular character of the treaties to be found in those periods. Let me suggest that the first period may be called the "Period of Adjustment," from the Treaty of Paris of 1783 which concluded the American War of Independence, down to the settlement of the Alabama Claims in the 1870's. The preoccupation here must be seen as part of the adjustment of the new United States to the remnant of old British North America, now the Canada of pre-Confederation and early Confederation. This adjustment was psychological, military, territorial, and economic, and the treaties in that period deal with the great boundary questions, pre-Revolutionary debts, fisheries, criminals, and trade, including the great experiment of reciprocity in 1854. In essence this was the time when British North America and the United States were feeling their way towards answering the question as to "who gets what" on this continent and how to determine the minimal conditions for the living together of a burgeoning sovereign and a dawdling colony.

The second period may be described as the "Period of Continental Stabilization," from the 1870's down to the negotiations over the Boundary Waters Treaty of 1909. Here the major questions of boundaries were concluded through settling the Alaska and Passamaquoddy Bay boundaries, the widening of common control over the movement of criminals, and the first modest ventures into some fisheries control over and above the rights acquired under the 1818 Treaty.

The third period may be called the "Period of Common Resource Conservation and Early Joint Management," and this is the period from the Boundary Waters Treaty of 1909 to the outbreak of the Second World War. It coincides with the emerging independence of Canada as an international person and as the leader of the movement from Empire to Commonwealth. It marks the breakthrough of American power from continental to global responsibilities which was to be firmly crystallized by the Second World War. It is a period during which the network of treaty relations, covering boundary waters, fisheries, taxation, extradition, and early questions of common defense, all pointed to such a formal intertwining of dealings with each other as to now suggest a cautious acceptance by both countries of those continental realities that would push them further along the road toward the common management of their common continental concerns.

The fourth period is the "Period of Wartime Continental Cooperation" from 1939 to 1946. Here the subject matter takes on a greater variety, the spirit of the relations is more intimate and the involvement more complete. Defense, trade, the common management of industrial resources for the purposes of war-making—are all indicative of the new dimension of mutual reliance and interdependence. Radio and broadcasting, air transport, already observed in prewar agreements, become almost annual additions to the list of note exchanges. I shall say more in a moment about the content of the obligations undertaken in this period. But clearly what had happened was the extension of the notion that many of the problems of Canadian-American wartime responsibility were but further projections of the idea of joint management of a common continent, an idea already maturing in fact if not in philosophy in the relations of the neighbors.

And, finally, the fifth period may be called the "Period of a Maturing Continental Partnership"—irascible but inevitable. The reaction of the postwar years expressing itself conflictingly in Canadian resentment and Canadian reliance is clearly evident in the broadening scope of joint action and joint responsibility side by side with dramatic moments of explosive irritation. Again the main concerns are trade, defense, certain special problems of the opening Arctic in consequence of defense, the intensity of double taxation burdens requiring special treaty treatment, and the further development of measures to deal with fisheries, trade, boundary waters, and other resources.

It is in this postwar period, of course, that Canadian self-consciousness as a people in the world begins to mature and take on a vigorous posture. Yet all of these events in Canadian–United States relations were set now in the context of a deeper global concern. Hitler's Germany and a defeated Japan had left the world scene as major aggressors only to be replaced by the manpower, ideology, and revolution, on a great scale of potential danger for the West, of the Union of Soviet Socialist Republics, Peiping China, and their satellite empire. Thus, Canadian continental interests had about them now the additional pressures of a Western alliance to protect North America and Western Europe against the rush of Soviet power. Moreover, simultaneously, other events in the Afro-Asian and Latin-American worlds invited further forms of Canadian external involvement, partly through the Commonwealth with its surface political intimacies and economic aid programs, and partly through a bilateral and United Nations approach to the growing north-south dilemma of developed and less-developed states facing each other across the abyss of affluence.

We must see, therefore, the postwar continental interests of both the United States and Canada in the setting of these wider regional and multilateral interests and obligations. Indeed, it is important to consider the continuing interpenetration of the regional and global obligations with the continental ones. For example, on a security level this is to be seen in the effect of membership in the United Nations, the North Atlantic Treaty Organization, and the Organization of American States (for the United States at least) on North American security. It is also to be seen in the effect of membership in the General Agreement on Tariffs and Trade, the Organization for European Economic Co-operation, the International Bank for Reconstruction and Development, and the International Monetary Fund on North American and other regional economic arrangements. Thus continental obligations and experiments with joint management and partnership somehow have had to be related to the wider duties assumed multilaterally by both states. And, indeed, this is one of the continuing concerns for both countries as a technical as well as a political matter—namely, the reconciliation of their bilateral continental needs and arrangements with existing multilateral duties and with others that undoubtedly have yet to come.

Yet despite these wider claims, the intensity of United States–Canadian treaty relations may be seen from a glance at the bilateral treaties affecting Canada as a whole, from 1935 to 1957, compared with the bilateral exchanges with the United States alone. I shall not detail the entire comparative list, but take it in five year periods. From 1935 to 1939 inclusive, Canada entered into a total of 86 bilateral agreements. In the same period the total number entered into between Canada and the United States alone is 18, almost one-fourth of the total. Between 1940 and 1945 inclusive—the war years—there were 139 bilaterals, of which 66 were entered into with the United States. Between 1946 and 1950 there were 124 bilaterals, of which 36 were Canadian–U.S. exchanges. And, finally, between 1951 and 1956 there were 139 bilaterals of which 47 were U.S.–Canadian. At the same time between 1940 and 1949 Canada entered into 121 general and multilateral treaties which, of course, inferentially affected her legal relations with the United States.

It will be evident that the volume of the United States–Canadian treaty relations, so striking a percentage of the total of all Canadian treaty relations, must be an index of the variety and depth of their common interests and intermingling.

It is now necessary to look at the content of the treaty structure between the United States and Canada—say, since 1925, and viewed as a whole. Some of the statistics here are again revealing. In that period there were no less than 63 treaties, agreements, exchanges of notes, etc., dealing with defense problems, 24 covering boundary waters, 17 concerned with civil aviation, 14 with varieties of problems of great lakes and high seas fishing, 12 with radio and television, 9 dealing with oil and pipe lines, 7 covering shipping matters, 12 dealing with trade including Hyde Park, the Joint Mobilization Committee and Postwar Economic Settlement, 6 concerned with exchanges of agricultural labor and machinery, 7 dealing with taxation, 4 with extradition, 4 with unemployment insurance, 5 with weather stations, and a variety of individual special engagements, including 3 for atomic energy and the settlements of issues concerning smuggling, boundaries, surplus war property, traffic accidents, prize cases, and other matters.

The striking volume of notes and agreements dealing with defense expresses the permanent reality of that situation. And in the postwar period scarcely a year goes by without the appearance of important new common security decisions embodied in an agreement.

Something of the flavor of the past five years alone, and therefore of the trends, can be obtained from the following summary: in 1956 we find defense, unemployment insurance, atomic energy, and boundary waters make up the list; in 1957 the Alaska pipeline, boundary waters, atomic energy, fisheries, and double taxation; in 1958 the

North American Air Defense Command, boundary waters, aerial refueling, and agricultural labor; in 1959 radio, boundary waters, commercial air routes, defense, atomic energy, and the Alaska pipeline; in 1960 atomic energy, satellite tracking stations, and a submarine loan; and finally, in 1961, most important, the Columbia River Basin Treaty.

Are there any particular formal lessons to be drawn from this wide United States–Canadian experience? That is to say, are there any treaty techniques here that are peculiar to the North American search for answers to the joint management of the common continent? Enough already is known of certain of the unique features of the common boundary waters and fisheries conservation experience to make unnecessary any further discussion, except to suggest that the uniqueness claimed for the International Joint Commission had at least some navigation precedents in the Danube and Rhine Commissions, although the subject matter of the control was quite different. And, certainly, while the triumph of the Canadian argument as to Columbia downstream benefits is a very considerable achievement, its real conceptual origins surely are in doctrines of "unjust enrichment" and varieties of riparian rights concepts already well known to private law.

Perhaps the most insistent lesson of treaty form in recent years is the clear shift in the method of obligation from formal treaties and agreements to exchanges of notes and even simple declarations. This more informal technique avoids constitutional and political difficulties, but of course the method is not well suited to situations where the ratification process is politically desirable and where implementation by municipal law seems necessary and is to involve extensive legislative enactment.

Indeed, it has been suggested that, in many parts of the world where conventional relations take place, exchanges of notes are now the instrument of choice for their simplicity and ease of technical management. Undoubtedly, a most striking illustration of the use of notes between Canada and the United States was the solution of the complex St. Lawrence Seaway problems by simple exchanges of notes on the one hand and orders of the International Joint Commission on the other—although it is a nice question whether the two countries shall long be able to delay some grand formal instrument for the management of the Seaway. It is no little irony that the most formal agreements on the Canadian side have been between the Federal Government and the province of Ontario.

Finally, it is worth thinking for a moment about the extent to which the whole contemporary defense structure—apart from NATO —rests upon this informal network of exchanges of notes. Indeed, there are critics of the North American Air Defense Command who are concerned not only with the substance of this aspect of the alliance but with this excessive informality resting upon notes as well as the unilateral instructions from the two governments to their respective armed services in the matter of flight procedures, identification routines, etc. It is not difficult to understand this concern, because the Canadian public finds itself more confused about its own defense policy and relations with the United States over matters of defense than perhaps on almost any other subject embracing common tribulations today.

It now remains to examine the areas of continuing contention and tension between Canada and the United States and to ask what this holds for the future—the future as treaty substance and the future as treaty form.

It seems to me that there remain, and may always be with the two North American partners, for as long as we can see, certain fundamental areas of actual and potential dispute—resources, trade, United States investment, defense, boundary waters, and, perhaps even in due course, immigration. The resources problem has five great natural groups: rivers, fish, energy (natural gas and oil, electric power), forest products, base metals. On some of these the two nations have evolved sensible bilateral policies, each feeding the needs and the sense of equity of the other. They have done well on boundary rivers, on fish conservation. But as Professor Saul Sinclair has recently pointed out in the case of fish, the Halibut, Sockeye, and Pink Salmon Conventions are all concerned with the biology of conservation but not with the hard economics of a shared industry.[2]

Considering the Paley Report on the decline of United States primary resources, the two nations have not yet begun to explore adequately the significance of Canada as a resource area for the future United States needs of natural gas, petroleum, base metals, and forest products. And Canadian energy policy is still undefined with respect

[2] Saul Sinclair, *License Limitations in British Columbia; A Method of Economic Fisheries Management*, Dept. of Fisheries (Ottawa, 1960).

to the export of electric power.[3] As to trade matters, generally some progress has appeared with respect to easing arbitrary interpretation for customs regulations, but the basic question of access for Canadian secondary industries to American markets remains unsolved, along with the erratic status of the American market for base metals, oil, and occasionally forest products. Above all of these hangs the continuing general Canadian fear of American surplus products deployed to interrupt the marketing of competing Canadian exports.

United States investment in Canada—already so dramatized that everyone knows that much of Canada's secondary industry and most of its primary metal and petroleum resource development have passed into American hands—clearly requires patience and careful thought on both sides. The proposed Canadian legislation to impose upon American subsidiaries disclosure of statements and the general debate over opening of subsidiaries to Canadian equity participation are all straws in the wind that blows in the direction more of a desire for partnership than for exclusion—however misinterpreted that "blowing" may be in the United States. Similarly, United States antitrust laws daring to be executed extraterritorially require less of informal undertaking—as at present—and more formal arrangements in order to avoid future irritations. And here too, the effect of United States regulations in the matter of trading with the Communist world are likely to raise issues chronically for Canadian subsidiaries unless agreement can be reached on formulas that meet the minimal needs of public opinion on both sides.

And then there is defense. Canadian opinion here oscillates between the growing sense of futility of a Canada lingering on the periphery of major decisions and a competing sense of the need to bear a proper share of the day's duties. To acquire atomic weapons or not, to permit American refuelings of Strategic Air Command planes over Canadian airspace or not, to have some control over the relations of the North American Air Defense Command to the Strategic Air Command or not, to relate the North American Air Defense Command to NATO more directly or not—all of these are issues which no treaty can solve until the time and the spirit and the right formulas all move into some favorable conjunction. And here too one might face the classical problem of jurisdiction in the Arctic—

---

[3] Since this paper was written there seems to have evolved a firm policy of permitting the export of electric energy under license from the National Energy Board.

its ice-cap, its waters, and its airspace where, in Canada, the assumption is today that the Canadian writ runs everywhere but in the Beaufort Sea and among the moving frozen blocks on the polar cap.

Apart from these bilateral questions there are peculiarly Canadian problems involving the future of its own constitutional position in the matter of treaties. It is widely known that some unfortunate interpretations of the British North American Act, flowing from the *Labour Conventions Case* of 1937, have led to the belief that Canada has a kind of "built-in Bricker amendment" with the Parliament of Canada unable to implement treaties if the subject matter already is within the jurisdiction of the provinces. Most of the discussion with respect to the law of treaties in Canada has tended to turn on this question, and the not inconsiderable literature on Canadian treaty-making powers is confined largely to the problem of implementation. It is, however, likely that the Supreme Court of Canada will take the first opportunity to undo the presumed effects of the *Labour Conventions Case,* and this prediction is based on the general drift in the court's position on many matters that suggest a high degree of realism in its approach to the modern state from civil rights to federal power.[4] Of course, the need for municipal implementation would not necessarily arise frequently, but already one or two issues are on the horizon which suggest that some contests are in the offing—notably the relation of federal power to the control of foreign investment and the difficulties presently arising out of the dispute between the Federal Government and British Columbia over the Columbia River Treaty. Indeed, Canadians are likely to discover that the means of federal-provincial dispute-settlement are more difficult to fashion than those required for interstate differences between the neighbors.

Some conclusions inevitably flow from this general analysis. Canada and all states now find in conventional international law the instruments of choice for much of their international dealings; and a continuing network of treaties, agreements, and notes marks the life of the two countries in the international order. To this extent, therefore, it is only natural that bilateral agreements of all kinds are indispensable to the solution of the problems arising from the forthcoming era of fractious partnership. Already there looms as one problem area the juridical framework required for a possible free-

---

[4] The new spirit of dynamic nationalism in Quebec may delay any further movements toward stronger central government, including the treaty implementing power.

trade area in the Atlantic or North American region. Something similar in its permanence may be necessary for common defense arrangements beyond NATO, if there is to be a long-term interlacing of security arrangements in North America. Again the resource requirements of the United States and Canadian sensitivity to a certain erratic quality in United States needs for these resources may have to be stabilized again within the framework of some administrative structure that provides joint machinery for a sensible approach to the long term development and export of Canadian base metals, forest products, and sources of energy. Equally, the United States antitrust laws will need definition in relation to American subsidiaries in Canada; while a gentlemen's agreement will be insufficient to prevent irritations in the future over surplus disposal of agricultural products or proposed Iron-Curtain or Chinese Mainland trade by American subsidiaries in Canada which are otherwise acting within the proper limits of Canadian law.

Then too, we have only begun to consider the significance of the potential legal obligations, as well as the general political meaning, of Canada in joining the Organization of American States. While the movement of populations to and fro across the verbally barbed frontier should remain easy, some sharper definitions than exist today may be necessary. In taxation and criminal law the standards of a common treaty approach already are well set. In the end what the two nations are searching for is the common management of a continent, a partnership unequal in power, but equal in spirit—an economic stability on both sides, a sense of participation in the great defense decisions and a recognition by the United States of the sincerity of the search in Canada for the "Canadian image." For though the shores of the shared Atlantic and Pacific are washed by the same waters, Canadians wish to stem those other tides, across the open land-frontier, that may inundate a slowly emerging national culture. It will take more than treaties, machinery, and doctrine to solve the problem of sharing a language, a culture, and a continent while preserving an image. But in the end if the Canadian way is not merely accepted but encouraged by the United States, as American leadership is not truly resented by Canada, then with Robert Browning, Canada may say to its great neighbor, in all good will— "Grow old along with me, the best is yet to be. . . ."

Canada–United States Treaties

and Agreements

Including Those between the United States and the United Kingdom Affecting Canada (Bilateral—Excluding Postal Arrangements) 1782-1960

Titles used in this list are taken from the first reference citation. A few pluri-lateral agreements are included.

Instruments indicated by an asterisk (*) are listed as in effect, in whole or part, in *Treaties in Force: A List of Treaties and Other International Agreements of the United States in Force on January 1, 1961*; Dept. of State Pub. 7132.

Abbreviations used in reference citations are as follows:

BSP   *British and Foreign State Papers*
CTS   *Canada Treaty Series*
EAS   U.S., *Executive Agreement Series*
For. Rel.   *Foreign Relations of the United States*
Malloy   W. H. Malloy, *comp., Treaties, Conventions, International Acts, Protocols and Agreements Between the United States of America and Other Powers 1776-1909*, 2 vols.; vol. 3 (*1910-1923*, C. F. Redmond, comp.); vol. 4 (*1923-1937*, E. J. Trenwith, comp.).
Miller   Hunter Miller, *Treaties and Other International Acts of the United States*, 8 vols.
Stat.   U.S., *Statutes at Large*
TF   U.S., *Treaties in Force*
TIAS   U.S., *Treaties and Other International Acts Series*
TS   U.S., *Treaty Series*
UST   *United States Treaties and Other International Agreements*

This list has been compiled mainly from the following sources: CTS, EAS, Miller, Malloy, TIAS, TS, and UST. No exhaustive check against *For. Rel.* or non-published sources has been made.

Signed	*Title*	*Reference*
1782, Nov. 30	PROVISIONAL ARTICLES Between the United States of America, and his Britannic Majesty. (Peace)	8 *Stat.* 54 TS 102 1 BSP 773

Signed	Title	Reference
1783, Jan. 20	ARMISTICE Declaring a cessation of hostilities between the United States and Great-Britain.	8 *Stat.* 58 TS 103 1 BS P 777
1783, Sept. 3	DEFINITIVE TREATY OF PEACE Between the United States of America and his Britannic Majesty.	8 *Stat.* 80 TS 104 1 BSP 779
*1794, Nov. 19	TREATY OF AMITY, COMMERCE AND NAVIGATION, Between His Britannic Majesty and the United States of America, by their President, with the Advice and Consent of their Senate. (Jay Treaty)	8 *Stat.* 116 TS 105 1 BSP 784
1796, May 4	EXPLANATORY ARTICLE. (To the Third Article of the Treaty of Nov. 19, 1794)	8 *Stat.* 130 TS 106 1 BSP 804
1798, March 15	EXPLANATORY ARTICLE, to be added to the treaty of Amity, Commerce and Navigation, between the United States and his Britannic Majesty. (To the Fifth Article of the Treaty of Nov. 19, 1794, relative to the St. Croix River)	8 *Stat.* 131 TS 107 1 BSP 806
1798, Oct. 25	Declaration of the Commissioners under Article 5 of the Jay Treaty. (St. Croix River)	2 Miller 430 1 BSP 807
1802, Jan. 8	CONVENTION Between the United States and Great-Britain. (Relative to Articles 6 and 7 of the Jay Treaty and Article 4 of the Definitive Treaty of Peace; Claims)	8 *Stat.* 196 TS 108 1 BSP 808
1813, May 12	Cartel for the exchange of prisoners of war between Great Britain and the United States of America.	2 Miller 557 1 BSP 1410
1814, Dec. 24	TREATY OF PEACE AND AMITY, Between his Britannic Majesty and the United States of America. (Treaty of Ghent)	8 *Stat.* 218 TS 109 2 BSP 357
*1815, July 3	A CONVENTION To regulate the Commerce between the Territories of the United States and of his Britannick Majesty.	8 *Stat.* 228 TS 110 3 BSP 78
*1817, April 28, April 29	ARRANGEMENT Between the United States and Great Britain, between Richard Rush, Esq., acting as Secretary of the Department of State, and Charles Bagot, His	8 *Stat.* 231 TS 110½ 5 BSP 1200

Signed	Title	Reference
	Britannic Majesty's Envoy Extraordinary, &c. (Naval Forces on the Great Lakes)	
1817, Nov. 24	DECISION Of the Commissioners under the fourth article of the Treaty of Ghent.	8 *Stat.* 250 TS 111 5 BSP 199
*1818, Oct. 20	CONVENTION WITH GREAT BRITAIN.	8 *Stat.* 248 TS 112 6 BSP 3
1822, June 18	DECISION Of the Commissioners under the 6th Article of the Treaty of Ghent.	8 *Stat.* 274 TS 113 9 BSP 791
1827, Aug. 6	CONVENTION WITH GREAT BRITAIN. (Continuing Article 3 of the Convention of Oct. 20, 1818)	8 *Stat.* 360 TS 116 14 BSP 975
1827, Aug. 6	RENEWAL OF COMMERCIAL CONVENTION WITH GREAT BRITAIN. (Continuing Convention of July 3, 1815)	8 *Stat.* 361 TS 117 14 BSP 973
1827, Sept. 29	CONVENTION Between the United States of America and Great Britain. (Arbitration of Northeastern Boundary)	8 *Stat.* 362 TS 118 14 BSP 1004
*1842, Aug. 9	A TREATY To settle and define the boundaries between the territories of the United States and the possessions of Her Britannic Majesty in North America; for the final suppression of the African slave trade; and for the giving up of criminals, fugitive from justice, in certain cases. (Webster-Ashburton Treaty)	8 *Stat.* 572 TS 119 30 BSP 360
*1846, June 15	TREATY BETWEEN THE UNITED STATES OF AMERICA AND HER BRITANNIC MAJESTY FOR SETTLEMENT OF BOUNDARY WEST OF THE ROCKY MOUNTAINS.	18(2) *Stat.* 320 TS 120 34 BSP 14
1850, April 19	CONVENTION BETWEEN THE UNITED STATES OF AMERICA AND HER BRITANNIC MAJESTY RELATIVE TO A SHIP-CANAL BY WAY OF NICARAGUA, COSTA RICA, THE MOSQUITO COAST, OR ANY PART OF CEN-	18(2) *Stat.* 322 TS 122 38 BSP 4

Signed	Title	Reference
	TRAL AMERICA. (Clayton-Bulwer Treaty)	
*1850, Dec. 9	PROTOCOL OF A CONFERENCE HELD AT THE FOREIGN OFFICE. (Cession of Horseshoe Reef)	18(2) *Stat.* 325 63 BSP 890
1853, Feb. 8	TREATY BETWEEN THE UNITED STATES OF AMERICA AND HER BRITANNIC MAJESTY FOR THE SETTLEMENT OF CLAIMS.	18(2) *Stat.* 326 TS 123 43 BSP 34
1854, June 5	RECIPROCITY TREATY BETWEEN THE UNITED STATES OF AMERICA AND HER BRITANNIC MAJESTY. (Canadian Reciprocity Treaty)	18(2) *Stat.* 329 TS 124 44 BSP 25
1854, July 17	CONVENTION BETWEEN THE UNITED STATES OF AMERICA AND HER BRITANNIC MAJESTY EXTENDING THE DURATION OF THE COMMISSION ON CLAIMS AUTHORIZED BY THE CONVENTION OF FEBRUARY 8, 1853.	18(2) *Stat.* 333 TS 125 44 BSP 29
1863, July 1	TREATY BETWEEN THE UNITED STATES OF AMERICA AND HER BRITANNIC MAJESTY FOR THE FINAL SETTLEMENT OF THE CLAIMS OF THE HUDSON'S BAY AND PUGET'S SOUND AGRICULTURAL COMPANIES.[1]	18(2) *Stat.* 346 TS 128 53 BSP 6
*1870, Feb. 24	DECLARATION APPROVING AND ADOPTING THE MAPS PREPARED BY THE JOINT COMMISSION OF THE NORTHWEST BOUNDARY FOR SURVEYING AND MARKING THE BOUNDARIES BETWEEN THE BRITISH POSSESSIONS AND THE UNITED STATES ALONG THE 49TH PARALLEL OF NORTH LATITUDE, UNDER THE FIRST ARTICLE OF THE TREATY OF 15TH JUNE, 1846.	1 Malloy 658 TS 129 63 BPS 1053
1870, May 13	CONVENTION BETWEEN THE UNITED STATES OF AMERICA AND	18(2) *Stat.* 348 TS 130

[1] For the Award of the Commissioners under this Treaty, dated Sept. 10, 1869, see 18 (2) *Stat.* 347.

Signed	Title	Reference
	HER BRITANNIC MAJESTY, RELATIVE TO NATURALIZATION.	60 BSP 36
1871, Feb. 23	CONVENTION BETWEEN THE UNITED STATES OF AMERICA AND HER BRITANNIC MAJESTY, SUPPLEMENTAL TO THE CONVENTION OF MAY 13, 1870, RELATIVE TO NATURALIZATION.	18(2) *Stat.* 354 TS 132 61 BSP 38
1871, May 8	TREATY BETWEEN THE UNITED STATES OF AMERICA AND HER BRITANNIC MAJESTY FOR AN AMICABLE SETTLEMENT OF ALL CAUSES OF DIFFERENCE BETWEEN THE TWO COUNTRIES. (Treaty of Washington)	18(2) *Stat.* 355 TS 133 61 BSP 40
1873, Jan. 18	ADDITIONAL ARTICLE TO THE TREATY WITH GREAT BRITAIN OF MAY 8, 1871, RESPECTING PLACES FOR HOLDING SESSIONS OF THE COMMISSIONERS UNDER THE TWELFTH ARTICLE THEREOF.	18(2) *Stat.* 368 TS 134 63 BSP 30
*1873, March 10	PROTOCOL OF A CONFERENCE AT WASHINGTON, MARCH 10, 1873, RESPECTING THE NORTHWEST WATER-BOUNDARY. (Haro Channel)	18(2) *Stat.* 369 TS 135 63 BSP 354
1873, June 7	PROTOCOL OF A CONFERENCE HELD AT WASHINGTON ON THE SEVENTH DAY OF JUNE, ONE THOUSAND EIGHT HUNDRED AND SEVENTY-THREE, RESPECTING THE TIME AT WHICH ARTICLES 18 TO 25, AND ARTICLE 30 OF THE TREATY OF MAY 8, 1871, SHOULD GO INTO EFFECT.	18(2) *Stat.* 372 TS 136 63 BSP 39
1874, May 28	PROTOCOL OF A CONFERENCE HELD AT WASHINGTON MAY 28, 1874 SETTING THE TIME AT WHICH ARTICLES 18 TO 25, AND ARTICLE 30 OF THE TREATY OF MAY 8, 1871, SHOULD GO INTO EFFECT WITH RESPECT TO NEWFOUNDLAND.	1 Malloy 727 TS 137 65 BSP 1283
1877,	Declaration between the United States and	20 *Stat.* 703

Signed	*Title*	*Reference*
Oct. 24	Great Britain. Trade-marks.	TS 138 68 BSP 12
1885, June 22	AGREEMENT BETWEEN THE UNITED STATES AND GREAT BRITAIN RESPECTING THE FISHERIES.	1 Malloy 729 TS 138-1 76 BSP 522
1888, Feb. 15	ORIGINAL MODUS VIVENDI PENDING THE RATIFICATION OF THE TREATY CONCERNING FISHERIES.	1 Malloy 738 TS 138-2 79 BSP 272
*1889, July 12	Extradition Convention between the United States of America and Her Britannic Majesty, supplementary to the Tenth Article of the Treaty concluded between the same High Contracting Parties on the ninth day of August, 1842.	26 *Stat.* 1508 TS 139 81 BSP 41
1891, June 15	AGREEMENT BETWEEN THE GOVERNMENT OF THE UNITED STATES AND THE GOVERNMENT OF HER BRITANNIC MAJESTY FOR A MODUS VIVENDI IN RELATION TO THE FUR SEAL FISHERIES IN BEHRING SEA.	27 *Stat.* 980 TS 140 84 BSP 492
1891, Dec. 18	AGREEMENT BETWEEN THE SECRETARY OF STATE OF THE UNITED STATES AND THE ENVOY EXTRAORDINARY AND MINISTER PLENIPOTENTIARY OF GREAT BRITAIN ON THE TEXT OF ARTICLES FOR INSERTION IN THE BERING SEA ARBITRATION AGREEMENT.	1 Malloy 744 TS 140-2
1892, Feb. 29	A Convention between the Governments of the United States and Her Britannic Majesty submitting to arbitration the questions which have arisen between those Governments concerning the jurisdictional rights of the United States in the waters of the Behring Sea.	27 *Stat.* 947 TS 140-1 84 BSP 48
1892, April 18	Convention between the Governments of the United States and Her Britannic Majesty for the renewal of the existing modus vivendi in Behring Sea.	27 *Stat.* 952 TS 140-3 84 BSP 62
1892, June 3	Treaty between the United States of America and the United Kingdom of Great Britain	27 *Stat.* 961 TS 141

Signed	*Title*	*Reference*
	and Ireland for the recovery of persons who may desert from the merchant vessels of either country while in the ports of the other.	84 BSP 67
1892, July 22	Convention between the United States of America and the United Kingdom of Great Britain and Ireland for a joint survey of the territory adjacent to the boundary line of the United States of America and the Dominion of Canada dividing the Territory of Alaska from the Province of British Columbia and the Northwest Territory of Canada.	27 *Stat.* 955 TS 142 84 BSP 70
1893, Aug. 15	AWARD OF THE TRIBUNAL OF ARBITRATION CONSTITUTED UNDER THE TREATY CONCLUDED AT WASHINGTON, THE 29TH OF FEBRUARY 1892, BETWEEN THE UNITED STATES OF AMERICA AND HER MAJESTY THE QUEEN OF THE UNITED KINGDOM OF GREAT BRITAIN AND IRELAND.	1 Malloy 751 TS 140-4 85 BSP 1158
1893, Aug. 15	DECLARATION MADE BY THE TRIBUNAL OF ARBITRATION AND REFERRED TO THE GOVERNMENTS OF THE UNITED STATES AND GREAT BRITAIN FOR THEIR CONSIDERATION.	1 Malloy 759 TS 140-5
1894, Feb. 3	Supplemental Convention between the United States of America and the United Kingdom of Great Britain and Ireland, extending, until December 31, 1895, the provisions of Article I, of the Convention of July 22, 1892, relative to British Possessions in North America.	28 *Stat.* 1200 TS 143 86 BSP 12
1896, Feb. 8	Convention between the United States and Great Britain, for the settlement of claims presented by Great Britain against the United States in virtue of the Convention of February 29, 1892.	29 *Stat.* 844 TS 144 88 BSP 8
1898, May 30	PROTOCOL OF THE CONFERENCES AT WASHINGTON IN MAY, 1898, PRELIMINARY TO THE APPOINTMENT	1 Malloy 770 TS 145

Signed	Title	Reference
	OF A JOINT COMMISSION FOR THE ADJUSTMENT OF QUESTIONS AT IS-SUE BETWEEN THE UNITED STATES AND GREAT BRITAIN, IN RESPECT TO THE RELATIONS OF THE FORMER WITH THE DOMINION OF CANADA.	
*1899, March 2	Convention between the United States of America and the United Kingdom of Great Britain and Ireland relating to the tenure and disposition of real and personal property.	31 *Stat.* 1939 TS 146 91 BSP 118
1899, Oct. 20	MODUS VIVENDI WITH GREAT BRIT-AIN, FIXING A PROVISIONAL BOUND-ARY LINE BETWEEN THE TERRI-TORY OF ALASKA AND THE DOMIN-ION OF CANADA ABOUT THE HEAD OF LYNN CANAL.	1 Malloy 777 TS 146½ 91 BSP 116
*1900, Dec. 13	Supplementary treaty of extradition between the United States and Great Britain.	32(2) *Stat.* 1864 TS 391 92 BSP 72
1901, Nov. 18	Treaty between the United States and Great Britain to facilitate the construction of a ship canal.	32(2) *Stat.* 1903 TS 401 94 BSP 46
1902, Jan. 13	Supplementary Convention between the United States and Great Britain, extending for a period of twelve months from July 28, 1901, the time within which British Colonies or Foreign Possessions may give their ad-hesion to the Convention for the tenure and disposition of real and personal property, signed at Washington on March 2, 1899.	32(2) *Stat.* 1914 TS 402 95 BSP 114
*1903, Jan. 24	Convention between the United States and Great Britain providing for the settlement of questions between the two countries with respect to the boundary line between the territory of Alaska and the British posses-sions in North America.	32(2) *Stat.* 1961 TS 419 96 BSP 84
1903, Oct. 20	DECISION OF THE ALASKAN BOUND-ARY TRIBUNAL UNDER THE TREA-TY OF JANUARY 24, 1903, BETWEEN THE UNITED STATES AND GREAT BRITAIN.	1 Malloy 792 98 BSP 152

Signed	Title	Reference
*1905, March 25	ALASKAN BOUNDARY.—EXCHANGE OF NOTES.—ACCEPTANCE OF THE REPORT OF THE COMMISSIONERS TO COMPLETE THE AWARD UNDER THE CONVENTION OF JANUARY 24, 1903, RESPECTING THE BOUNDARY LINE BETWEEN ALASKA AND THE BRITISH NORTH AMERICAN POSSESSIONS.	1 Malloy 796 TS 476 98 BSP 155
*1905, April 12	Supplementary convention between the United States and Great Britain for the extradition of criminals.	34(3) *Stat.* 2903 TS 458 98 BSP 385
*1906, April 21	Convention between the United States and Great Britain providing for the surveying and marking out upon the ground of the 141st degree of west longitude where said meridian forms the boundary line between Alaska and the British Possessions in North America.	34(3) *Stat.* 2948 TS 452 99 BSP 177
1906, Oct. 6, Oct. 8	MODUS VIVENDI BETWEEN THE UNITED STATES AND GREAT BRITAIN IN REGARD TO INSHORE FISHERIES ON THE TREATY COAST OF NEWFOUNDLAND.	1 Malloy 805 TS 485 100 BSP 578
1907, Sept. 4, Sept. 6	MODUS VIVENDI BETWEEN THE UNITED STATES AND GREAT BRITAIN IN REGARD TO INSHORE FISHERIES ON THE TREATY COAST OF NEWFOUNDLAND.	1 Malloy 811 TS 488 100 BSP 588
1908, April 4	Arbitration convention between the United States and Great Britain.	35(2) *Stat.* 1960 TS 494 101 BSP 208
1908, April 11	Convention between the United States and Great Britain relating to fisheries in United States and Canadian waters.	35(2) *Stat.* 2000 TS 498 101 BSP 224
*1908, April 11	Convention between the United States and Great Britain relating to the Canadian international boundary.	35(2) *Stat.* 2003 TS 497 101 BSP 210
*1908, May 18	Treaty between the United States and Great Britain concerning reciprocal rights for Unit-	35(2) *Stat.* 2035 TS 502

Signed	Title	Reference
	ed States and Canada in the conveyance of prisoners and wrecking and salvage.	101 BSP 226
1908, July 15, July 23	AGREEMENT EFFECTED BY EXCHANGE OF NOTES CONCERNING NEWFOUNDLAND FISHERIES.	1 Malloy 832 TS 504 102 BSP 908
*1909, Jan. 11	Treaty between the United States and Great Britain relating to boundary waters between the United States and Canada.	36(2) *Stat.* 2448 TS 548 102 BSP 137
1909, Jan. 27	Special agreement between United States and Great Britain relating to North Atlantic Coast fisheries.	36(2) *Stat.* 2141 TS 521 102 BSP 145
1909, July 22, Sept. 8	AGREEMENT EFFECTED BY EXCHANGE OF NOTES CONCERNING NEWFOUNDLAND FISHERIES.	1 Malloy 844 TS 533 102 BSP 909
*1910, May 21	Treaty between the United States and Great Britain fixing the boundary line in Passamaquoddy Bay.	36(2) *Stat.* 2477 TS 551 103 BSP 319
1910, Aug. 18	Special agreement between the United States and Great Britain for the submission of outstanding pecuniary claims to arbitration.	37(2) *Stat.* 1625 TS 573 103 BSP 322
1911, Jan. 12	MINUTES OF CONFERENCES HELD AT WASHINGTON THE 9TH, 10TH, 11TH AND 12TH OF JANUARY, 1911, AS TO THE APPLICATION OF THE AWARD DELIVERED ON THE 7TH SEPTEMBER, 1910, IN THE NORTH ATLANTIC COAST FISHERIES ARBITRATION TO EXISTING REGULATIONS OF CANADA AND NEWFOUNDLAND.	3 Malloy 2627 TS 553
1911, Jan. 14	MINUTES OF CONFERENCES HELD AT WASHINGTON THE 13TH AND 14TH OF JANUARY, 1911, AS TO THE OBJECTIONS OF THE UNITED STATES TO EXISTING LAWS AND FISHERY REGULATIONS OF CANADA AS RECORDED IN PROTOCOL XXX OF THE PROCEEDINGS UPON THE NORTH ATLANTIC COAST FISHERIES ARBITRATION.	3 Malloy 2628 TS 554

Signed	Title	Reference
1911, Feb. 7	Treaty between the United States and Great Britain providing for the preservation and protection of fur seals.	37(2) *Stat.* 1538 TS 563 104 BSP 202
1912, July 20	Agreement between the United States and Great Britain adopting with certain modifications the rules and method of procedure recommended in the award of September 7, 1910, of the North Atlantic Coast Fisheries Arbitration.	37(2) *Stat.* 1634 TS 572 105 BSP 284
1913, May 31	Arbitration agreement between the United States and Great Britain extending the duration of the convention of April 4, 1908.	38(2) *Stat.* 1767 TS 587 106 BSP 820
1914, June 2	AGREEMENT EFFECTED BY EXCHANGE OF NOTES RELATIVE TO PRESERVATION OF THE STATUS QUO WITH RESPECT TO THE PROTECTION OF OIL INTERESTS IN MEXICO.	3 Malloy 2639 107 BSP 568
1914, June 24	AGREEMENT EFFECTED BY EXCHANGE OF NOTES RELATIVE TO THE PRESERVATION OF THE STATUS QUO WITH RESPECT TO MINES OR MINING RIGHTS IN MEXICO.	3 Malloy 2640 107 BSP 569
*1914, Sept. 15	Treaty between the United States and Great Britain for the advancement of general peace.	38(2) *Stat.* 1853 TS 602 108 BSP 384
1915, Nov. 3	AGREEMENT EFFECTED BY EXCHANGE OF NOTES EXTENDING THE TIME FOR THE APPOINTMENT OF THE COMMISSION UNDER ARTICLE II OF THE TREATY OF SEPTEMBER 15, 1914, FOR THE ADVANCEMENT OF PEACE.	3 Malloy 2644 TS 602-A 109 BSP 865
*1916, Aug. 16	Convention between the United States and Great Britain for the protection of migratory birds.	39(2) *Stat.* 1702 TS 628 110 BSP 767
1918, June 3	Arbitration agreement between the United States and Great Britain extending the duration of the convention of April 4, 1908.	40(2) *Stat.* 1627 TS 635 111 BSP 568
1918, June 3	Convention between the United States and Great Britain providing for military service	40(2) *Stat.* 1624 TS 634

Signed	Title	Reference
	of citizens of the United States in Canada and of Canadians in the United States.	111 BSP 572
*1921, Oct. 21	Supplementary convention between the United States and Great Britain, providing for the accession of the Dominion of Canada to the real and personal property convention of March 2, 1899.	42(2) *Stat.* 2147 TS 663 114 BSP 414
*1922, May 15	Supplementary extradition convention between the United States and Great Britain.	42(2) *Stat.* 2224 TS 666 116 BSP 508
1923, March 2	Convention between the United States and Great Britain for the preservation of the halibut fishery of the Northern Pacific Ocean.	43(2) *Stat.* 1841 TS 701 117 BSP 382
1923, June 23	Agreement between the United States and Great Britain further extending the duration of the arbitration convention of April 4, 1908.	43(2) *Stat.* 1695 TS 674 117 BSP 372
1924, Jan. 23	Convention between the United States and Great Britain for prevention of smuggling of intoxicating liquors.	43(2) *Stat.* 1761 TS 685 119 BSP 467
*1924, June 6	Convention between the United States and Great Britain in respect of Canada, to suppress smuggling.	44(3) *Stat.* 2097 TS 718 119 BSP 593
*1925, Jan. 8	Convention between the United States and Great Britain in respect of Canada for extradition of offenses against narcotic laws.	44(3) *Stat.* 2100 TS 719 121 BSP 931
*1925, Feb. 24	Treaty between the United States and Great Britain in respect of boundary between the United States and Canada.	44(3) *Stat.* 2102 TS 720 121 BSP 933
*1925, Feb. 24	Treaty and protocol between the United States and Great Britain in respect of Canada, to regulate the level of the Lake of the Woods.	44(3) *Stat.* 2108 TS 721 121 BSP 939
*1925, Sept. 18, Sept. 23, Oct. 1	RADIO BROADCASTING. ARRANGEMENT WITH CANADA.	4 Malloy 4250 TS 724A
*1928, Aug. 2, Sept. 17	Exchange of notes between the United States and the Dominion of Canada for relief from double income tax on shipping profits.	47(2) *Stat.* 2580 EAS 4 1928 CTS 9

Signed	Title	Reference
*1928, Oct. 2, Dec. 29 1929, Jan. 12	ARRANGEMENT EFFECTED BY EX-CHANGE OF NOTES BETWEEN THE UNITED STATES AND THE DOMIN-ION OF CANADA—Governing Radio Communications Between Private Experimental Stations.	TS 767-A 1929 CTS 2
*1929, Feb. 26, Feb. 28	RADIO STATIONS—ARRANGEMENTS RELATIVE TO THE ASSIGNMENT OF HIGH FREQUENCIES TO RADIO STA-TIONS ON THE NORTH AMERICAN CONTINENT, EFFECTED BY EX-CHANGE OF NOTES BETWEEN THE UNITED STATES, CANADA, CUBA AND NEWFOUNDLAND.	4 Malloy 4787 TS 777-A
1929, Aug. 22, Oct. 22	Exchange of notes between the United States and the Dominion of Canada concerning the admission of civil aircraft, the issuance of pilots' licenses, and the acceptance of certificates of air worthiness for aircraft imported as merchandise.	47(2) *Stat.* 2575 EAS 2 1929 CTS 13
*1929, Oct. 10, Oct. 23	Exchange of notes between the United States and the Dominion of Canada concerning quarantine inspection of vessels entering Puget Sound and waters adjacent thereto or the Great Lakes via the St. Lawrence River.	47(2) *Stat.* 2573 EAS 1 1929 CTS 14
1930, May 9	Convention between the United States of America and the Dominion of Canada for the preservation of the halibut fishery of northern Pacific Ocean and Bering Sea.	47(2) *Stat.* 1872 TS 837 1931 CTS 3
*1930, May 26	Convention between the United States of America and Canada and protocol of exchange of ratifications concerning the sockeye salmon fisheries.	50(2) *Stat.* 1355 TS 918 1937 CTS 10
1932, May 5	Arrangement between the United States of America and the Dominion of Canada concerning radio broadcasting.	47(2) *Stat.* 2704 EAS 34
1932, Sept. 15, Sept. 16	EXCHANGE OF NOTES Constituting an Agreement between CANADA AND THE UNITED STATES OF AMERICA granting RECIPROCAL "BLANKET" PERMISSION FOR THE PERIOD OF ONE	1932 CTS 4

Signed	Title	Reference
	YEAR FROM JULY 1, 1932, FOR FLIGHTS OF MILITARY AIRCRAFT.	
1933, June 7, June 10	EXCHANGE OF NOTES PROLONGING FOR ONE YEAR AND MODIFYING THE AGREEMENT OF SEPTEMBER 15-16, 1932, CONCERNING FLIGHTS OF MILITARY AIRCRAFT BETWEEN CANADA AND THE UNITED STATES OF AMERICA.	1933 CTS 9
*1933, Dec. 9	Convention between the United States of America and the Dominion of Canada concerning Load Lines.	49(2) *Stat.* 2685 TS 869 1934 CTS 10
*1934, April 23, May 2, May 4	Arrangement between the United States of America and the Dominion of Canada governing radio communications between private experimental stations and between amateur stations.	48(2) *Stat.* 1876 EAS 62 1934 CTS 5
1934, May 21, June 2, June 12, June 20	EXCHANGE OF NOTES PROLONGING FOR ONE YEAR AND MODIFYING THE AGREEMENT OF SEPTEMBER 15-16, 1932, CONCERNING FLIGHTS OF MILITARY AIRCRAFT BETWEEN CANADA AND THE UNITED STATES OF AMERICA.	1934 CTS 9
*1935, April 15	Convention between the United States of America and the Dominion of Canada relative to the establishment of a tribunal to decide questions of indemnity and future regime arising from the operation of smelter at Trail, British Columbia.	49(2) *Stat.* 3245 TS 893 1935 CTS 20
*1935, July 29, Sept. 19	Arrangement relating to visits of consular officers to citizens of their own country serving sentences in penal institutions. Exchange of notes.	1961 TF 25 *For. Rel.,* 1935, II, 57
*1935, Sept. 20, Nov. 6	Arrangement relating to the level of Lake Memphremagog. Exchange of notes.	1961 TF 23 *For. Rel.,* 1935, II, 53
1935, Sept. 23, Sept. 24, Nov. 5	EXCHANGE OF NOTES PROLONGING FOR ONE YEAR AND MODIFYING THE AGREEMENT OF SEPTEMBER 15-16, 1932, CONCERNING FLIGHTS OF	1935 CTS 9

Signed	Title	Reference
	MILITARY AIRCRAFT BETWEEN CANADA AND THE UNITED STATES OF AMERICA.	
1935, Nov. 15	Agreement, supplementary proclamation, and related notes between the United States of America and the Dominion of Canada respecting reciprocal trade.	49(2) *Stat.* 3960 EAS 91 1936 CTS 9
1936, June 29	EXCHANGE OF NOTES PROLONGING FOR ONE YEAR THE AGREEMENT OF SEPTEMBER 15-16, 1932, AS AMENDED IN 1935, CONCERNING FLIGHTS OF MILITARY AIRCRAFT BETWEEN CANADA AND THE UNITED STATES OF AMERICA.	1936 CTS 10
1936, Dec. 30	Convention between the United States of America and Canada concerning income taxation.	50(2) *Stat.* 1399 TS 920 1937 CTS 13
1937, Jan. 29	Convention between the United States of America and Canada revising the convention for the preservation of halibut fishery of Northern Pacific Ocean and Bering Sea.	50(2) *Stat.* 1351 TS 917 1937 CTS 9
1937, March 2, March 10, Aug. 17, Sept. 8, Sept. 20, Oct. 9	Agreement between the United States of America and Canada regarding the exchange of information concerning issuance of radio licenses.	51 *Stat.* 314 EAS 109
1937, June 7, June 10	EXCHANGE OF NOTES PROLONGING FOR ONE YEAR THE AGREEMENT OF SEPTEMBER 15-16, 1932, AS AMENDED IN 1935, CONCERNING FLIGHTS OF MILITARY AIRCRAFT BETWEEN CANADA AND THE UNITED STATES OF AMERICA.	1937 CTS 8
*1937, Dec. 3, Dec. 28; 1938, Jan. 24	Reciprocal arrangement between the United States of America and Canada relative to admission to practice before patent offices.	52 *Stat.* 1475 EAS 118 1937 CTS 19
1937,	EXCHANGE OF NOTES CONCERNING	1938 CTS 20

Signed	Title	Reference
Dec. 28; 1938, Feb. 15, Feb. 25	THE ISSUE OF APPENDIX CERTIFI-CATES OF TONNAGE TO UNITED STATES PASSENGER VESSELS BE-TWEEN CANADA AND THE UNITED STATES OF AMERICA.	
*1938, April 29, Aug. 24, Oct. 22; 1939, Sept. 2, Oct. 18; 1940, Jan. 10, March 4	Arrangement between the United States of America and Canada for the reciprocal rec-ognition of load line regulations for vessels engaged in international voyages on the Great Lakes.	54(2) Stat. 2300 EAS 172 1940 CTS 3
*1938, June 9, July 11, July 18, Aug. 22, Sept. 27, Oct. 4, Nov. 16, Dec. 20	Arrangement between the United States of America and Canada respecting radio com-munications between Alaska and British Columbia.	53(3) Stat. 2092 EAS 142 1938 CTS 22
1938, June 18, June 20	EXCHANGE OF NOTES PROLONGING FOR ONE YEAR THE AGREEMENT OF SEPTEMBER 15-16, 1932, AS AMENDED IN 1935, CONCERNING FLIGHTS OF MILITARY AIRCRAFT BETWEEN CANADA AND THE UNITED STATES OF AMERICA.	1938 CTS 7
*1938, July 28	Arrangement between the United States of America and Canada respecting air naviga-tion.	53(3) Stat. 1925 EAS 129 1938 CTS 8
*1938, July 28	Arrangement between the United States of America and Canada relating to issue of cer-tificates of competency or licenses for the piloting of civil aircraft.	53(3) Stat. 1937 EAS 130 1938 CTS 9
*1938, July 28	Arrangement between the United States of America and Canada for the acceptance of certificates of airworthiness for export.	53(3) Stat. 1941 EAS 131 1938 CTS 10

Signed	Title	Reference
*1938, Sept. 15	Convention between the United States of America and Canada respecting emergency regulation of level of Rainy Lake and of other boundary waters in the Rainy Lake watershed.	54(2) *Stat.* 1800 TS 961 1940 CTS 9
1938, Oct. 28, Dec. 10	Arrangement between the United States of America and Canada regarding radio broadcasting.	53(3) *Stat.* 2042 EAS 136 1941 CTS 4
1938, Nov. 17	Agreement between the United States of America and Canada respecting reciprocal trade.	53(3) *Stat.* 2348 EAS 149 1939 CTS 8
*1939, Feb. 20	Arrangement between the United States of America and Canada respecting the use of radio for civil aeronautical services.	53 (3)*Stat.* 2157 EAS 143 1939 CTS 5
1939, March 7, April 5, June 22	Arrangement between the United States of America and Canada concerning visits in uniform by members of defense forces.	53(3) *Stat.* 2439 EAS 157 1939 CTS 13
*1939, June 9, June 10	EXCHANGE OF NOTES RELATING TO THE APPLICATION AND INTERPRETATION OF THE RUSH-BAGOT AGREEMENT.	1940 CTS 12 TIAS 1836 61(4) *Stat.* 4069
1939, June 22, June 23	EXCHANGE OF NOTES PROLONGING FOR ONE YEAR THE AGREEMENT OF SEPTEMBER 15-16, 1932, AS AMENDED IN 1935, CONCERNING FLIGHTS OF MILITARY AIRCRAFT BETWEEN CANADA AND THE UNITED STATES OF AMERICA.	1939 CTS 9
1939, Aug. 18	Arrangement between the United States of America and Canada relating to air transport services.	54(2) *Stat.* 1805 EAS 159 1939 CTS 10
1939, Nov. 30	Proclamation by the President of the United States issued on November 30, 1939, pursuant to article III of the reciprocal trade agreement between the United States of America and Canada signed November 17, 1938, respecting allocation of tariff quota on heavy cattle during the calendar year 1940.	54(2) *Stat.* 2290 EAS 170
1939,	Supplementary agreement between the Unit-	54(2) *Stat.* 2413

Signed	Title	Reference
Dec. 30	ed States of America and Canada amending with regard to fox furs and skins the agreement of November 17, 1938, respecting reciprocal trade.	EAS 184
1940, Feb. 29	Agreement between the United States of America and Canada concerning the establishment of a Board of Inquiry for the Great Lakes Fisheries.	54(2) *Stat.* 2409 EAS 182 1940 CTS 2
*1940, June 18	Agreement between the United States of America and Canada respecting exemptions from exchange control measures.	54(2) *Stat.* 2317 EAS 174 1940 CTS 5
*1940, Aug. 18	DECLARATION BY THE PRIME MINISTER OF CANADA AND THE PRESIDENT OF THE UNITED STATES OF AMERICA REGARDING THE ESTABLISHING OF A PERMANENT JOINT BOARD ON DEFENCE.	1940 CTS 14
*1940, Sept. 6	Treaty between the United States of America and Canada amending in their application to Canada certain provisions of the treaty for the advancement of peace between the United States of America and Great Britain signed September 15, 1914.	55(2) *Stat.* 1214 TS 975 1941 CTS 9
1940, Sept. 23, Oct. 18	EXCHANGE OF NOTES BETWEEN CANADA AND THE UNITED STATES OF AMERICA CONSTITUTING AN AGREEMENT REGARDING PERMISSION FOR UNITED STATES COAST GUARD VESSELS ON THE GREAT LAKES TO ENTER CANADIAN TERRITORIAL WATERS IN CERTAIN CIRCUMSTANCES.	1940 CTS 15
*1940, Oct. 14, Oct. 31, Nov. 7	Agreement between the United States of America and Canada respecting Great Lakes–St. Lawrence Waterway.	54(2) *Stat.* 2426 EAS 187 1940 CTS 11
*1940, Oct. 30, Nov. 2	ARMAMENT OF NAVAL VESSELS TO BE INCAPABLE OF IMMEDIATE USE. Exchange of Notes. (Understanding regarding Rush-Bagot Agreement.)	61(4) *Stat.* 4077 TIAS 1836 1940 CTS 12
1940,	Arrangement between the United States of	54(2) *Stat.* 2422

Signed	Title	Reference
Nov. 29, Dec. 2	America and Canada giving effect to article III of the air transport arrangement signed August 18, 1939, respecting air transport services.	EAS 186 1940 CTS 13
1940, Nov. 30	Proclamation by the President of the United States of America issued November 30, 1940, pursuant to article III of the reciprocal trade agreement between the United States of America and Canada signed November 17, 1938, respecting allocation of tariff quota on heavy cattle during the calendar year 1941.	54(2) *Stat.* 2445 EAS 190
1940, Dec. 13	Supplementary agreement between the United States of America and Canada amending with regard to fox furs and skins the agreement of November 17, 1938 respecting reciprocal trade.	55(2) *Stat.* 1319 EAS 216 1941 CTS 10
1941, March 17, June 6, June 17	Arrangement between the United States of America and Canada respecting joint committees on economic cooperation.	55(2) *Stat.* 1444 EAS 228
*1941, March 27	Agreement and exchange of notes between the United States of America and Great Britain respecting leased naval and air bases, and protocol between the United States of America, Great Britain, and Canada concerning the defense of Newfoundland.	55(2) *Stat.* 1560 EAS 235 1941 CTS 2
*1941, April 20	DECLARATION BY THE PRIME MINISTER OF CANADA AND THE PRESIDENT OF THE UNITED STATES OF AMERICA REGARDING CO-OPERATION FOR WAR PRODUCTION.	1941 CTS 14
1941, May 20	Arrangement between the United States of America and Canada respecting the temporary diversion for power purposes of additional waters of the Niagara River above the Falls.	55(2) *Stat.* 1276 EAS 209 1941 CTS 7
1941, May 28	EXCHANGE OF NOTES REGARDING WHEAT MARKETING BETWEEN CANADA AND THE UNITED STATES OF AMERICA.	1941 CTS 6
1941,	EXCHANGE OF NOTES BETWEEN	1941 CTS 20

Signed	Title	Reference
July 22, Aug. 7, Sept. 5, Oct. 20	CANADA AND THE UNITED STATES OF AMERICA PROVIDING FOR RECIPROCAL RELAXATION OF THE LOAD LINE REGULATIONS FOR SHIPS MAKING VOYAGES ON LAKES AND RIVERS.	
*1941, Aug. 28, Sept. 4	Arrangement between the United States of America and Canada respecting visits in uniform by members of defense forces.	55(2) *Stat.* 1551 EAS 233 1941 CTS 11
1941, Oct. 27, Nov. 27	Supplementary arrangement between the United States of America and Canada respecting an additional temporary diversion for power purposes of waters of the Niagara River above the Falls.	55(2) *Stat.* 1380 EAS 223 1941 CTS 15
*1941, Nov. 10	Agreement between the United States of America and Canada respecting the temporary raising of level of Lake St. Francis during low-water periods.	56(2) *Stat.* 1833 EAS 291 1941 CTS 19
*1942, Feb. 26, March 9	EXCHANGE OF NOTES BETWEEN CANADA AND THE UNITED STATES OF AMERICA RELATING TO THE APPLICATION AND INTERPRETATION OF THE (RUSH-BAGOT) AGREEMENT CONCERNING THE NAVAL FORCES ON THE GREAT LAKES.	1942 CTS 3 TIAS 1836 61(4) *Stat.* 4080
*1942, March 4	Convention and protocol between the United States of America and Canada respecting double taxation.	56(2) *Stat.* 1399 TS 983 1942 CTS 2
*1942, March 6, March 12	Agreement between the United States of America and Canada respecting unemployment insurance benefits.	56(2) *Stat.* 1451 EAS 244 1942 CTS 4
*1942, March 17, March 18	Agreement between the United States of America and Canada respecting a military highway to Alaska.	56(2) *Stat.* 1458 EAS 246 1942 CTS 13
1942, March 18, March 20	Agreement between the United States of America and Canada respecting transfers of citizens and former citizens between armed forces.	56(2) *Stat.* 1455 EAS 245 1942 CTS 5
1942, March 30,	Agreement between the United States of America and Canada respecting application	56(2) *Stat.* 1477 EAS 249

Signed	Title	Reference
April 6, April 8	of the Selective Training and Service Act of 1940, as amended, to Canadians in the United States, and reciprocal treatment of American citizens in Canada.	1942 CTS 7
*1942, May 4, May 9	Agreement between the United States of America and Canada respecting the southern terminus of Alaska Highway.	57(2) *Stat.* 1373 EAS 380 1942 CTS 22
*1942, June 27, June 29	Agreement between the United States of America and Canada respecting the Canol Project.	57(2) *Stat.* 1413 EAS 386 1942 CTS 23
*1942, July 21, Oct. 29, Nov. 9	Agreement between the United States of America and Canada respecting importation privileges for government officials and employees.	57(2) *Stat.* 1379 EAS 383 1942 CTS 20
*1942, Aug. 14, Aug. 15	Agreement between the United States of America and Canada respecting the Canol Project pipeline.	57(2) *Stat.* 1416 EAS 387 1942 CTS 24
*1942, Aug. 26, Sept. 10	Agreement between the United States of America and Canada respecting flight strips along Alaska Highway.	57(2) *Stat.* 1375 EAS 381 1942 CTS 26
1942, Sept. 30	EXCHANGE OF NOTES BETWEEN CANADA AND THE UNITED STATES OF AMERICA RESPECTING MILITARY SERVICE OF UNITED STATES CITIZENS RESIDING IN CANADA.	1942 CTS 14
*1942, Oct. 5, Oct. 9	EXCHANGE OF NOTES BETWEEN CANADA AND THE UNITED STATES OF AMERICA EXTENDING TO OCTOBER 1, 1943 THE AGREEMENT FOR THE TEMPORARY RAISING OF THE LEVEL OF LAKE ST. FRANCIS OF NOVEMBER 10, 1941.	1942 CTS 18 EAS 291 56(2) *Stat.* 1832
*1942, Nov. 2, Nov. 4	Agreement between the United States of America and Canada respecting workmen's compensation and unemployment insurance in connection with construction projects in Canada.	56(2) *Stat.* 1770 EAS 279 1942 CTS 16
*1942, Nov. 28, Dec. 7	Agreement between the United States of America and Canada respecting the Haines-Champagne section of Alaska Highway.	57(2) *Stat.* 1377 EAS 382 1942 CTS 21

Signed	Title	Reference
*1942, Nov. 30	Exchange of notes between the United States of America and Canada respecting post-war economic settlements.	56(2) *Stat.* 1815 EAS 287 1942 CTS 17
1942, Dec. 8, Dec. 19	Agreement between the United States of America and Canada respecting fur seals.	58(2) *Stat.* 1379 EAS 415 1942 CTS 25
*1942, Dec. 28; 1943, Jan. 13	Agreement between the United States of America and Canada respecting the Canol Project exploratory wells.	57(2) *Stat.* 1418 EAS 388 1943 CTS 18
*1943, Jan. 18, Feb. 17, March 13	Agreement between the United States of America and Canada respecting Canol Project areas.	57(2) *Stat.* 1420 EAS 389 1943 CTS 19
*1943, Jan. 27	Agreement between the United States of America and Canada respecting the post-war disposition of defense installations and facilities.	57(2) *Stat.* 1429 EAS 391 1943 CTS 2
*1943, Feb. 22, Feb. 23	Agreement between the United States of America and Canada respecting the lease of White Pass and Yukon railway.	57(2) *Stat.* 1423 EAS 390 1943 CTS 3
1943, March 4	Arrangement between the United States of America and Canada respecting air transport services, continuing in effect the arrangement of November 29 and December 2, 1940 giving effect to article III of the arrangement signed August 18, 1939.	57(2) *Stat.* 923 EAS 314 1943 CTS 4
1943, March 26	Agreement between the United States of America, Canada, and the United Kingdom of Great Britain and Northern Ireland respecting industrial diamonds.	57(2) *Stat.* 931 EAS 317
*1943, April 10	Agreement between the United States of America and Canada respecting access to Alaska Highway.	57(2) *Stat.* 1274 EAS 362 1943 CTS 17
1943, May 24, Aug. 13	Agreement between the United States of America and Canada respecting jurisdiction over prizes.	58(2) *Stat.* 1210 EAS 394 1943 CTS 13
1943, May 25,	Agreement between the United States of America and Canada respecting waiver of	57(2) *Stat.* 1021 EAS 330

Signed	Title	Reference
May 26	claims arising as a result of collisions between vessels of war.	1943 CTS 12
1943, June 12; 1944, Jan. 26, Feb. 21	EXCHANGE OF NOTES BETWEEN CANADA AND THE UNITED STATES OF AMERICA RENEWING CANADA'S PERMISSION TO PAN-AMERICAN AIRWAYS INCORPORATED TO FLY OVER CANADA BETWEEN JUNEAU (ALASKA) AND SEATTLE (WASHINGTON).	1944 CTS 2
*1943, July 19	Agreement between the United States of America and Canada respecting the Alaska Highway.	57(2) Stat. 1023 EAS 331 1943 CTS 10
*1943, Aug. 6, Aug. 9	Agreement between the United States of America and Canada respecting Provincial and municipal taxation on United States defense projects in Canada.	57(2) Stat. 1065 EAS 339 1943 CTS 11
1943, Sept. 3, Nov. 11	Agreement between the United States of America and Canada concerning application of the agreement of May 25 and 26, 1943 respecting waiver of claims arising as a result of collisions between vessels of war.	57(2) Stat. 1301 EAS 366
*1943, Oct. 5, Oct. 9	Agreement between the United States of America and Canada respecting the temporary raising of the levels of Lake St. Francis during low-water periods, continuing in effect the agreement of November 10, 1941 as continued by the agreement of October 5 and 9, 1942.	57(2) Stat. 1366 EAS 377 1943 CTS 15
1943, Nov. 5, Nov. 25; 1944, Jan. 17	Agreement between the United States of America and Canada respecting radio broadcasting stations.	58(2) Stat. 1238 EAS 400 1944 CTS 1
*1944, Feb. 25, March 3	Agreement between the United States of America and Canada respecting the Upper Columbia River Basin.	58(2) Stat. 1236 EAS 399
*1944, March 1, March 23	Agreement between the United States of America and Canada respecting claims arising out of traffic accidents involving vehicles of United States and Canadian armed forces.	60(2) Stat. 1948 TIAS 1581 1944 CTS 10

Signed	Title	Reference
1944, May 1	EXCHANGE OF NOTES BETWEEN CANADA AND THE UNITED STATES OF AMERICA CONSTITUTING AN AGREEMENT FOR A TEMPORARY ADDITIONAL DIVERSION OF WATER AT NIAGARA FOR POWER PURPOSES.	1944 CTS 13
*1944, June 7	Agreement between the United States of America and Canada respecting revision of Canol projects.	58(2) *Stat.* 1384 EAS 416 1944 CTS 16
*1944, June 8	Convention between the United States of America and Canada respecting double taxation, estate taxes and succession duties.	59(2) *Stat.* 915 TS 989 1944 CTS 17
*1944, June 23, June 27	Agreement between the United States of America and Canada respecting payment for certain defense installations.	58(2) *Stat.* 1290 EAS 405 1944 CTS 19
1944, July 19, July 22	EXCHANGE OF NOTES BETWEEN CANADA AND THE UNITED STATES OF AMERICA RENEWING CANADA'S PERMISSION TO PAN AMERICAN AIRWAYS INCORPORATED TO FLY OVER CANADA BETWEEN JUNEAU (ALASKA) AND SEATTLE (WASHINGTON).	1944 CTS 21
*1944, July 21, Aug. 5	Agreement between the United States of America and Canada respecting sockeye salmon fisheries.	59(2) *Stat.* 1614 EAS 479 1944 CTS 22
1944, Aug. 29, Sept. 8	EXCHANGE OF NOTES BETWEEN CANADA AND THE UNITED STATES OF AMERICA AMENDING CANADA'S PERMISSION TO PAN AMERICAN AIRWAYS INCORPORATED TO FLY OVER CANADA BETWEEN JUNEAU (ALASKA) AND SEATTLE (WASHINGTON).	1944 CTS 23
*1944, Aug. 31, Sept. 7	Agreement between the United States of America and Canada continuing in effect the agreement of November 10, 1941, respecting the temporary raising of the level of Lake St. Francis during low-water periods.	58(2) *Stat.* 1437 EAS 424 1944 CTS 26
1944, Sept. 1, Sept. 2	EXCHANGE OF NOTES BETWEEN CANADA AND THE UNITED STATES OF AMERICA RECORDING CANADA'S PERMISSION TO PAN AMERICAN AIR-	1944 CTS 24

Signed	Title	Reference
1944, Sept. 1, Sept. 2	WAYS INCORPORATED TO FLY INTO, THROUGH AND AWAY FROM CANADA AND TO USE THE AIRPORT AT BOTWOOD (NEWFOUNDLAND) IN CONNECTION WITH THE OPERATION OF ITS ATLANTIC SERVICES. EXCHANGE OF NOTES BETWEEN CANADA AND THE UNITED STATES OF AMERICA RECORDING CANADA'S PERMISSION TO AMERICAN EXPORT AIRLINES INCORPORATED TO FLY INTO, THROUGH AND AWAY FROM CANADA AND TO USE THE AIRPORTS AT BOTWOOD AND GANDER LAKE (NEWFOUNDLAND) IN CONNECTION WITH THE OPERATION OF ITS ATLANTIC SERVICES.	1944 CTS 25
*1944, Nov. 22, Dec. 20	Agreement between the United States of America and Canada amending the agreement of January 27, 1943 respecting postwar disposition of defense installations and facilities.	58(2) Stat. 156 EAS 444 1944 CTS 35
1944, Dec. 28, Dec. 30	EXCHANGE OF NOTES BETWEEN CANADA AND THE UNITED STATES OF AMERICA CONSTITUTING AN AGREEMENT CONCERNING THE ACQUISITION OF LAND FOR UNITED STATES DEFENCE PROJECTS IN CANADA.	1944 CTS 34
1945, Feb. 13	Agreement between the United States of America and Canada respecting flights of military aircraft.	62(3) Stat. 394 TIAS 2056 1945 CTS 1
1945, Feb. 17	Agreement between the United States of America and Canada respecting air transport services.	59(2) Stat. 135 EAS 457 1945 CTS 2
*1945, Feb. 26	Agreement between the United States of America and Canada respecting an arrangement for evaluation of all facilities of the Canol Project.	61(4) Stat. 367 TIAS 1695 1945 CTS 3
*1945, May 7,	Agreement between the United States of America and Canada respecting cooperation	61(4) Stat. 395 TIAS 1752

Signed	Title	Reference
May 15	in the reconversion of industry in the transition from war to peace, continuing the principles of the Hyde Park Declaration of April 20, 1941.	1948 CTS 1
*1945, Aug. 31, Sept. 6	Agreement between the United States of America and Canada respecting waiver by Canada of certain rights relating to crude oil facilities of the Canol Project.	61(4) *Stat.* 3679 TIAS 1696
1945, Nov. 15	Agreed declaration by the President of the United States of America, the Prime Minister of the United Kingdom, and the Prime Minister of Canada respecting atomic energy.	60(2) *Stat.* 1479 TIAS 1504 1945 CTS 13
*1945, Dec. 21; 1946, Jan. 3	Canol Project: Agreement between the United States of America and Canada respecting the disposition of storage and loading facilities at Prince Rupert.	60(2) *Stat.* 1930 TIAS 1565 1946 CTS 1
*1946, March 30	Agreement between the United States of America and Canada respecting transfer of defense installations and equipment.	60(2) *Stat.* 1741 TIAS 1531 1946 CTS 12
*1946, July 11, July 15	EXCHANGE OF NOTES BETWEEN CANADA AND THE UNITED STATES OF AMERICA CONCERNING THE DISPOSAL OF WAR SURPLUSES AND RELATED MATTERS.	1946 CTS 31 60(2) *Stat.* 1751 TIAS 1531
*1946, Sept. 3, Sept. 27	Agreement between the United States of America and Canada respecting patent rights in connection with RDX and other explosives.	61(3) *Stat.* 2949 TIAS 1628 1946 CTS 51
*1946, Sept. 28, Nov. 13, Nov. 15	Agreement between the United States of America and Canada respecting waiver of certain claims involving government vessels.	61(3) *Stat.* 2520 TIAS 1582 1946 CTS 42
*1946, Nov. 7, Dec. 30; 1947, March 5, March 6	Arrangement between the United States of America and Canada respecting disposal of crude oil facilities of the Canol Project.	61(4) *Stat.* 3681 TIAS 1697 1946 CTS 41
*1946, Nov. 18, Dec. 6	Understandings between the United States of America and Canada regarding the Rush-Bagot Agreement of April 28 and 29, 1817,	61(4) *Stat.* 4082 TIAS 1836 1946 CTS 40

Signed	*Title*	*Reference*
	respecting naval forces on the American Lakes.	
*1947, Jan. 8, Oct. 15	Agreement between the United States of America and Canada respecting allocation of FM channels in radio broadcasting.	61(4) *Stat.* 3800 TIAS 1726 1947 CTS 30
*1947, Jan. 9	Agreement between the United States of America and Canada respecting surplus property disposal operations.	61(3) *Stat.* 2738 TIAS 1603 1947 CTS 3
*1947, Feb. 12	JOINT STATEMENTS BY THE GOVERNMENTS OF CANADA AND OF THE UNITED STATES OF AMERICA REGARDING DEFENCE COOPERATION BETWEEN THE TWO COUNTRIES.	1947 CTS 43
1947, March 18	Agreement between the United States of America and Canada respecting termination of the reciprocal trade agreement signed December 13, 1940, relating to fox furs and skins.	61(3) *Stat.* 3054 TIAS 1638
1947, April 10, April 12	Agreement between the United States of America and Canada amending the agreement of February 17, 1945, respecting air transport services.	61(3) *Stat.* 2869 TIAS 1619 1947 CTS 11
1947, June 25, Aug. 20	Interim arrangement between the United States of America and Canada respecting mobile radio transmitting stations.	61(4) *Stat.* 3349 TIAS 1670 1947 CTS 25
*1947, Aug. 13, Oct. 23	Agreement between the United States of America and the United Kingdom of Great Britain and Northern Ireland respecting the delimitating of the area within Newfoundland territorial waters adjacent to the United States Naval Base at Argentia.	61(4) *Stat.* 4065 TIAS 1809
*1947, Oct. 30	Agreement and accompanying letters between the United States of America and Canada rendering inoperative the Trade Agreement of November 17, 1938, and supplementing the General Agreement on Tariffs and Trade of October 30, 1947.	61(4) *Stat.* 3695 TIAS 1702
1947, Dec. 24; 1948,	Arrangement between the United States of America and Canada respecting engineering standards applicable to the allocation of	62(3) *Stat.* 2652 TIAS 1802 1948 CTS 7

Signed	Title	Reference
April 1, April 13	standard broadcasting stations (540-1600 kcs.).	
1947, Dec. 26	Agreement between the United States of America and Canada amending the provisional agreement of December 8 and 19, 1942, respecting fur seals.	62(2) *Stat.* 1821 TIAS 1686 1947 CTS 36
*1948, Jan. 24, March 2	Agreement between the United States of America and Canada respecting the transfer of defense installations and equipment, extending and modifying the agreement of March 30, 1946.	62(3) *Stat.* 3912 TIAS 1981 1948 CTS 8
*1948, March 1, March 31	Agreement between the United States of America and Canada respecting the operation and maintenance of a land line communication system between Edmonton, Alberta, and Fairbanks, Alaska.	62(3) *Stat.* 3883 TIAS 1966 1948 CTS 6
*1948, March 4, April 30	Agreement between the United States of America and Canada respecting sanitary practices in the shellfish industries.	62(2) *Stat.* 1898 TIAS 1747 1948 CTS 10
*1948, April 9, April 14	Agreement between the United States of America and Canada respecting the transfer of defense installations and equipment, extending and modifying the agreement of March 30, 1946. Supplementary exchange of notes.	62(3) *Stat.* 3914 TIAS 1981 1948 CTS 8
1948, April 22, April 29	EXCHANGE OF LETTERS BETWEEN CANADA AND THE UNITED STATES OF AMERICA PROVIDING FOR THE RENEWAL OF THE ARRANGEMENT OF 1942 FOR THE EXCHANGE OF AGRICULTURAL LABOUR AND MACHINERY.	1948 CTS 35
1948, Nov. 23	Agreement between the United States of America and Canada respecting control of exports of potatoes from Canada to the United States.	62(3) *Stat.* 3717 TIAS 1896 1948 CTS 33
1948, Dec. 23	EXCHANGE OF NOTES BETWEEN CANADA AND THE UNITED STATES OF AMERICA CONSTITUTING AN AGREEMENT FOR AN ADDITIONAL TEMPORARY DIVERSION OF WATER	1948 CTS 20

Signed	*Title*	*Reference*
	IN THE NIAGARA AREA FOR POWER PURPOSES.	
*1949, Jan. 24, Jan. 31	Agreement between the United States of America and Canada respecting air search and rescue operations.	63(3) *Stat.* 2328 TIAS 1882 1949 CTS 2
*1949, March 14	Agreement between the United States of America and Canada respecting the settlement of certain war accounts and claims.	63(3) *Stat.* 2432 TIAS 1925 1949 CTS 9
1949, April 5, April 7	EXCHANGE OF LETTERS BETWEEN CANADA AND THE UNITED STATES OF AMERICA PROVIDING FOR THE RENEWAL OF THE ARRANGEMENT OF 1942 FOR THE EXCHANGE OF AGRICULTURAL LABOUR AND MACHINERY.	1949 CTS 6
*1949, April 12	Agreement between the United States of America and Canada respecting a Joint Industrial Mobilization Committee.	63(3) *Stat.* 2331 TIAS 1889 1949 CTS 8
*1949, June 4	Agreement between the United States of America and Canada respecting the use by civil aircraft of Stephenville and Argentia military air bases in Newfoundland.	63(3) *Stat.* 2486 TIAS 1933 1949 CTS 15
*1949, June 4	Agreement between the United States of America and Canada respecting air transport services, superseding the agreement of February 17, 1945, as amended.	63(3) *Stat.* 2489 TIAS 1934 1949 CTS 14
*1949, June 17, June 18	DEFENSE INSTALLATIONS AND EQUIPMENT. Agreement effected by exchange of notes.	2 UST 2272 TIAS 2352 1949 CTS 16
1949, June 20	EXCHANGE OF NOTES BETWEEN CANADA AND THE UNITED STATES OF AMERICA TERMINATING THE AGREEMENT OF NOVEMBER 23, 1948 CONCERNING THE EXPORT OF POTATOES AND SEED POTATOES TO THE UNITED STATES.	1949 CTS 17
*1949, Nov. 17; 1950, Jan. 24	CLAIMS. Agreement supplementing the convention of April 15, 1935. Effected by exchange of notes.	3 UST 539 TIAS 2412 1951 CTS 35

Signed	Title	Reference
*1950, Feb. 27	NIAGARA RIVER, WATER DIVERSION. Convention.	1 UST 694 TIAS 2130 1950 CTS 3
*1950, March 24	HALIBUT FISHING VESSELS. Convention.	1 UST 536 TIAS 2096 1950 CTS 5
*1950, June 8, June 22	PACIFIC OCEAN WEATHER STATIONS. Agreement effected by exchange of notes.	1 UST 569 TIAS 2103 1951 CTS 36
*1950, June 12	DOUBLE TAXATION. Convention modifying and supplementing the convention and accompanying protocol of March 4, 1942.	2 UST 2235 TIAS 2347 1951 CTS 22
*1950, June 12	DOUBLE TAXATION. Convention modifying and supplementing the convention of June 8, 1944.	2 UST 2247 TIAS 2348 1951 CTS 23
1950, June 29, July 6	EXCHANGE OF LETTERS BETWEEN CANADA AND THE UNITED STATES OF AMERICA PROVIDING FOR THE RENEWAL OF THE ARRANGEMENT OF 1942 FOR THE EXCHANGE OF AGRICULTURAL LABOUR AND MACHINERY.	1950 CTS 11
*1950, Sept. 25; 1951, Feb. 16	PACIFIC OCEAN WEATHER STATIONS. Agreement effected by exchange of notes.	2 UST 720 TIAS 2228 1951 CTS 37
*1950, Oct. 26	INDUSTRIAL MOBILIZATION. Agreement effected by exchange of notes.	1 UST 716 TIAS 2136 1950 CTS 15
*1951, Feb. 8	TELECOMMUNICATIONS (Operation of Certain Radio Equipment or Stations). Convention.	3 UST 3787 TIAS 2508 1952 CTS 7
1951, March 15, March 16	EXCHANGE OF AGRICULTURAL LABOUR AND MACHINERY. Agreement effected by Exchange of Letters.	1951 CTS 4
*1951, March 27	CIVIL DEFENSE COOPERATION. Agreement effected by exchange of notes.	2 UST 717 TIAS 2227 1951 CTS 3
*1951,	EXCESS U.S. PROPERTY. Agreement ef-	2 UST 1566

Signed	Title	Reference
April 11, April 18	fected by exchange of notes.	TIAS 2298 1951 CTS 9
*1951, July 31, Sept. 11	UNEMPLOYMENT INSURANCE BENEFITS. Agreement amending the agreement of March 6 and 12, 1942. Effected by exchange of notes.	3 UST 2812 TIAS 2452 1951 CTS 14
*1951, Aug. 1	DEFENSE. Continental Radar Defense System. Agreement effected by Exchange of Notes.	5 UST 1721 TIAS 3049 1951 CTS 31
1951, Oct. 9, Dec. 12; 1952, Feb. 7	WEATHER STATIONS. Exchange of Notes.	1952 CTS 36
*1951, Oct. 26	EXTRADITION. Supplementary convention supplementing the convention of December 13, 1900 between the United States of America and the United Kingdom.	3 UST 2826 TIAS 2454 1952 CTS 12
*1952, Jan. 22, Feb. 22	WEATHER STATIONS. Agreement amending the agreement of February 16, 1951. Effected by exchange of notes.	3 UST 3062 TIAS 2488 1952 CTS 33
1952, Feb. 7, March 1	FUR SEALS. Agreement effected by exchange of notes.	3 UST 3900 TIAS 2521 1952 CTS 26
*1952, Feb. 13, March 19	LEASED BASES IN NEWFOUNDLAND. Agreement modifying the agreement of March 27, 1941, between the United States of America and the United Kingdom of Great Britain and Northern Ireland. Effected by exchange of notes.	3 UST 4271 TIAS 2572
*1952, Feb. 21	TELECOMMUNICATIONS. (Agreement for the Promotion of Safety on the Great Lakes by means of Radio).	3 UST 4926 TIAS 2666 1952 CTS 25
1952, April 15, April 16	EXCHANGE OF AGRICULTURAL LABOUR AND MACHINERY. Agreement effected by Exchange of Letters.	1952 CTS 6
*1952, April 23, June 23	TELEVISION. Agreement effected by exchange of notes.	3 UST 4443 TIAS 2594 1952 CTS 13

Signed	Title	Reference
*1952, April 28, April 30	DEFENSE. Application of NATO Status of Forces Agreement to United States Forces at Leased Bases. Agreement effected by Exchange of Notes.	5 UST 2139 TIAS 3074
1952, May 9	HIGH SEAS FISHERIES OF THE NORTH PACIFIC OCEAN. Convention with Annex and Protocol. (Japan also signatory).	4 UST 380 TIAS 2786 1953 CTS 3
*1952, June 30	BOUNDARY WATERS. St. Lawrence Seaway. Exchange of Notes.	1952 CTS 30 TIAS 3053 5 UST 1784
*1952, Nov. 4, Nov. 8	DEFENSE. Agreement effected by exchange of notes.	3 UST 3741 TIAS 2503 1952 CTS 27
*1952, Dec. 5	DEFENSE. Agreement effected by exchange of notes.	3 UST 5295 TIAS 2730 1952 CTS 22
*1953, March 2	PRESERVATION OF HALIBUT FISHERY OF NORTHERN PACIFIC OCEAN AND BERING SEA. Convention.	5 UST 5 TIAS 2900 1953 CTS 14
*1953, March 9, March 17	MOBILE RADIO TRANSMITTING STATIONS. Understanding effected by Exchange of Notes. Providing for Conditional Cancellation of Interim Arrangement of June 25 and August 20, 1947.	5 UST 2840 TIAS 3138 1953 CTS 1
*1953, May 1, July 31	DEFENSE. Communications Facilities in Newfoundland. Agreement amending Agreement of November 4 and 8, 1952. Effected by Exchange of Notes.	4 UST 1474 TIAS 2810 1953 CTS 25
*1953, June 26, June 30	NAVIGATION. Transfer of Loran Stations in Newfoundland to the Canadian Government. Agreement effected by Exchange of Notes.	4 UST 2174 TIAS 2865 1953 CTS 12
*1953, June 30	DEFENSE. Haines-Fairbanks Oil Pipeline Installation. Agreement effected by Exchange of Notes.	4 UST 2223 TIAS 2875 1953 CTS 20
*1953, Nov. 12	JOINT UNITED STATES–CANADIAN COMMITTEE ON TRADE AND ECONOMIC AFFAIRS. Agreement effected by Exchange of Notes.	5 UST 314 TIAS 2922 1953 CTS 18

Signed	Title	Reference
*1953, Nov. 12	SAINT LAWRENCE SEAWAY. Establishment of Saint Lawrence River Joint Board of Engineers. Agreement effected by Exchange of Notes.	5 UST 2538 TIAS 3116 1953 CTS 21
*1954, May 1, May 3	NAVIGATION. Loran Station on Cape Christian, Baffin Island. Agreement effected by Exchange of Notes.	5 UST 1459 TIAS 3019 1954 CTS 6
*1954, June 4, June 28	PACIFIC OCEAN WEATHER STATIONS. Agreement effected by Exchange of Notes.	5 UST 2765 TIAS 3132 1954 CTS 12
*1954, Aug. 17	SAINT LAWRENCE SEAWAY. Agreement effected by Exchange of Notes.	5 UST 1784 TIAS 3053 1954 CTS 14
*1954, Sept. 10	GREAT LAKES FISHERIES. Convention.	6 UST 2836 TIAS 3326 1955 CTS 19
*1954, Sept. 13	CONSTRUCTION OF REMEDIAL WORKS AT NIAGARA FALLS. Agreement effected by Exchange of Notes.	5 UST 1979 TIAS 3064 1954 CTS 7
*1955, March 31, June 8	Defense: Communications Facilities in Newfoundland. Agreement amending the agreement of November 4 and 8, 1952, as amended. Effected by exchange of notes.	6 UST 2269 TIAS 3296 1955 CTS 9
*1955, April 19; 1956, Jan. 26	Status of Canadian Forces Stationed in the Federal Republic of Germany. Agreement effected by exchange of notes.	7 UST 203 TIAS 3495 1956 CTS 26
*1955, May 5	ESTABLISHMENT IN CANADA OF WARNING AND CONTROL SYSTEM AGAINST AIR ATTACK. Agreement effected by exchange of notes.	6 UST 763 TIAS 3218 1955 CTS 8
*1955, June 8	Trade: Withdrawal of Concession and Grant of Compensatory Concessions Under General Agreement on Tariffs and Trade. Agreement.	6 UST 6231 TIAS 3474 1955 CTS 13
*1955, June 13	Defense: Radar Stations in the Newfoundland–Labrador Area. Agreement effected by exchange of notes.	6 UST 6045 TIAS 3452 1955 CTS 29
*1955, June 15	ATOMIC ENERGY. Agreement (Civil Uses).	6 UST 2595 TIAS 3304 1955 CTS 15

Signed	Title	Reference
*1955, June 15	ATOMIC ENERGY. Agreement (Information for Mutual Defense Purposes).	6 UST 2607 TIAS 3305 1955 CTS 16
*1955, June 15	Defense: Radar Stations in British Columbia, Ontario, and Nova Scotia. Agreement effected by exchange of notes.	6 UST 6051 TIAS 3453 1955 CTS 30
*1955, July 21	Financial Arrangements for Furnishing Certain Supplies and Services to Naval Vessels. Agreement effected by exchange of notes.	6 UST 3043 TIAS 3351 1955 CTS 20
*1955, Sept. 22	Defense: Establishment of a Petroleum Products Pipeline in Newfoundland. Agreement effected by exchange of notes.	6 UST 3899 TIAS 3392 1955 CTS 18
*1955, Nov. 22, Dec. 20	Air Transport Services. Agreement amending schedule 2 of the agreement of June 4, 1949.	6 UST 6065 TIAS 3456 1955 CTS 28
*1955, Dec. 20; 1956, April 23	Unemployment Insurance: Canadian Employees of the United States Armed Services in Canada. Agreement effected by exchange of notes.	8 UST 1879 TIAS 3933 1956 CTS 13
*1956, April 18, April 19	Defense: Construction and Operation of Housing Units in Newfoundland. Agreement effected by exchange of notes.	7 UST 731 TIAS 3552 1956 CTS 6
*1956, June 26	Atomic Energy: Cooperation for Civil Uses. Agreement amending agreement of June 15, 1955.	8 UST 275 TIAS 3771 1957 CTS 8
*1956, July 23, Oct. 26; 1957, Feb. 26	Saint Lawrence Seaway: Navigation Improvements of the Great Lakes Connecting Channels. Arrangement effected by exchange of notes.	8 UST 279 TIAS 3772 1957 CTS 9
*1956, Aug. 8	Double Taxation: Taxes on Income. Convention modifying and supplementing the convention of March 4, 1942, as modified and supplemented.	8 UST 1619 TIAS 3916 1957 CTS 22
1956, Sept. 24	Disposition of Rights in Atomic Energy Inventions. Agreement (United Kingdom also signatory).	7 UST 2526 TIAS 3644 1956 CTS 20
*1956,	Relocation of Roosevelt Bridge. Agreement	7 UST 2865

Signed	*Title*	*Reference*
Oct. 24	effected by exchange of notes.	TIAS 3668 1956 CTS 24
*1956, Nov. 7, Dec. 4	Saint Lawrence Seaway: Deep-Water Dredging in Cornwall Island Channels. Exchange of notes.	7 UST 3271 TIAS 3708
*1956, Nov. 30; 1957, April 8, April 9	Saint Lawrence Seaway: Navigation Improvements of the Great Lakes Connecting Channels. Agreement effected by exchange of notes.	8 UST 637 TIAS 3814 1957 CTS 4
*1956, Dec. 28	Sockeye and Pink Salmon Fisheries. Protocol amending the convention of May 26, 1930.	8 UST 1057 TIAS 3867 1957 CTS 21
*1957, Jan. 16, Jan. 17	Defense: Maintenance of Haines–Fairbanks Pipeline. Agreement effected by exchange of notes.	8 UST 23 TIAS 3732 1957 CTS 1
1958, April 3, April 11	BOUNDARY WATERS. (Peace Bridge.) Exchange of Notes.	1958 CTS 10
*1958, May 12	North American Air Defense Command. Agreement effected by exchange of notes.	9 UST 538 TIAS 4031 1958 CTS 9
*1958, June 20	Defense: Aerial Refueling Facilities. Agreement effected by exchange of notes.	9 UST 903 TIAS 4051 1958 CTS 15
*1958, Aug. 29, Sept. 2	Establishment of Canada–United States Ministerial Committee on Joint Defense. Agreement effected by exchange of notes.	9 UST 1159 TIAS 4098 1958 CTS 22
1958, Oct. 23, Oct. 31	LABOUR. (Seasonal Movement of Woods Workers.) Exchange of Notes.	1958 CTS 28
1958, Dec. 9; 1959, Jan. 7	RADIO. (Operation of TV Station at Scranton, Pa.) Exchange of Notes.	1959 CTS 2
*1959, Feb. 27	Saint Lawrence Seaway: Navigation Improvements of the Great Lakes Connecting Channels. Agreement effected by exchange of notes.	10 UST 383 TIAS 4199 1959 CTS 6
*1959,	Saint Lawrence Seaway: Tariff of Tolls.	10 UST 323

Signed	*Title*	*Reference*
March 9	Agreement effected by exchange of notes.	TIAS 4192 1959 CTS 5
*1959, April 9	Air Transport Services. Agreement amending the agreement of June 4, 1949, as amended.	10 UST 773 TIAS 4213 1959 CTS 8
*1959, April 13	Establishment in Canada of Warning and Control System Against Air Attack: Communications Facilities at Cape Dyer, Baffin Island. Agreement effected by exchange of notes.	10 UST 739 TIAS 4208 1959 CTS 9
*1959, May 1	Defense: Short Range Tactical Navigation (TACAN) Facilities. Agreement effected by exchange of notes.	10 UST 790 TIAS 4218 1959 CTS 10
*1959, May 22	Atomic Energy: Cooperation for Mutual Defense Purposes. Agreement.	10 UST 1293 TIAS 4271 1959 CTS 16
*1959, July 13	Establishment of Ballistic Missile Early Warning System. Agreement effected by exchange of notes.	10 UST 1260 TIAS 4264 1959 CTS 12
*1959, Aug. 17, Aug. 20	Defense: Maintenance of Haines–Fairbanks Pipeline. Agreement extending the agreement of January 16 and 17, 1957.	10 UST 1701 TIAS 4320 1959 CTS 21
*1960, March 31	Canol Project: Disposal of Pipeline Facilities in Canada. Agreement effected by exchange of notes.	11 UST 2486 TIAS 4631 1960 CTS 10
*1960, June 11	Atomic Energy: Cooperation for Civil Uses. Agreement amending the agreement of June 15, 1955, as amended and modified.	11 UST 1780 TIAS 4518 1960 CTS 17
*1960, June 14	Defense: Joint Upper Atmosphere Research Facilities at Fort Churchill, Manitoba. Agreement effected by exchange of notes.	11 UST 1801 TIAS 4524 1960 CTS 12
*1960, July 20, Aug. 23, Aug. 31	Defense: Loan of Vessel. Agreement effected by exchange of notes.	11 UST 2214 TIAS 4593 1960 CTS 22
*1960, Aug. 24	Tracking Stations. Agreement effected by exchange of notes.	11 UST 2084 TIAS 4564 1960 CTS 19

Bibliographical Note

TREATY TEXTS

Texts of Canada–United States treaties are to be found in a number of sources. On the Canadian side, two volumes have been compiled under official auspices: *Treaties and Agreements Affecting Canada in Force between His Majesty and the United States of America with Subsidiary Documents 1814-1913* (Ottawa, 1915) and *Treaties and Agreements Affecting Canada in Force between His Majesty and the United States of America with Subsidiary Documents 1814-1925* (Ottawa, 1927). The *Canada Treaty Series* commences with volume for 1928 and is current. Texts of treaties concluded prior to the 1920's appear in British sources, particularly the *British Treaty Series; British and Foreign State Papers;* and *Handbook of Commercial Treaties* (issued in 1913 and 1931).

In the United States treaties were published in the *Statutes at Large* until 1950. Thereafter texts have been published in *United States Treaties and Other International Agreements* (usually cited as UST). In the *Statutes at Large,* Volume 8 contains a compilation of treaties covering the period 1778-1845; and Volume 18, Part 2, contains a compilation up to the year 1871. A complete list of all the treaties and other international agreements published in the *Statutes at Large* is given in Volume 64, Part 3. International agreements are also published by the Department of State in pamphlet form in the *Treaties and Other International Acts Series* (usually cited TIAS). This series, TIAS, began in 1946 and is in continuation of two earlier series, the *Treaty Series* (usually cited TS) and the *Executive Agreement Series* (usually cited EAS). *Treaties and Other International Acts of the United States of America,* edited by Hunter Miller, covers treaties of the period 1776-1863; this eight-volume work, issued 1931-1948, contains extensive notes as well as treaty texts. *Treaties, Conventions, International Acts, Protocols and Agreements between the United States of America and Other Powers, 1776-1909,* compiled by William M. Malloy, was issued in two volumes in 1910; Volume 3 covering the period 1910-1923, compiled by C. F. Redmond, appeared in 1923; and Volume 4, compiled by E. J. Trenwith, covering the period 1923-1937, was published in 1938.

Texts of treaties concluded since World War I are also contained in the *League of Nations Treaty Series,* and the *United Nations Treaty Series.*

DIPLOMATIC RELATIONS

General works on diplomatic history and relations which provide perspective and background for treaty questions arising between Canada and the United States, and earlier between Britain and the United States affecting Canada, include: G. P. deT. Glazebrook, *A History of Canadian External Relations,* rev. ed. (Toronto, 1950); R. B. Mowat, *The Diplomatic Relations of Great Britain and the United States* (London, 1925); J. N. Mathews, *American Foreign Relations* (New York, 1928); Samuel F. Bemis, *A Diplomatic History of the United States* (New York, 1936); Thomas A. Bailey, *A Diplomatic History of the American People,* 3rd ed. (New York, 1952); Fred Alexander, *Canadians and Foreign Policy* (Toronto, 1960). The survey volumes, *Canada in World Affairs* (Toronto, 1941—), published under the auspices of the Canadian Institute of International Affairs, furnish Canadian background for the period since the beginning of the Second World War. To be noted also is H. L. Keenleyside *et al., The Growth of Canadian Policies in External Affairs* (Durham, N. C., 1961); this volume contains a useful bibliographical note by Gaddis Smith.

Works dealing more closely with Canada–United States relations include: R. A. Falconer, *The United States as a Neighbour from a Canadian Point of View* (Cambridge, 1925); J. M. Callahan, *American Foreign Policy in Canadian Relations* (New York, 1937); H. F. Angus, ed., *Canada and Her Great Neighbour* (New Haven, 1938); John MacCormac, *Canada: America's Problem* (New York, 1940); E. W. McInnis, *The Unguarded Frontier* (Garden City, N. Y., 1942); and H. L. Keenleyside and G. S. Brown, *Canada and the United States* (rev. ed.; New York, 1952). J. B. Brebner, *North Atlantic Triangle* (New Haven, 1945); and E. W. McInnis, *The Atlantic Triangle and the Cold War* (Toronto, 1959) explore relations of the North American nations and Britain in the context of postwar problems.

The literature dealing with specific aspects of relations from the eighteenth century on is extensive. Books and monographs to be mentioned include: T. C. Pease, ed., *Anglo-French Boundary Disputes in the West, 1749-1763* (Springfield, Ill., 1936); Max Savelle, *Diplomatic History of the Canadian Boundary* (New Haven, 1940); N. V. Russell, *The British Régime in Michigan and the Old Northwest, 1760-1796* (Northfield, Minn., 1939); Bradford Perkins, *The First Rapprochement; England*

and the U.S., 1795-1805 (Philadelphia, 1955); J. W. Pratt, *Expansionists of 1812* (New York, 1925); F. A. Updyke, *The Diplomacy of the War of 1812* (Baltimore, 1913); J. M. Callahan, *The Neutrality of the American Lakes and Anglo-American Relations* (Baltimore, 1898); H. S. Burrage, *Maine in the Northeastern Boundary Controversy* (Portland, Maine, 1919); A. B. Corey, *The Crisis of 1830-1842 in Canadian-American Relations* (New Haven, 1941); Bernard De Voto, *The Year of Decision, 1846* (Boston, 1943); M. C. Jacobs, *Winning Oregon* (Caldwell, Ida., 1938); Frederick Merk, *Albert Gallatin and the Oregon Problem* (Cambridge, Mass., 1950); L. B. Shippee, *Canadian-American Relations 1849-1874* (New Haven, 1939); H. G. MacDònald, *Canadian Public Opinion on the American Civil War* (New York, 1926); J. M. Callahan, *The Alaska Purchase and Americo-Canadian Relations* (Morgantown, W. Va., 1908); Lionel M. Gelber, *The Rise of Anglo-American Friendship* (London, 1938); C. S. Campbell, Jr., *Anglo-American Understanding, 1898-1903* (Baltimore, 1957); John S. Galbraith, *The Establishment of Canadian Diplomatic Status at Washington* (Berkeley, Cal., 1951); F. W. Howay, W. N. Sage, and H. F. Angus, *British Columbia and the United States* (Toronto, 1942).

Periodical writings on particular facets of Canadian–United States relations continue to increase in volume; the following will provide a sample of items for the period through the nineteenth century: W. R. Manning, "The Nootka Sound Controversy," *Am. Hist. Assn., Ann. Rept.*, 1904; C. M. Gates, "The West in American Diplomacy, 1812-1815," *Miss. Valley Hist. Rev.*, XXVI (1940), 499-510; W. H. Goodman, "The Origins of the War of 1812: A Survey of Changing Interpretations," *Miss. Valley Hist. Rev.*, XXVIII (1941), 171-186; L. M. Hacker, "Western Land Hunger and the War of 1812," *Miss. Valley Hist. Rev.*, X (1924), 365-395; J. W. Pratt, "Western Aims in the War of 1812," *Miss. Valley Hist. Rev.*, XII (1925), 36-50; G. R. Taylor, "Agrarian Discontent in the Mississippi Valley Preceding the War of 1812," *Jour. of Pol. Econ.*, XXXIX (1931), 471-505; A. C. Glueck, Jr., "The Riel Rebellion and Canadian-American Relations," *Can. Hist. Rev.*, XXXVI (1955), 199-221; O. E. Tiffany, "The Relations of the United States to the Canadian Rebellion of 1837-1838," *Buffalo Hist. Soc. Pub.*, VIII (1905), 1-147; D. F. Warner, "Drang Nach Norden: The U.S. and the Riel Rebellion," *Miss. Valley Hist. Rev.*, XXXIX (1953), 693-712; Alastair Watt, "The Case of Alexander McLeod," *Can. Hist. Rev.*, XII (1931), 145-167; C. P. Stacey, ed., "A Private Report of General Winfield Scott on the Border Situation in 1839," *Can. Hist. Rev.*, XXI (1940), 407-414; M. B. Hamer, "Luring Canadian Soldiers into Union Lines during the War between the States," *Can. Hist. Rev.*, XXVII (1946), 150-162;

H. A. Davis, "The Fenian Raid on New Brunswick," *Can. Hist. Rev.*, XXXVI (1955), 316-334.

An introduction to the changing tones in relations during the first several decades of the twentieth century may be obtained from a volume mentioned earlier, H. L. Keenleyside *et al.*, *The Growth of Canadian Policies in External Affairs* (Durham, N. C., 1961), particularly the essays by Gaddis Smith, "Canadian External Affairs During World War I" (pp. 33-58) and James Eayrs, "'A Low Dishonest Decade': Aspects of Canadian External Policy, 1931-1939" (pp. 59-80). The widening range of questions arising between the two countries and the increasing amount of discussion thereof are illustrated by: Alexander Brady, "Canadian-American Relations," *Int. Affairs*, XXVIII (1952), 190-195; Melvin Conant, "Canada and Continental Defence: An American View," *Int. Jour.*, XV (1960), 219-228; John S. Conway, "Canadian-American Relations: Co-operation or Conflict," *Int. Jour.*, XIII (1958), 204-212; G. Ferguson, "Canada and the 'Atlantic Alliance,'" *Int. Jour.*, XII (1957), 83-89; G. V. Ferguson, "Likely Trends in Canadian-American Political Relations," *Can. Jour. Econ. Pol. Sci.*, XXII (1956), 437-448; J. Douglas Gibson, "The Changing Influence of the United States on the Canadian Economy," *Can. Jour. Econ. Pol. Sci.*, XXII (1956), 421-436; E. J. Hanson, "Natural Gas in Canadian-American Relations," *Int. Jour.*, XII (1957), 186-198; John W. Holmes, "Canada and the United States in World Politics," *For. Affairs*, XL (1961), 105-117; Tom Kent, "The Changing Place of Canada," *For. Affairs*, XXXV (1957), 581-592; Peyton V. Lyon, "Problems of Canadian Independence," *Int. Jour.*, XVI (1961), 250-259; Edgar McInnis, "The English Speaking Triangle: Some Considerations," *Int. Jour.*, XII (1957), 243-249; L. B. Pearson, "Canada's Northern Horizon," *For. Affairs*, XXXI (1953), 581-591; G. Rosenbluth, "Changes in Canadian Sensitivity to United States Business Fluctuations," *Can. Jour. Econ. Pol. Sci.*, XXIII (1957), 480-503. To these may be added the various reports and statements issued by the Canadian-American Committee, sponsored by the National Planning Association (U.S.) and the Private Planning Association of Canada.

TREATY RELATIONS

Primary Materials. Selected correspondence and other documents bearing on treaty relations appear in a variety of published sources. The basic United States source is the series *The Foreign Relations of the United States* (1861—). This series runs about two decades behind events. Current materials will be found in *The Department of State Bulletin*. Also useful is *American Foreign Policy: Current Documents*, published annually by the Department of State in continuation of *A Decade of American Foreign Policy: Basic Documents 1941-1949* and *American Foreign Policy, 1950-1955: Basic Documents*. Materials covering the pre-American Civil War period are collected in *American State Papers: Foreign Relations* (6 vols.) and in William R. Manning, ed., *Diplomatic Correspondence of the United States: Canadian Relations 1784-1860* (4 vols., Washington, 1940-1945). Valuable information is available in the documents and reports published by the United States Congress; these include papers transmitted to Congress relative to diplomatic and treaty problems, hearings of the Senate Committee on Foreign Relations on particular treaties, and Senate executive reports on treaties submitted to it for approval. The volumes previously noted, *Treaties and Other International Acts of the United States of America*, edited by Hunter Miller, contain in addition to treaty texts, accounts of the negotiations of individual treaties, but these accounts vary in scope. Another series earlier cited, *British and Foreign State Papers*, contains correspondence and other documents relating to treaties and treaty problems. The Canadian Department of External Affairs publishes a Monthly Bulletin entitled *External Affairs*. Parliamentary debates and sessional papers of both the British and Canadian Parliaments provide a wealth of material, although Canadian sessional papers are no longer published. Since World War II, the *Minutes of Proceedings and Evidence* of the Standing Committee on External Affairs of the Canadian House of Commons have been regularly published. Norman Mackenzie and Lionel H. Laing, *Canada and the Law of Nations* (Toronto, 1938) is a convenient collection of legal decisions involving specific treaties.

Secondary Materials. On the whole, there is fairly wide selection of writings on specific treaties, but it is uneven. Some treaties seem to have attracted, for one reason or another, greater attention than others.

On the Treaty of 1794, the standard work is Samuel F. Bemis, *Jay's Treaty* (New York, 1923). A. L. Burt, *United States, Great Britain and British North America* (New Haven, 1940) presents valuable supplementary material to Bemis's study. Facts of the Jay negotiations and their impact are explored in Bradford Perkins, ed., "Lord Hawkesbury and the Jay-Grenville Negotiations," *Miss. Valley Hist. Rev.*, XL (1953), 291-304; Joseph Charles, "The Jay Treaty: The Origins of the American Party System," *Will. & Mary Quar.*, XII, 3d ser. (1955), 581-630.

The Webster-Ashburton Treaty is discussed in E. D. Adams, "Lord Ashburton and the Treaty of Washington," *Am. Hist. Rev.*, XVII (1912), 764-782; Frederick Merk, "The Oregon Question in the Webster-Ashburton Negotiations," *Miss. Valley Hist. Rev.*, XLIII (1956), 379-404.

The Oregon Treaty is the subject of a considerable body of periodical writings: G. V. Blue, "France and the Oregon Question," *Oregon Hist. Quar.*, XXXIV (1933), 39-54, 144-163; R. C. Clark, "British and American Tariff Policies and Their Influence on the Oregon Boundary Treaty," Pac. Coast Branch of Am. Hist. Assn., *Proc.*, 1926, pp. 32-50; H. S. Commager, "England and the Oregon Treaty of 1846," *Ore. Hist. Quar.*, XXVIII (1927), 18-38; N. A. Graebner, "Maritime Factors in the Oregon Compromise," *Pac. Hist. Rev.*, XX (1951), 331-345; D. W. Howe, "The Mississippi Valley in the Movement for Fifty-four Forty or Fight," Miss. Valley Hist. Assn., *Proc.*, V (1919), 99-116; J. P. Martin, "Free Trade and the Oregon Question, 1842-1846," *Facts and Factors in Economic History: Articles by Former Students of Edwin Francis Gay* (Cambridge, Mass., 1932), pp. 470-491; Joseph Schafer, "The British Attitude toward the Oregon Question, 1815-1846," *Am. Hist. Rev.*, XVI (1911), 273-299; and to these must be added the following articles by Frederick Merk: "The British Corn Crisis of 1845-46 and the Oregon Treaty," *Agric. Hist.*, VIII (1934), 95-123; "British Government Propaganda and the Oregon Treaty," *Am. Hist. Rev.*, XL (1934), 38-62; "British Party Politics and the Oregon Treaty," *Am. Hist. Rev.*, XXXVII (1932), 667-672; "The Genesis of the Oregon Question," *Miss. Valley Hist. Rev.*, XXXVI (1950), 583-612; "The Oregon Pioneers and the Boundary," *Ore. Hist. Quar.*, XXVIII (1927), 366-388.

On the Clayton-Bulwer Treaty, see R. W. Van Alstyne, "British Diplomacy and the Clayton-Bulwer Treaty, 1850-1860," *Jour. of Mod. Hist.*, XI (1939), 149-183.

The Reciprocity Treaty of 1854 is the subject of studies by D. C. Masters, *The Reciprocity Treaty of 1854* (London, 1937); C.C. Tansill, *The Canadian Reciprocity Treaty of 1854* (Baltimore, 1922), and C. D. Allin and G. M. Jones, *Annexation, Preferential Trade and Reciprocity* (Toronto, 1912).

The Treaty of 1870 dealing with naturalization is discussed by R. L. Morrow, "The Negotiation of the Anglo-American Treaty of 1870," *Am. Hist. Rev.*, XXXIX (1934), 663-681.

The Treaty of Washington receives attention in Goldwin Smith's *The Treaty of Washington, 1871: A Study in Imperial History* (Ithaca, N. Y. 1941); see also Caleb Cushing, *The Treaty of Washington* (New York, 1873); R. C. Clark, "The Diplomatic Mission of Sir John Rose, 1871," *Pac. Northwest Quar.*, XXVII (1926), 227-242.

On the Boundary Waters Treaty of 1909, see A. O. Gibbons, "Sir George Gibbons and the Boundary Waters Treaty of 1909," *Can. Hist. Rev.*, XXXIV (1953), 124-138; Chirokaikan J. Chacko, *The International Joint Commission between the United States and the Dominion of Canada* (New York, 1932); L. M. Bloomfield and Gerald F. Fitzgerald, *Boundary Waters Problems of Canada and the United States: The International Joint Commission 1912-1958* (Toronto, 1958); Robert D. Scott, "The Canadian-American Boundary Waters Treaty: Why Article II?," *Can. Bar. Rev.*, XXXVI (1958), 511-547; Robert A. MacKay, "The International Joint Commission between the United States and Canada," *Am. Jour. Int. Law*, XXII (1928), 292-318.

Writings on the Alaskan Boundary Settlement include: T. A. Bailey, "Theodore Roosevelt and the Alaska Boundary Settlement," *Can. Hist. Rev.*, XVIII (1937), 123-130; J. A. Garraty, ed., "Henry Cabot Lodge and the Alaskan Boundary Tribunal," *New Eng. Quar.*, XXIV (1951), 467-494; S. R. Tompkins, "Drawing the Alaska Boundary," *Can. Hist. Rev.*, XXVI (1945), 1-24.

On the abortive attempt at reciprocity in 1911, see L. E. Ellis, *Reciprocity, 1911* (New Haven, 1939) and "The Northwest and the Reciprocity Agreement of 1911," *Miss. Valley Hist. Rev.*, XXVI (1939), 55-66.

After World War I, treaty ties between Canada and the United States increased markedly in number and scope. The following references will provide introductions to various treaty problem areas. On fisheries, see Charles B. Selak, Jr., "The United States–Canadian Great Lakes Fisheries Convention," *Am. Jour. Int. Law*, L (1956), 122-129; E. Walenberg, "Columbia River Fish Compact," *Oregon Law Rev.*, XVIII (1939), 88-107. Taxation problems are discussed in M. B. Carroll, "Foreign Trade Advantage in Canadian-American Convention," *Taxes*, XXIII (1945), 148-150; R. W. V. Dickerson, "Taxation and Foreign Investment by Canadian Corporations," *Univ. Brit. Col. Law Rev.*, I, no. 4 (1961), 483-498; M. M. Kassell, "Appraisal of Canada–U.S. Tax Treaty," *Trusts and Estates*, LXXX (1945), 105-107. Boundary water problems have attracted considerable attention; see Jacob Austin, "Canadian–U.S. Practice and Theory Respecting the International Law of International Rivers: A Study of the History and Influence of the Harmon Doctrine," *Can. Bar Rev.*, XXXVII (1959), 393-445; Clyde Eagleton, "Use of the Waters of International Rivers," *Can. Bar Rev.*, XXXIII (1955), 1018-1034; James Simsarian, "The Diversion of Waters Affecting the United States and Canada," *Am. Jour. Int. Law*, XXXII (1938), 488-518; H. A. Smith, "The Chicago Diversion," *Can. Bar Rev.*, VIII (1930), 330-343; Gerald F. Fitzgerald, "Legal Aspects of the Power Development of the Saint John River Basin," *Univ. New Brun. Law Jour.*, XII (1959), 7-38; William F. Ryan, "Saint John River Power Development: Some International Law Problems," *Univ. New Brun. Law Jour.*, XI (1958), 20-25. On Columbia River developments, see C. B. Bourne, "Columbia River Diversion: The Law Determining Rights of Injured Parties," *Univ. Brit. Col. Legal Notes*, II (1958), 610-622; Maxwell Cohen, "Columbia River Treaty—A Comment," *McGill Law Jour.*, VIII (1962), 212-215 and "Some Legal and Policy Aspects of the Columbia River Dispute," *Can. Law Rev.*, XXXVI (1958), 25-41; Charles E. Martin, "The Diversion of Columbia River Waters," *Proc. Am. Soc. Int. Law*, 1957, 2-10. A comprehensive treatment of the St. Lawrence River developments is William R. Willoughby, *The Saint Lawrence Waterway* (Madison, Wisc., 1961); see also E. Borchard, "The St. Lawrence Waterway and Power Project," *Am. Jour. Int. Law*, XLIII (1949), 411-434; P. C. Jessup, "Great Lakes–St. Lawrence Deep Water Way Treaty," *Am. Jour. Int. Law*, XXVI (1932), 814-819; H. J. Lawford, "Treaties and Rights of Transit on the St. Lawrence," *Can. Bar Rev.*, XXXIX (1961), 577-602. Problems of extradition are thoroughly discussed in G. V. La Forest, *Extradition to and from Canada* (New Orleans, 1961). Aspects of defense questions are reflected in H. L. Keenleyside, "The Canada–United States Permanent Joint Board on Defence, 1940-1945," *Int. Jour.*, XVI (1960), 50-77; L. B. Pearson, "NATO: Retrospect and Prospects," *Int. Jour.*, XIV (1959), 79-84; Ronald S. Ritchie, "Problems of a Defence Policy for Canada," *Int. Jour.*, XIV (1959), 202-212. A symposium issue of the *University of British Columbia Law Review* (Vol. I, no. 3, 1960) discusses extraterritorial application of domestic law and the effect of existing uses on apportionment of international rivers; useful is Kurt H. Nadelmann *et al.*, "A Round Table on Selected Problems in Legal Relations between Canada and the United States," *Am. Jour. Comp. Law*, XI (1962), 283-322.

INDEX

Acheson, Dean, 17 n.
Act concerning corporations and labour unions, Canada (1962), 144, 145
Advancement-of-Peace Treaty (1914), 5, 26
Advisory Opinion on Reservations to the Genocide Convention, 4
Agreements and treaties (1782-1960), list of, 196-231
Aitken, H. G. J., 171 n., 177 n.
Alabama Claims, vii, 8, 9, 187
Alaska: boundary of, 4, 103, 187; oil in, 168; pipeline, 190
Alaskan Boundary Arbitration (1903), 10-11, 78
Albania, 77
Alberta: gas development in, 169 n., 170-175 *passim*; nickel in, 156; oil development in, 166, 167
Alberta Oil and Gas Conservation Board, 179
Alberta Petroleum and Natural Gas Conservation Board, 174
Allen, James, 87 n., 97
Alverstone, Lord, 10-11
Amery, Leopold, 89 n.
Amory, Thomas C., 30 n.
Anaconda Copper Mining Co., 158, 172, 173, 174
Anglin, C. J. C., 32 n.
Antarctica, treaty concerning (1959), 3 n.
Antitrust policy, conflict over U. S., x, 142-144
Arctic, 93, 112, 114, 193
Argue, H., 137 n.
Armstrong, Donald, 151 n.
Arrow River and Tributaries Slide and Boom Co., Re (1932), 32 n., 182 n.
Ashburton-Webster Treaty (1842); *see* Webster-Ashburton Treaty
Ashland Oil and Refining Co., 167
Asquith, H. H., 98
Atomic Energy, Agreement for Co-operation on Civil Uses of (1955), 5, 6, 162, 184

Atomic Energy Authority, United Kingdom, 164
Atomic Energy Commission, U. S., 161, 162, 163-165
Austin, Jacob, 16 n., 18 n., 32 n., 37 n.
Austin, John, 73
Australia: lead in, 159; military policy of, 84, 87-92 *passim*, 93 n., 95 n., 97 n., 108
Aylesworth, A. B., 10

Baghdad Pact (1955), 99 n.
Bahia de Nipe Cases (1961), 150 n.
Banco Nacional de Cuba v. Sabbatino (1961, 1962), 150 n.
Bank of Nova Scotia, 137, 149
Barton, Edmund, 88 n.
Batista, Fulgencio, 138
Battle of Britain, 105
Bay of Fundy, 29, 30, 46, 47, 49
Bennett, E. F., 59, 61
Bennett, Wallace F., 66
Bering Sea Arbitration, 9-10, 78
Berlin Blockade, 92
Beyers, C. F., 98 n.
Bibliography: of diplomatic relations, 233-235; of treaty relations, 235-239; of treaty texts, 232-233
Bidwell, P. W., 155 n., 158 n., 169 n., 170 n.
Bismarck, Otto von, 148 n.
Bloomfield, L. M., 32 n.
Board of Transport Commissioners, 165
Bogotá Conference (1960), 22-23
Bonner's Ferry, 68
Borden, Robert, 15, 87, 95
Borden Commission, 181
Botha, Louis, 87, 90 n., 98
Boti, Regino, 137
Boundary waters: and Boundary Water Treaty (q.v.), 32-34; freedom of navigation on, 30-32; and International Joint Commission (q.v.), 33, 35-37; international law applied to, 14-19; problems of, viii, ix (*see also* Chicago Diversion, Columbia River